Drug Lord

A TRUE STORY

DRUG LORD

The Life and Death
of a Mexican Kingpin

DEMAND
PUBLICATIONS
S E A T T L E

TERRENCE E. POPPA

Second edition, third printing

Poppa, Terrence E.
    Drug lord : the life and death of a Mexican kingpin :
a true story / Terrence E. Poppa. — 2nd ed., rev. and
updated.
    p. cm.
    Includes index.
    English ed. first published in 1990 by Pharos Books,
New York City.
    Preassigned LCCN: 98-72519
    ISBN: 0-9664430-0-4

    1. Acosta, Pablo, d. 1987. 2. Narcotics dealers—
Mexico—Biography. 3. Narcotics, Control of—Mexico—
Case studies. 4. Drug traffic—Mexico—Case studies. 5.
Drug traffic—United States—Case studies. 6. Political
corruption—Mexico. I. Title.

HV5805.A25P67 1998   363.45'092[B]
                                             QBI98-1145

Printed in the United States of America

Cover photo by Terrence Poppa

Demand Publications
2608 Second Avenue, Suite 2450
Seattle, WA 98121
Email: publisher@druglord.com
Web: http://www.druglord.com
Order desk: 1-888-622-7311

To Linda Bejarano, Victor Manuel Oropeza, Yolanda Figueroa and the hundreds of journalists of this hemisphere who have been murdered, kidnapped, tortured, threatened or persecuted for seeking the truth

Drug Lord is a true story. Though some names have been omitted and several changed to protect the innocent, the characters and scenes are real. The dialogue was taken word for word from interviews with participants, including the chief participant of them all, Pablo Acosta.

TABLE OF CONTENTS

PART III: Death of a Drug Lord

FOREWORD

Many books have been published during the last several decades about drug trafficking and drug traffickers. Few have risen above the limitations of the true crime genre. For the most part, these works offer little more than insights into the greed of particular individuals. It is refreshing therefore when a book comes along that goes beyond the narrow focus of an individual morality play, and offers perspectives and conceptual tools for understanding the activity's destructive origin. One such book is this one.

Drug Lord is a riveting portrait of Pablo Acosta, the scarfaced Mexican *padrino* who controlled crime along 250 miles of the Rio Grande. It is a linear work that traces the drug lord's rise from humble beginnings, his rapid ascension to power through murder and treachery, his smuggling of sixty tons of cocaine a year into the United States, his struggles to defend his expanding empire against rivals, the betrayals and over-indulgence that fostered his downfall, and his dramatic death at the hands of the same police system that had been giving him protection.

This story of a Mexican drug trafficker would be worthy even if it had been limited to biography—it is in fact the first inside look at a Mexican drug trafficking organization ever published. But Poppa's book is much more. By following the life and career of Pablo Acosta, the granddaddy of Mexican cocaine traffickers and mentor of Amado Carrillo Fuentes, the future "Lord of the Skies," Poppa lays out a brutal truth that many in Washington D.C. still refuse to believe. Namely, that drug trafficking in Mexico is controlled from the top by key agencies of government, political institutions and key officials among the elite. The drug kingpins, despite their riches and violence, are merely pawns. They are the front men and the fall guys, the expendable employees. They are like Aztec princes of old who were allowed to have their time in the sun but whose hearts were cut out in ritualized sacrifice when the glory days were over.

The success of Pablo Acosta in reaching the pinnacle of organized crime power was not simply the product of violent individual entrepreneurship and gang leadership ability, but was actually the result of a license, a franchise given out by Mexican state and federal government officials to drug traffickers in return for a large percentage of the take and other services. Thus, Poppa was among the first to understand that this was not the work of a few bad-apple politicians and policemen, but was the product of an embedded system of organized corruption that runs from Mexico City through the state capitals and government officials down to the regions where the traffickers operate. These concessions were zoned out along administrative and jurisdictional lines. It was a system known as *la plaza* and is useful to quote what the author has to say about this at length here, for it forms the conceptual fabric of the entire book:

For decades Mexican informants tried to explain the idea to their law enforcement contacts in the United States. When somebody had the *plaza*, it meant that he was paying an authority or authorities with sufficient power to ensure that he would not be bothered by police or by the military. The protection money went up the ladder, with percentages shaved off at each level up the chain of command until reaching the Grand Protector or the Grand Protectors in the scheme.

To stay in the good graces of his powerful patrons, the *plaza* holder had a dual obligation: to

generate money for his protectors and to lend his
intelligence gathering abilities by fingering the independent operators—those narcotics traffickers
and drug growers who tried to avoid paying the
necessary tribute. The independents were the ones
who got busted by the Mexican Federal Judicial
Police, the Mexican equivalent of the FBI, or by
the army, giving Mexico statistics to show it was
involved in authentic drug enforcement. That most
of the seized narcotics were then recycled—sold to
the favored groups or outrightly smuggled by police groups—was irrelevant. The seizures were in
fact made and there were headlines to prove it.

Sometimes, the authorities would protect their
man from rivals; other times they would not, preferring a variety of natural selection to determine
who should run the *plaza*. If the authorities arrested or killed the *plaza* holder, it was usually because
he had stopped making payments, or because his
name had started to appear in the press too frequently and the trafficker had become a liability.
Sometimes international pressure became so strong
that the government was forced to take action
against a specific individual—regardless of how
much money he was generating.

It was a system that enabled the Mexican political and police structures to keep a lid on drugs and
profit handsomely from it at the same time.

This, in a few clear and concise paragraphs, is the history
of drug trafficking in Mexico for at least the last half of this
century, if not longer. Because of such insights, graphically
illustrated in the life and death of Pablo Acosta, Poppa's book
rises far above the level of anything that has ever been written
about the subject. It is a deft allegory, a bold paradigm, a cou-
rageous denunciation that cuts through the smokescreen of
official posturing, blanket denials and sophisticated cover-ups.

As allegory, it shows that Mexico's drug kingpins are, in

truth, simply replaceable cogs used and exploited by an official system of political and governmental corruption and control. Replace Pablo Acosta's name with that of any drug trafficker, past or present, and it is the same story. Change the name of Ojinaga—Pablo Acosta's town—to Mexico, and you have the big picture.

Thus Poppa's *Drug Lord* is the biography of Rafael Caro Quintero, the Guadalajara drug thug who was arrested after American pressure over the murder of DEA agent Enrique Camarena. It is the history of Miguel Angel Felix Gallardo or of Juan Garcia Abrego, traffickers who lost their *plaza* franchises and their freedom after changes in Mexican political administrations. It is the profile of Rafael Aguilar Guajardo, a trafficker-turned-Mexican federal security police commander who was assassinated two days after he threatened to reveal his high-level Mexican government contacts. It is the career of Amado Carrillo Fuentes, the infamous cocaine trafficker who died recently under surgery after indicating he was shifting his operations from Mexico to Chile. It is the story-in-the-making of the Arrellano Felix brothers, Benjamin and Ramon, of the so-called Tijuana cartel, currently the big names in drug trafficking today. The names are many, but the story remains the same.

These insights and the tenacious bravery that it took to uncover the truth easily rank Poppa as one of the most remarkable journalists of the last decade. Indeed, the history of the origin of this book is almost as gripping as the book itself. A prize winning journalist and a Pulitzer Prize finalist, Poppa arrived as a border reporter and a correspondent for Scripps Howard News Service in 1984, a time of political turmoil in Mexico and fear that a revolt in northern Mexico was just around the corner. He explored the election-rigging practices of the Institutional Revolutionary Party, known as the PRI, the party that emerged from the Mexican Revolution that has monopolized power even to this day. Very quickly, Poppa began to see the connections between crime and the institutionalized power system. He wrote numerous reports about the theft of American automobiles by Mexican federal and state police agencies, providing photographic and documentary evidence. Later, he began to see the connections between the traffickers and the PRI's federal and state police agencies. The entrenched interests quickly took note of the unwanted exposure. Soon, he was being portrayed on a state-controlled Mexican television station as a CIA spy. Reams of "Wanted" posters bearing his photo and branding him as an "anti-Mexican agitator" were being handed out from Mexican state police agencies. Each published report brought fresh threats against the author, threats that culminated in the kidnapping and torture of an American freelance news photographer, Al Gutierrez, by one of the border traffickers and a promise to kill Poppa in reprisal for stories that he had written.

In response, the author's news organization bought him a handgun and sent him on the road, getting him out of Dodge while things cooled down. Poppa used the time to explore the growing cocaine trafficking corridor that was appearing through north-central Mexico. He ended up in the stronghold and hideout of Pablo Acosta, then one of the most powerful drug traffickers of northern Mexico, feared for his reputation for killing rivals and then dragging their bodies behind his Bronco through the desert until there was not much left except a shredded torso. Poppa spent two days with Acosta, tape-recording hours and hours of interviews with the fearsome trafficker. Between drags from crack-laced Marlboros and swigs of El Presidente brandy, Acosta spoke of murders, smuggling and protection. When the newspaper reports based on the meeting were published, an embarrassed Mexico City sent a squad of crack federal police after Acosta. They trapped the drug lord five months later and killed him in a machine-gun battle reminiscent of Vietnam for its intensity.

A few months later, Poppa wrote one of the most comprehensive newspaper series ever written up to that time about the nature of crime in Mexico and its ties to the government, a report that led to an invitation to testify before the U.S. Senate Subcommittee on Investigations. Simultaneously, two of the most notorious traffickers named in the series, Rafael Aguilar

Guajardo and Gilberto Ontiveros, put up $250,000 in cocaine to have Poppa kidnapped, taken into Mexico and killed. This threat was picked up by an informant of the U.S. Customs Service. Federal agents warned Poppa of the threat and advised him to take precautions. Poppa, in turn, reported the threat to a United States senator who turned to the U.S. Customs Commissioner for help. The threat was investigated from Washington and the information was determined to have come from one of the service's best-placed sources in Mexico. Several days later, Poppa was invited to the Customs enforcement office in El Paso where he was shown a memorandum that had been sent to every enforcement office along the border, giving the American feds instructions to inform their counterparts in Mexico that the United States intended to shut down the border from San Diego to Brownsville if there were any further threats against the reporter. Two days later, Customs learned that the traffickers had withdrawn the contract. It was at that point that Poppa quit newspaper reporting to begin an investigation into the Pablo Acosta organization, work that led him into the heart of the biggest cocaine corridor ever created in the Western Hemisphere. The result is this book.

The author was on the trail of one of the worthiest stories of our times, that the real problem facing the United States as a drug crime victim is a governmental system south of the border of exploitation and corruption that controls and manipulates the traffickers for the benefit of the system. The result has been a flooding of North America with drugs and the pervasive misery and social disruptions drug abuse has caused. At the time this book first came out, the north-central Mexican state of Chihuahua was already being used as the main corridor for bringing cocaine to the United States. The governorship of Chihuahua under Fernando Baeza Melendez, the Fifth Military Zone in Chihuahua City, the federal police headquarters there and the state police agencies throughout Chihuahua, not to mention the key federal agencies such as Customs, were securely under the control of this embedded protection system. It is estimated that 400 tons of cocaine were flown into northern Mexico from Colombia during the first two years of this operation. Of that, twenty-two tons were discovered in 1989 a warehouse in Sylmar, just north of Los Angeles. Many of these facts have subsequently come to light.

The history of the last seven years, therefore, has been the history of the corroboration this unique work. Hardly a month goes by without some new revelation. Many of the people in Poppa's book continue to make the news, such as Guillermo Gonzalez Calderoni, the Mexican federal police commander who hunted down and killed Pablo Acosta. This top-ranking Mexican federal police commander later defected to the United States. In exchange for safe harbor here, he passed on information to the FBI about his government's drug trafficking involvement, including details of the fabulous wealth the brother of the Mexican president at the time was amassing thanks to protection he was giving to a Gulf Coast trafficker, and the scheming by this presidential sibling to buy up state-owned port facilities on the Gulf of Mexico to facilitate drug shipments by sea. Poppa was the first to meet and write about Amado Carrillo Fuentes, Pablo Acosta's partner and successor who eventually became the most powerful of the Mexican drug traffickers of the 1990s until his freakish death in 1997 while undergoing plastic surgery. Scandals involving Mexican generals on Carrillo Fuentes' payroll have made the headlines.

In light of all of these revelations, it is indeed interesting to listen to the self-serving speeches of Mexican presidents blaming the drug trafficking problem on consumption in the United States. The most recent example is President Ernesto Zedillo's demand that the United States make "reparations" to Mexico to make up for the "filthy mess" drug consumption in the United States supposedly caused down there. Poppa's book is a valuable tool for correctly interpreting these grotesque distortions. Such rhetoric is likely to grow in frequency and hysteria the more the truth about the mafia nature of the Mexican system comes out.

The mills of the gods grind slowly, but they grind fine.

Things are changing in Mexico. The major parties and institutions and elites and their embedded systems of corruption are still in place but cracks in the structure are showing. The Institutional Revolutionary Party is now as decrepit and faltering as was the Communist Party of the Soviet Union a decade ago. Federal elections in 1997 created new coalitions in the Mexican Congress and for the first time have opened the door to investigating and cracking the system of corruption and its connections to trafficking. Whether this opportunity can be successfully exploited, however, remains to be seen. For the elites and institutions of Mexico, particularly the military, which is likely to fill and control any vacuums in drug trafficking, are extremely powerful. We are likely to see many traffickers and drug lords like Pablo Acosta come and go, and *plaza* franchises change hands all along the border before we see real change in the Mexican system. Thus, while Poppa's book tells a story at one point in time, it is still as relevant and important reading today was when it was first written. For, while the players change, the play continues. And sad to say, most Americans and many policy makers in Washington still do not understand.

Drug Lord is an exciting and important book that can help change this. I urge you to read on.

—*Peter A. Lupsha, professor emeritus and senior scholar, Latin American Institute, University of New Mexico*

Part One

La Plaza

*A*costa directs his organization from Ojinaga with an iron fist and does not tolerate rebellion either overt or covert. If a leak is suspected, or if a member or associate fails to act as expected, they are removed quickly and permanently. He has a strict enforcement policy, which is killing the delinquent customer.

Acosta takes a personal and active interest in any bad business practices, or talking by his enemies and competitors. His killings are very flamboyant and are done in a distinctive manner as an example to others. He is a vicious and extremely dangerous person who has little regard for human life if it stands in the way of his operation.

Although he is small in stature, he does not hesitate to become involved in a gun battle with his peers or with law enforcement personnel. Acosta has put out several contracts on competitors and has been implicated in two murders in Hobbs, New Mexico, and four in Mexico.

His organization has been linked to at least twenty murders since 1982, and the total may even be double that number. Reports are that he has begun to arm his members with Teflon coated ammunition capable of penetrating body armor-type bulletproof vests worn by law enforcement officers. Acosta himself is known to wear a bulletproof vest and usually travels with or is followed by heavily armed bodyguards.

Intelligence (unconfirmed) indicates that Pablo Acosta and his organization have "high level" protection that reaches from Mexico City to the governor of Chihuahua (Oscar Ornelas). At the local level in Northern Chihuahua and Ojinaga he is believed to be protected by the Mexican general in charge of the area. The MFJP (Mexican Federal Judicial Police) in the Ojinaga area has been reportedly composed of some of his men and directly controlled by him through one of its comandantes. In other cases some of his other men were reported to have MFJP credentials to color their activities and cover their carrying weapons in public.

From the introduction to a confidential 223-page U.S. Drug Enforcement Administration report, *The Pablo Acosta Organization*, April 1986

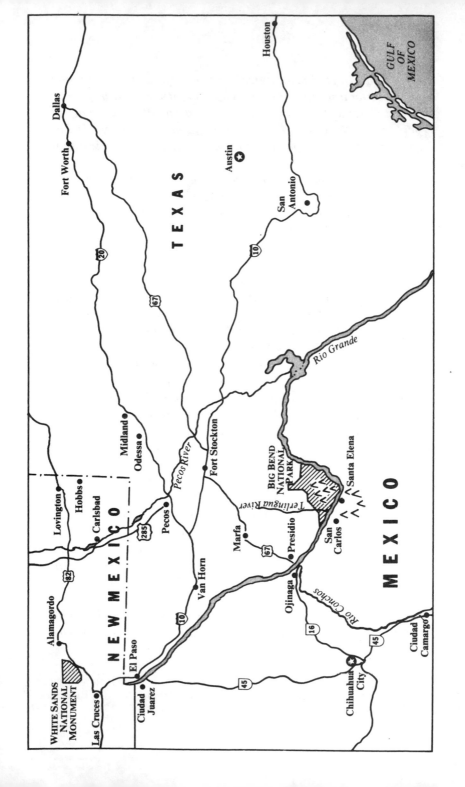

Chapter One

OJINAGA

When you first see Ojinaga from the American side, it is after you drive through rugged mountains on a two-lane highway from Marfa and begin the long descent into the Rio Grande basin. There, ten miles in the bluey distance, lies the town on a plain on the Mexican side of the river. From the distance one sees huge dust devils swirling across the scorched fields outside of town. Plumes of black smoke from the municipal dump billow high into the sky. Ojinaga looks like a town under siege.

Like the villages still in existence upstream and downstream, Ojinaga had once been little more than a collection of adobe hovels at the edge of the Rio Grande. It was through this parched border town that John Reed, the impassioned chronicler of violent change, entered Mexico for his reportage on the Mexican Revolution. He described the Ojinaga of those savage days as a town of "white dusty streets piled high with filth and fodder."

The later Ojinaga grew under the stimulus of trade, legal and illegal. As isolated from authority on the Mexican side as Presidio—its little sister on the American side, Ojinaga became an ideal route for smugglers pushing contraband of all kinds. During Prohibition, it was bootleg liquor and *sotol*, a potent cactus moonshine. During the Second World War, airmen and soldiers based at a bomber field outside of Marfa gave a boost to bordertown commerce by spending freely in the downtown shops and in the cantinas of the red light district.

Following the war, heroin began coming through in greater and greater amounts. Smuggled from the slopes of Sinaloa on Mexico's west coast, where peasants learned that opium poppies brought a higher price than corn, the gum extracted from the poppy made its way through the sierras of Chihuahua to clandestine laboratories in the mountains above the mining town of Parral to transform it into heroin. From there the heroin was brought to the United States via Ojinaga. There was never any shortage of people willing to smuggle the refined product into the United States.

The Ojinaga that Pablo Acosta came to dominate was born of the ashes of Domingo Aranda, an old-time smuggler and drug dealer who was burned to death one day on the banks of the Rio Grande.

Aranda was one of the most successful of the heroin smugglers and was possibly the first drug lord of the region. At least, he was the first of the succession of *padrinos* who are remembered today. A tall, broad-shouldered peasant from rural Ojinaga, Aranda got his start as a *contrabandista* during World War II, escorting mule trains laden with tires, sugar, coffee and just about anything else that happened to be rationed or was in short supply in the United States during those years. With forty, fifty, or even one hundred mules, these caravans plodded through the lunar canyons of the Texas Big Bend under the cover of darkness to avoid U.S. Customs patrols. Smugglers made use of olden signaling methods to communicate over long distances. Ranchers in the Big Bend area knew what it meant when they saw bonfires on mountaintops late at night or the distant flashes of mirrors by day.

After the war Domingo Aranda moved from Ojinaga and settled in Portales, a farm town on the plains of southeastern New Mexico. Rationing ended with the war and like other out-of-work contrabanders he took up smuggling black tar—the brown, clayey, poorly refined heroin coming out of the Parral mountains. With his sons as apprentices, Aranda ran the heroin from the sierras to the Rio Grande, then followed the old contraband routes north across private ranch roads and unpaved county roads. In the United States, he avoided detection by distributing only to trusted Mexican pushers who in turn sold chiefly to Mexican addicts. From his modest home in Portales, he developed distribution networks in Albuquerque and as far north as Chicago.

By the standards of the early 1960s, he was a very successful drug trafficker.

At first, Domingo Aranda specialized in heroin. But as the anti-war generation began to emerge in the United States, he took advantage of the new opportunity and branched into marijuana.

Aranda might have continued operating his business from the New Mexico farm community indefinitely if he had not killed one of his business partners there in 1969, forcing him to flee back to Ojinaga. The story police learned was that Aranda shot Pancho Carreon in self-defense during an argument that started over a card game. They were drinking heavily and the joking took an insulting turn: Carreon supposedly made a crude remark about Aranda's sister. When Aranda jumped to his feet and threatened to kill him, Carreon lunged across the table with a knife. As he fell back, Aranda whipped out a .25-caliber pistol from his boot and shot Carreon in the mouth, severing an artery. Carreon choked to death on his own blood.

Aranda made a run for it back to Mexico, basing his operation from then on in Ojinaga.

The Ojinaga of 1969 was a struggling border town of ten thousand people. Like most Mexican towns, Ojinaga had the usual cluster of historic buildings around a quaint central square with a church at one end. The tidy, comfortable homes of the well-to-do were on paved side streets. Farther from the center began the unpaved roads that wound through neighborhoods full of the sagging, eroded adobe homes of the less fortunate.

At the time, telephone numbers were three digits and operators used plug-in switchboards. Older telephone operators there tell of the misdirected calls they frequently got from the United States, evidence of the remoteness of the border town.

"*No, señor*, this is not Okinawa," the operators would patiently explain. "Okinawa is in Japan. You have reached Ojinaga, Mexico. *O-hee-na'-ga, May'-hee-co!*"

The few phones reserved for international calls at the downtown telephone company hung from the walls. In self-imposed exile to avoid prosecution for the killing of Pancho Carreon, Aranda transformed the musty telephone office into his operations center. Telephone operators still remember how Aranda used to come early in the morning and spend several hours leaning against the wall or sitting on a chair. He had a way of bending his head down and sticking a finger in one ear whenever the noise in the crowded room got too loud. The operators could often hear Aranda's loud voice but they never really could decipher the veiled language. He always paid for the expensive calls from a thick wad of dollars and pesos he pulled from his pocket. "Cattle broker" he told anyone curious enough to inquire about his occupation.

About 1968, before the killing of his partner and his own flight to Mexico, Domingo Aranda brought some new blood into the organization.

Manuel Carrasco was a tall, square-faced *campesino* from the Ojinaga area who first went to Portales as a migrant laborer. Born in 1934 in a village outside of Ojinaga, he had married one of Aranda's nieces. Like so many of the farm workers from the adobe hamlets surrounding Ojinaga, Carrasco did seasonal work in the cotton fields of West Texas and New Mexico before heading back home to Ojinaga to work the family corn field. At first Aranda had Carrasco "mule" loads of heroin whenever he was on his way back to Portales, then gave him more responsibility by letting him run some deliveries of heroin or marijuana all the way to Chicago.

Manuel Carrasco was bright, ambitious. During his trips to Chicago and other big cities, he could see that the market in the United States went far beyond the vision of his *jefe*. Aranda was myopic. The 60s counterculture seemed hell-bent on smoking, snorting or injecting every mind-altering substance known to pharmacopoeia. And they were paying real money for it, particularly on the coasts and in the big cities. With some hustle, a man could make himself a fortune just supplying run-of-the-mill drugs like heroin and marijuana.

Yet Manuel could see that his uncle-in-law was content to supply one or two or three distributors in each of the communities he dealt in. After working a few years under Domingo Aranda's tutelage, Carrasco started making separate deals with some of Aranda's customers and forging connections with other buyers. Before long he was operating an organization that was completely independent of Aranda and was expanding his distribution network to California and Arizona.

Over time, Carrasco also managed to connect with Aranda's marijuana and heroin suppliers in Parral, a mining town in southeastern Chihuahua. But he later set up heroin laboratories of his own in mountain hideaways southwest of Chihuahua City. State police in New Mexico who tracked Carrasco's rise believe his organization became sophisticated enough to fly *goma*, the opium poppy extract, from the growing fields of Sinaloa to his laboratories in the nearly inaccessible mountain regions of Chihuahua. Then he flew the refined product to desert landing sites around Ojinaga.

With his better organizational skills and boundless ambition, Carrasco in a few years came to dominate narcotics through Ojinaga.

Domingo Aranda, meanwhile, suffered financial reverses when several valuable drug shipments were busted in the United States. Like a roll of the dice in the board games that force a player back to the starting point, these misfortunes were so great that he ended up having to seek work from Manuel Carrasco, his former runner.

Then one day in 1973 Aranda was murdered and his body was torched on the banks of the Rio Grande outside of Ojinaga, a crime that horrified Ojinaga for its ruthlessness and signaled the beginning of a new era.

According to one explanation cited for the murder, Aranda was killed by Pancho Carreon's sons to avenge the shooting of their father years earlier in New Mexico. The Carreon sons had put out a contract for Aranda. But while he was still in control of Ojinaga crime, no one dared act on it. When Manuel Carrasco became the crime godfather of Ojinaga, Aranda could not be killed without the drug *don's* consent. To get the Ojinaga drug lord to hand him over, the Carreon sons convinced Carrasco that Aranda was skimming off his loads.

Another version was that Aranda had learned of a stash of large-denomination greenbacks Manuel kept under his bed, hidden in a compartment built into the box spring. Aranda was eager to re-establish himself but needed capital. He made the mistake of bringing a Chihuahua State cop with him to steal the money. The *judicial*, as Mexican state and federal police are called, told his *comandante*. The *comandante,* a friend of Carrasco's, told Carrasco.

Whatever the motive, one evening in 1973 Carrasco set up the murder by asking Aranda to help him bring a load of marijuana to the river's edge down by El Mulato, a village across the river from Redford, Texas, where some buyers were supposedly waiting for the shipment. The two men drove down the valley with the marijuana in the back of Carrasco's truck. It was late at night. When they arrived at the riverbank, they saw some men milling around in front of the headlights of a pickup truck parked by the water. As they walked up to the group, Aranda recognized one of the Carreon sons. Aranda realized too late that it was a setup.

The way the incident was told to New Mexico state narcotics agents, Domingo Aranda ran as fast as a sixty-year-old man could run, but that was not fast enough. A shot was fired. Aranda was hit in the spine. He staggered and fell, face down.

The men drew five gallons of gasoline from one of the trucks. They dug a small ditch around Aranda's writhing body. The wounded smuggler begged for his life as the men piled branches on him and then poured the gasoline. "Manuel, what you're doing isn't human," Aranda pleaded. Carrasco struck a match and flicked it. The exploding gasoline sent flames shooting high above. If there were cries of agony, they could not have been heard above the roar of the blaze as the pyre sucked up air like a gigantic blast furnace.

Someone had brought some six-packs of Budweiser. They stood around drinking in the light of the fire. When the flames died down, they buried what was left of Aranda, loaded the marijuana into the back of the Carreon truck, secured the load under tarpaulins and drove across the shallow river, avenged.

Domingo Aranda's body was later found buried under a few inches of sand. American police who saw the Polaroids said nothing was left of the trafficker but a charred torso with stumps where the limbs had been. Later, it was rumored that a finger and an ear had been chopped off and sent to Aranda's family in Portales.

Even before the murder, Manuel Carrasco had earned the nickname *La Vibora*—The Snake. Some attribute it to his business methods; others say it was because his eyes had once turned yellow from hepatitis and the coloration had reminded someone of a desert rattlesnake.

Carrasco's parting words to his accomplices following Aranda's death were: "That is what will happen to anyone who tries to cross The Snake."

The murder of Domingo Aranda sealed *La Vibora*'s control over the region's crime on both sides of the border. With the flick of a match, he became the first of a line of powerful and often brutal drug lords of the northern Chihuahua desert.

Chapter Two

COUP d'ETAT

The people of Ojinaga became aware of how powerful Carrasco had become when nothing was done about the murder of Domingo Aranda. Following the killing, Carrasco's influence with authority seemed if anything to be on the upswing. When a new general took over the Ojinaga garrison, Carrasco was frequently seen with him in public. A former cavalry officer with a fondness for racehorses, the general soon was trotting around town mounted on a thoroughbred, a gift from the drug lord. On occasions Manuel Carrasco was also seen with an escort of soldiers. It was clear he was not being taken to jail.

The brigadier had a glass eye, giving rise to jokes that the handicap made him the right man for the job: How much easier to turn a blind eye to all of *La Vibora*'s drug smuggling! The word in Ojinaga was that Carrasco was paying a total of $100,000 a month for protection. No one knew for sure who was the recipient of this alleged sum of money. But the townspeople drew their own conclusions.

The year after Aranda's murder, the people of Ojinaga saw the extent of Manuel Carrasco's power when the city government fell under his influence.

By that year, the border town was in deplorable condition. In less than ten years, it had doubled in size to twenty thousand people, swelled by economic refugees from rural Chihuahua and from the interior of Mexico. Basic municipal services such as electricity, sewage and running water, not to mention paved streets, had not kept pace with the growth. When it rained the streets were churned into mud pits; the rest of the time they were as dusty as the Sahara. Ramshackle squatter neighborhoods were springing up in the southeast part of town. Starvation was evident in some of the outlying villages, while malnutrition was becoming a serious health problem in town. Tax money was not accounted for, at least not to the people. Corrupt government, spawned by the control of Mexico's political system by a single party ever since 1929, was getting the blame.

It was election time and campaigns were gearing up for the mayoral race. Citizens of Ojinaga were given an open invitation to attend a convention sponsored by the National Action Party, a center-right opposition party most commonly called the PAN for its acronym in Spanish, to select an opposition candidate. The party was one of a half-dozen opposition political parties appearing on the ballots in those days, most of them to the left. With its center-right, Catholic-inspired philosophy with similarities to European Christian democracy, this was the only one that the ruling party viewed as a serious challenge in northern Mexico.

The party's adherents taught that Mexico's problems stemmed from a lack of political alternatives and a lack of control by the governed. Though opposition parties were formally allowed to compete in Mexican elections, the political process was largely a charade. Opponents were rarely allowed to win. Even so, the National Action Party taught that democracy in Mexico could eventually be achieved when enough citizens became aware of their civic and human rights and organized for action.

The slate of nominees for the PAN candidate for mayor consisted of a journalist, two merchants and a rancher. The convention took place on a warm Sunday afternoon in February at a popular dance hall on the east slope of downtown Ojinaga. Peasants in cotton shirts and sweat-soaked straw hats rubbed shoulders with merchants in tan *guayaberas* and expensive Resistol hats. Mechanics with grease still under their fingernails sat next to the manicured wives of attorneys.

A fiery speech by one of the opposition party leaders, Antonio Vazquez, an attorney, was typical of the political oratory of the day:

"People of Ojinaga," he began. "Once again a group of free men and women has come together with the goal of achieving an orderly participation in the political life of our community. We cannot take a distance from the great and serious problems that we see all around us in our economic, social, family and work life. For years, we have been submerged in a political, social and economic existence that has been plagued with vices and irregularities. It is a secret to no one that the purpose for which the Revolution was fought, for fair elections, has been violated across the land.

"We all know how we are manipulated. We know that workers, to get jobs or to keep them, must belong to government unions. And we all know that the peasants, to keep the land the government has allowed them to work, must belong to the official union. And we all know what that means when elections come along. They will vote to keep their jobs and keep their land.

"Another of our most pressing concerns is the corruption we see every day among government officials. We see them working their little rackets together. And since we are on the subject, why not add as well that they have formed an alliance with organized crime. And this with the idea of obtaining riches and privileges, leading to a twisted idea of what politics should be all about.

"Fellow citizens, those who are running Mexico today have forgotten that only power that seeks the common good is legitimate power. Political activity has as its goal to satisfy the needs of the people, and not to satisfy the shameless and seemingly limitless greed of the official party."

The speeches continued for several hours. Finally came a show of hands. The winner on the first round was Ernesto Poblano. He was not the most eloquent of the candidates, but he was by far the best known of the four. A merchant originally from a village on the Rio Conchos south of Ojinaga, he had sponsored baseball teams in and around Ojinaga. He had been an accountant in a customs brokerage firm in town before opening a hardware store. He soon became the president of the Chamber of Commerce—all by the time he was twenty seven.

With his selection began the most intensive opposition-party campaign Ojinaga had ever seen. Mexican elections are usually accompanied by charges of ballot-box stuffing, doctored tally sheets, multiple voting by government supporters, deletion of the names of government opponents from voter registration lists, the theft of ballot boxes and numerous other vote-rigging techniques. This election was no different. But of the 6,500 ballots counted, Poblano *still* won by a hundred and fifty votes. Even more surprising, the government recognized the victory—the only one of sixty-seven municipal elections it conceded to an opposition party that year in Chihuahua, and one of the few ever conceded up to that time in Mexico.

But the jubilation soon faded. Even before the new administration took over, rumors spread that Poblano had been laundering money for Manuel Carrasco. Rumors further alleged that Carrasco had given Poblano the capital to buy the hardware store. Another allegation accused Poblano of having first gone secretly to the official party to seek the nomination for mayor but had been told the position was going to a longstanding party loyalist.

The PAN municipal committee held a closed-door meeting with Poblano one month before the October 1974 inauguration day. The mayor-elect was adamant: These were malicious rumors designed to smear him and hurt the opposition party's credibility even before it was able to take office. Poblano convinced the party leadership the charges were unfounded. He was sworn in as mayor.

Several months after the reformist administration was sworn in, however, suspicions about the mayor's ties to *La Vibora* resurfaced when Carrasco began paying frequent visits to Poblano's office. Soon, the young mayor began calling each of the department heads individually into his office to engage them in conversations that at first touched on the problems facing the municipality. But these meetings invariably turned to discussion about drug trafficking. The officials were left with the impression Poblano was trying to feel them out. Carrasco himself was present during at least one of these sessions. As the mayor quizzed a top administrator, the drug lord sat on a sofa with his cowboy hat on his lap, listening politely and smiling ironically now and then, but did not participate in the conversation.

The mayor said to the administrator, "We have to recognize that drug trafficking is a good business, and also that there is nothing that can really be done about it. And anyway, all of the drugs are going to the United States."

The administrator replied: "Yes, but some of it always remains in Mexico where it is consumed. But the fact remains that there can never be any moral or ethical justification for that kind of activity."

The mayor and Manuel Carrasco exchanged smiles. The mayor went on, "Maybe not, but it can be seen as having an historical justification, as the vengeance of a vanquished country that lost half of its territory in a war with the United States—and is still being exploited by the United States."

After the unusual series of meetings, few in the new administration doubted any longer that the young mayor had sold out and possibly had done so long before becoming the opposition-party candidate. Perhaps that was why the government allowed the opposition party to win—he was already their man. Poblano's fellow party members began to press him to resign. He refused.

Meanwhile, the garrison commander made it a point of behaving abusively with the administration's police chief. On several occasions his troops pistol-whipped several of the municipal policemen, leading to a complaint with the governor's office and the commanding general of the Fifth Military Zone in Chihuahua City. The complaints were ignored.

Several months later, the other shoe fell. Following an audience in Chihuahua City with the governor, the mayor publicly resigned from the opposition party and joined the

Institutional Revolutionary Party, the official party. He announced the switch on the radio and published his reasons for it in the weekly papers.

It was like a car bomb going off outside City Hall. The city administration crumbled into a dusty heap, along with the hopes of people who had believed their participation could make a difference. The opposition police chief resigned in protest. All twenty city policemen joined him. Then Poblano demanded the resignation of the city administrator and all the other officials who did not agree with the new political alignment. A new group of people took over City Hall and a new batch of policemen filled the municipal station.

Poblano set about transforming Ojinaga into a drug trafficker's town, with all the trappings. A horse race *aficionado*, he organized some of the biggest match races the town had ever seen. He took it upon himself to invite narco-chieftains from all over Chihuahua for the big events, promising them stable accommodations and riders. He personally invited professional riders, many of them from Albuquerque where horse racing was also a passion. A simple phone call with Poblano's promise of $2,000 for a day's riding was enough to bring a stream of important jockeys to Ojinaga.

It was easy to identify *los narcos*, as drug traffickers are called in Spanish. They had flat semiautomatics stuffed in their waistbands. The more important ones wore bulletproof vests and had two or three bodyguards walking in step with them. They placed the biggest bets—sometimes as much as $50,000—in greenbacks. They ran the best horses, which they brought to the racegrounds in expensive trailers.

The big events were fiestas—thousands of people, makeshift stands serving *carne asada*, corn tortillas and beer. Mariachi groups strolled up and down the grounds. The racetrack was a three-hundred-yard conditioned straightaway equipped with a mechanical two-horse starting gate. The horses would break out of the gate and run between wires strung all the way down the narrow racecourse. At the finish line were judges selected by Poblano with cameras clicking in case of disputes.

The government sent additional soldiers from Chihuahua City for the big races. The troops were not there to shake anybody down for weapons or try to stop the illegal betting. They were there to prevent tempers from flaring and to make sure that no simmering private feuds turned into public blood-baths. With so much weaponry, it could get very ugly.

Ojinaga had never been much to look at. It was poor, it was miserable. In the summer, the town was unbearably hot; in the winter, unbearably cold. Nevertheless, the people of Ojinaga fondly called their town The Pearl of the Desert for its glimmering whiteness against an expanse of pale brown plains and barren red mountains.

It was a pearl that had fallen to the drug traffickers, a booty that in a few short years would belong to Pablo Acosta.

Chapter Three

CONTRABANDISTAS

T he saga of the Acosta family is the story of tens of thousands of Mexican borderland families who learned to survive by their wits in the midst of harsh political, economic and geographic circumstances. When the desert farms failed to produce enough food, migrant farm work in the United States or petty smuggling, sometimes both, allowed many of the *campesino* families to survive.

The Acostas were of a peasant family that had originated in the infertile northeastern desert of Chihuahua and had wandered back and forth across the border for generations in search of work. Pablo's grandfather, Lucas Acosta, was born in 1888 in Fort Stockton, a small West Texas ranching and farming community. Lucas was one of twenty-six children, all but eleven of whom died from disease and hunger. By the time Lucas came along, some of the Acostas had acquired homesteads and settled for good in Fort Stockton.

But Lucas was of the old nomadic stock. For a while he sweated in the mercury mines of Terlingua, on the American side of the Rio Grande, where his first son, Cornelio—Pablo's father—was born in 1906. Even before the Mexican Revolution broke out in 1910 with its promises of land and liberty, Lucas squatted on a ranch 100 miles downstream from Ojinaga, near the village of Santa Elena, on a stony chunk of desert that had been ignored by its pre-revolutionary landowner because of its remoteness. The farm was the site of a natural spring that bubbled refreshingly from the ground.

Pablo's grandfather was a practical man. The farm, which came to be known as *El Chupadero de Lucas*—Lucas' Watering Hole, was an ideal location for someone who did not want to get caught up in the fratricidal chaos of the Revolution. Federal troops and the insurgents decimated one another and reduced anything that stood in their path to rubble during ferocious clashes in towns and villages along the Rio Grande. When the thundering of the Revolution came too close, Lucas took his family to the north side of the river. He was, after all, an American citizen by birth.

The mineral-rich waters of the spring allowed Lucas to raise a few cows and goats and plant corn and beans to feed his children, who soon numbered ten. When not working his own land, he took Cornelio and his other older children on wagon rides to Fort Stockton to sell mesquite wood cut from bushes that grew thirty feet high alongside the Rio Grande.

Smuggling was also part of the Acosta life-style, one of the tactics of survival in the unforgiving borderlands. Lucas knew the routes across the barren plains and mountains of the Texas Big Bend and used them. When the Prohibition era began, Lucas found it profitable to buy jugs of *sotol*, a cactus moonshine, from bootleggers in the mountains of Chihuahua and Coahuila and smuggle them on the backs of mules up to Fort Stockton. The trip took more than a week. Typical of the smugglers of the time, he moved only at night through deep arroyos and gloomy canyons to avoid detection.

When Prohibition ended, Lucas brought Cornelio with him to work in the mountains to harvest candelilla plants and transform the cuttings into wax, an ingredient of chewing gum, cosmetics and shoe polish. It was not illegal to smuggle the amber-colored wax into the United States; it was just illegal to smuggle it out of Mexico.

The candelilla work that Lucas taught Cornelio was dirty and dangerous. It required standing over the smoky fires and the choking fumes of hot sulfuric acid needed to extract the wax from the tenacious mountain plant.

After a day of sweaty labor, in the chill of the night around a campfire, Lucas also taught Cornelio, then a teenager, lessons about economics and risk-taking. Both men were illiterate but far from ignorant. The wax industry was tightly controlled by a union in Coahuila, Lucas explained. One had to be a member of the union to be able to work candelilla. The poor could get a permit, all right, but then they had to join the government-controlled Candelilla Workers Union and sell all the wax to the union buyers. Yet across the river, the Americans paid twice what the union offered for each pound of wax. "Who should make the extra money?" Lucas asked. "The poor candelilla worker, or the Mexican government which turns around and sells much of the wax to the Americans anyway?"

Lucas and Cornelio spent one or two weeks at a time in the mountains gathering candelilla plants and extracting the wax. They worked at night to escape detection by the *forestales*, the Mexican rangers who enforced candelilla laws. To protect the union's interests in candelilla, the government sent in these well-armed agents to patrol in trucks. The rangers pulled a trailer with saddled horses. Whenever they spotted smoke in the mountains, they mounted up and fell upon the sooty peasants like U.S. Treasury agents upon Appalachian bootleggers.

With methodical fury the *forestales* would shoot all the burros between the eyes, pepper the 55-gallon storage drums with bullets, burn the wooden packsaddles, torch the stick huts and confiscate the wax. Then the raiders would take their prisoners tied together in chains to Saltillo, Coahuila. The penalty for illegal harvesting of candelilla was a jail sentence that ranged from six months to two years, depending on who was chief and who was Indian. What angered the peasants most was that the *forestales* sometimes kept the wax for themselves.

The Mexican G-men would also stake out the routes used by smugglers and pounce on them as they came down from the mountains. But Lucas, who knew the mountains better than anyone, showed Cornelio how to outsmart the agents and get the wax safely to the general stores at Cerro Chino, Castolon or Lajitas, hamlets on the American side that welcomed the wax traders.

Pablo Acosta would later proudly tell how his father and Macario Vazquez, the most famous of the candelilla smugglers, once shot it out with *forestales* in the mountains above the river village of Santa Elena. No one was killed or even wounded in the exchange, and Macario and Cornelio got through with their wax. But the Mexican rangers learned to fear the two men. If there was a lesson Pablo Acosta learned from the stories, it was the utility of inspiring fear.

When the Acosta men returned to *El Chupadero* with their money and wild tales, Pablo would sit with his thin arms wrapped around his legs, chin on his knees, eagerly listening to the stories. Like any boy, he was thrilled by the accounts of cunning and valor, and he visualized himself on horseback fighting the *forestales*. He longed to accompany the men on their journeys.

It was near this small river farm that had nurtured two generations of Acostas that Pablo was born, on January 26, 1937. His mother Dolores was taken to the nearby village of Santa Elena to give birth in an adobe shack attended by village women. By the time he was five, Pablo was one of eight children, and at times there were as many as thirty people living in the farm's two stone hovels. Dolores Acosta had not only Pablo and her other children to care for. When the men left, sometimes for months to work in fields near Fort Stockton or Lovington, she also had to watch over a swarm of Cornelio's younger brothers and sisters. The men took with them the children who were old enough for fieldwork but left everyone else behind.

Dolores delegated responsibility. She cooked on the cast-iron stove fueled with mesquite wood and took care of the girls and the most recently born. Hermenegilda, one of Cornelio's younger sisters, took care of Pablo and Pablo's older brother Juan.

Pablo was Hermenegilda's favorite. One of her evening duties was to round up the small herd of cows and goats that managed to wander away from the farm to nibble on the dried-out desert grass in the surrounding hills. Hermenegilda often carried Pablo on her shoulders as the two gaily skipped up the hills after the vagrant *animalitos*. Pablo always took a goat's jawbone with him as a toy pistol. As they walked through the mesquite-covered hills herding the animals, he would pretend to shoot at the goats, at the shadows cast by the mesquite and yucca and at the jackrabbits scared out of hiding by their approach.

The boy also liked to draw attention to himself. He frequently ran away from the house to hide in one of the arroyos just so everyone would have to come looking for him.

Hermenegilda was always anxious about Pablo and Juan. The brothers were always getting into trouble. Pablo's mother once scolded Hermenegilda: "Why waste your tears on them? They're going to do what they want, no matter what. I don't have the energy to worry about them. God will look after them." When Hermenegilda got married and moved away, Pablo cried bitterly. "Who is going to take care of me?" he sniffed.

About 1948, a plague of hoof and mouth disease began decimating livestock on both sides of the border. Though the Acosta livestock was healthy, the Mexican government pressured the family to destroy the animals. In exchange, the family was promised land at Providencia, a government *ejido*—communal farm—on the highlands of the Sierra Ponce fifteen miles farther south of *El Chupadero de Lucas*.

Pablo's father decided on the move in part from the loss of the animals, but also out of concern for his children's education. He was unable to read and understood the disadvantages. The nearest school was in Providencia where he had been sending Pablo and Juan for several years so they could learn to read and write. The brothers rode a burro up to the highland village. During the week, they stayed with relatives while attending school, and then returned to *El Chupadero* on the weekend.

Providencia was a collection of stone barracks that had been part of a military garrison used by one faction or another during the revolutionary years. The government finally abandoned the garrison and turned it into an *ejido*. Settlers moved in. Like *El Chupadero*, Providencia had a natural spring that gushed from the ground, providing water for cooking and washing, for growing beans and corn and for watering their small herd of goats.

The four other families living there at the time had no objection to a fifth moving in, especially a family with so many children. The one-room school was entitled to a government teacher as long as the enrollment did not drop below a certain number. The numerous Acosta children kept the enrollment well above the cutoff point.

The Acostas moved into one of the dilapidated stone buildings, a low three-room stone hut with a dirt floor and a roof so low one risked a lump on the head by standing up abruptly. The chinks between the rocks were plastered with mud. The roof was held up with cottonwood beams covered with a thick carpet of sotol stocks tied together with strips of yucca leaves. On top of that was a layer of caliche—hard desert clay—mixed with straw to keep out the rain.

Ejidos like Providencia were a product of the Revolution, created when the government tried to adapt much of post-revolutionary Mexico's agricultural land to a pre-Colombian system of land use. Under the system, *campesinos* could use the land but not own it. If they failed to work their parcel for a period of two years, it reverted to the government. In theory, the system was intended to prevent the accumulation of land into big properties, one of the causes of the Mexican Revolution. But as a system of agricultural production, it was a dismal failure and generated much of the rural poverty in which the Acosta family was caught up.

During the late 1940s, when Cornelio would work in the United States he would take all of the older children with him: Carmen, Aurora, Maria, Juan and Pablo. They stayed with family members somewhere along the migration trail. They would spend three months in the *limpia,* the weeding of the cotton fields. Because of the nature of migrant life, the Acosta family was separated for at least six months of the year.

The transition of Cornelio's family from Mexico to the United States was slow but progressive. By the early 1950s, family members had settled into communities along the migrant trail. If they went back to Mexico, it was only to visit.

It *was* hard to go home again. When he became an adult, Juan Acosta journeyed back to *El Chupadero de Lucas* and tried to lay claim to it. But the government had already taken it over and converted it into an *ejido*.

By 1958, Pablo had been on the migrant trail nine years with his father, brother and sisters. They worked on farms around Fort Stockton, Odessa and Lovington.

In October of that year, Cornelio was murdered in Fort Stockton. Pablo and his father had gone into Sandy's Lounge outside town for a beer. As they leaned against the bar talking someone tapped Pablo's father on the shoulder and said, "Hey, Cornelio, someone needs to talk to you out front."

Leaving Pablo in the bar, Cornelio walked out with the other man to the gravel parking lot where several cars and pickup trucks were parked at an angle. Seconds later, a gunshot rang out. Pablo ran out to find his father lying face up in the gravel with a bullet hole through his forehead. The son sprinted after a pickup truck he saw racing out of the parking lot but he was only able to get close enough to read the license plate.

Fort Stockton police traced the truck to a ranch hand named Pablo Baiza and arrested him. During the trial, the motive for the murder became clear: the Acosta and the Baiza clans had been killing each other back and forth in a blood feud that had started years before. Cornelio was the latest casualty on the Acosta side.

Travis Crumpton, Baiza's attorney, was a flamboyant West Texas barrister. Outlining the history of the feud, he explained that an Acosta had killed a Baiza clansman years before back in the village of Santa Elena. The killer hung the body from the rafters of an adobe hut, then locked a couple of hungry dogs inside. The attorney waved photos that the jury never got to see, but which presumably showed what was left of the body.

Crumpton went on with the family histories: "The two families emigrated and settled in West Texas; but they were rural Mexicans and didn't leave their feuding behind. There were more killings on both sides. Cornelio may or may not have had anything to with these killings, but *that's not the point*," Crumpton argued.

The lawyer leaned against the rail and encouraged the jurors to put themselves into the mind of the defendant. "Pablo Baiza was honor-bound to avenge his family's name. And so one day someone ran to him and told him that Cornelio Acosta was inside Sandy's Lounge. Pablo Baiza just did what he was expected to do by tradition."

Pablo Baiza had put an *"X"* on all the court documents that required his signature. He was a hard-working hand at the MacDonald Ranch down by Gervin. His face was sunburnt and his hands callused and gnarled from years of roping and branding cattle and sheep, mending fences and other strenuous ranch chores. Most of the twelve men of the jury were ranchers and knew a good, reliable worker when they saw one. Rancher MacDonald, Baiza's boss, even testified as to his worker's good character and first-rate performance on the job.

Pablo Acosta testified too, how he ran out of Sandy's Lounge to find his father with a bullet hole in his forehead and how he ran after the pickup truck and took down the killer's license plate.

The jury convicted Baiza of murder with "malice aforethought" and recommended five years probation, which was granted. Baiza had served three months in jail—all of it while waiting to come to trial.

The outcome of the trial did not do anything to lessen the motivation for the feud. Pablo Acosta never told anyone if he planned revenge on his own, but kinfolk on each side continued to trade threats for years. A Baiza was murdered not long after, in another Fort Stockton bar.

Even before his father's death, Pablo had been turning into a rowdy. His rap sheet showed him at age twenty charged with drunken driving and disorderly conduct in Lovington, a New Mexico farming community where he had lived on and off since 1949. Cleto, one of Pablo's paternal uncles, and Cleto's wife Saturnina lived in a narrow, aluminum-skin trailer on Chaves Street, on the east side of the Union Pacific railroad tracks that divided the Anglo community from the small but growing number of migrant Mexican families settling inside the city limits. Pablo lived in farmworker housing during the week, and in a small wooden shack behind the trailer on the weekend.

During this time, Pablo worked on farms in the spring, summer and fall and labored in the cotton gins in the winter, cleaning and baling cotton. Pablo was quiet young man—unless he got drunk. With a few drinks in him he was ready to whip anybody. The murder of his father aggravated his behavior; so did the treatment he encountered.

Hispanics in New Mexico were setting trends in the 1950s by making headway into state and national politics, but this came about in spite of tensions between the old against the new that could pop up in telling incongruities. The time a middle-aged Hispanic man sat down in a steakhouse in Tatum, a ranching town twenty miles up the road from Lovington, is still remembered. He asked for a menu but was bluntly told "Listen, feller. We don't serve Messkins here." The restaurant owner did not realize until later that the man he refused service was Dennis Chaves, then a United States senator from New Mexico.

Immigrants felt the tensions even more. For *braceros,* documented seasonal workers, haircuts could not be had from downtown Lovington barbershops, only from the Mexican *peluqueros* on the other side of the tracks. Mexicans did not shop in Anglo stores for fear of hostile stares and rude treatment. The barriers were invisible but as forceful as a magnetic field.

This hostility may account for Pablo Acosta's arrest in March 1961 at the Steakhouse, a popular restaurant and bar in Lovington where Mexicans did not go. By then Pablo had had a half-dozen run-ins with the law for drinking and fighting. Pablo was cocky and defiant and he went into the Steakhouse bar with an "I'll-show-you" attitude. He began drinking, got into a fistfight, and ended up throwing a pitcher of beer through a plate-glass window. A black-and-white

Polaroid taken of him at the Lovington Police Department showed a young man wearing a white T-shirt, with slicked back hair and a defiantly tipsy smirk on his face. He was fined $25 and given a ten-day suspended sentence.

None of the misdemeanors weighed heavily enough to prevent him from being formally granted United States citizenship. Usually, when he went back to Mexico to visit, it was simple enough to return to the United States just by wading across the river at Santa Elena or at some other village along the river. But in 1960 he was stopped by American immigration when he crossed the international bridge between Ojinaga

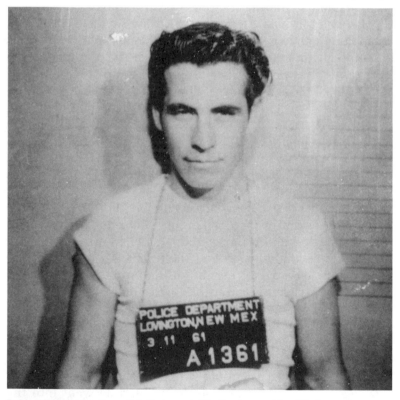

Pablo Acosta at the time of his first arrest. The Lovington, New Mexico, police report reads, "Subject threw a pitcher of beer through a plate glass window at the Smokehouse bar. Fined $25.00 and given a 10-day suspended sentence." (Photo courtesy of the Lovington Police Department)

and Presidio. Pablo could not prove he was a citizen or a permanent resident, so the Immigration and Naturalization Service deported him.

To avoid future border-crossing difficulties, he applied for recognition as an American citizen. In his application he argued that he had a right to citizenship by virtue of his father's birth in the United States. He had the documents to prove that his father was born in the mining town of Terlingua, Texas, on September 16, 1906. An INS judge in New Mexico agreed with him. In January 1964 Pablo Acosta was issued a certificate recognizing him as a citizen of the United States.

Pablo worked on New Mexico farms during the heyday of a local oil boom that caused labor shortages in agriculture and construction, fueling a migration of workers from Mexico. A vast pool of the gooey gold was discovered in the region in 1950 and soon wells were being drilled everywhere. Anglo workers abandoned the farms in droves for higher paying oil-field jobs. Cotton was booming at the same time. The corrugated-iron factories that housed the cotton gins could churn out a million or more bales in the fall and winter months. The scale of the cotton production and the shortage of labor created by the oilfields drew thousands of workers from Mexico. Documented workers were brought in by the truckload from Ojinaga and other border towns to work at the huge farms. More came illegally.

On Saturday afternoons the cotton farmers in the Lovington area had the workers driven into town in open trucks. The dusty field hands were dropped off in front of La Poblanita, a tortilla factory owned by a long-established Mexican-American family. With a café and pool hall in front, showers and a bunkhouse in back, it was the most popular place in town for the new immigrants.

Besides the café, the only entertainment in Lovington for Mexican workers was provided by a Spanish-language movie theater, the few east-side bars and an occasional dance. Many of the farmhands drove into town for the afternoon. They made purchases for the week and drove back to the farm the same day. The single men, including Pablo, stayed the night and partied. Occasionally the drinking led to fighting and the fighting led to arrests.

One Saturday night in April 1964 Pablo got into a gunfight in front of La Poblanita, his most serious trouble to date, and the first of many gunfights that would mark his life. It started as an argument with several other young men over a girl. Pablo challenged, "You want to fight about it? You follow me out of town and we'll fight."

Instead of following, one of the young men fired a shot while Pablo was backing out of the parking lot, creasing his cheek. Pablo fired back through the rear window of his car with a .22-caliber rifle. He hit one of the men in the chest.

It was considered the most sensational shooting in Lovington in a long time. At least twenty-four bullets flew, many of them wildly, The "affray" was written up *in The Lovington Daily Leader* with the headline GUN BATTLE LEADS TO FOUR ARRESTS.

Pablo was charged with assault with a deadly weapon and spent several months in jail waiting for trial. His aunts brought him fresh fruit and occasionally spicy Mexican dishes at the old county jail. Finally the charge was reduced to illegal use of a firearm and he was given a ninety-day sentence. He ended up serving thirty days.

It was about that time that Pablo married Olivia Baeza, a plump Mexican girl from Ojinaga whom he had met in Odessa, a Texas agricultural and oil town. They were married at the Catholic church in downtown Ojinaga. The entire town was invited to the wedding and to the reception in an *ejido* outside Ojinaga enlivened with mariachis and horse races. The newlyweds returned to the United States, settling in Odessa.

Besides fieldwork, construction was about the only kind of work available for someone like Pablo, an immigrant with the equivalent of a fourth-grade education

Pablo did not have anything to do with drug smuggling during that time, though trafficking on a relatively small scale had been taking place in the region for decades. The scale of

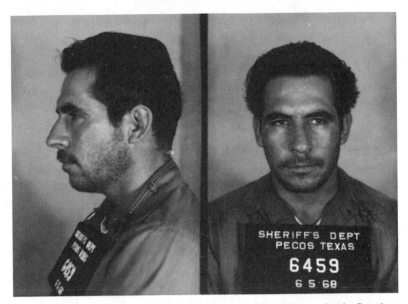

On May 28, 1968, Acosta smuggled narcotics into the United States for the first time. He was caught near Marfa, Texas, with one ounce of heroin attached to his upper arm. He was tried in the federal court in Pecos, Texas, and spent the next five years at at Fort Leavenworth. (Photo courtesy of the Reeves County Sheriff's Department)

the activity at that time can be gauged from the local newspapers. Several days after the Poblanita shootout, *The Lovington Daily Leader* carried a story about a major drug bust in Lovington. In bold eight-column headlines it screamed the news: *Five* pounds of marijuana had been seized in the biggest sting ever in Lovington and several members of a Mexican narcotics ring had been arrested.

That was 1964. The ruinous affair between Americans and drugs was just barely under way. The cadres of dealers and suppliers, like the armies of users, had not even been recruited. They stood in the shadows, waiting for a future nobody could have predicted.

Pablo's call came several years later while working on construction sites in oil-booming Odessa. He became friendly with some construction workers from Ojinaga who boasted about supplementing their incomes through small-time smuggling. Pablo was now the main support for his mother and younger brothers and sisters. He had his own family to support as well. Money was tight.

Many of the construction workers had come from *campesino* families like Pablo's, families that had smuggled contraband of one kind or another, in one direction or another, over the generations. Odessa was still the border. Smuggling was still a way of life. It sounded so easy! It was just a matter of bringing a stash back to Odessa after a weekend visit to relatives in Ojinaga.

One day Pablo drove down to Ojinaga with the intention of smuggling drugs back into the United States; it was all arranged. All he had to do was drive down to Ojinaga to pick it up. He had never smuggled anything before. It was a new and exciting experience. He could feel the adrenaline rush as they secured the heroin to his upper arm. He was a runner, a mule, and he was going to transport it and—when it was delivered—collect his fee. He knew what would happen if he was caught.

He was about to get caught.

It was May 28, 1968. While Pablo was being readied in Ojinaga with the heroin, someone else across the bridge in Presidio was tipping off American authorities. The informant rushed into the U.S. Customs enforcement office behind the international port of entry, barely a hundred yards from Ojinaga. The informant did not know the name of the drug courier, but he gave a description of the smuggler, the car he would be driving and the license plate number. The informant was not sure if the drug runner would pick up the heroin in Ojinaga or Presidio, but he would soon find out, he told his American contacts.

Three hours later the U.S. Customs informant was back at the enforcement office to report an urgent development: the Mexican smuggler had already met an Ojinaga dealer somewhere in Presidio. The smuggler was already at this moment driving north on Highway 67.

It took a customs officer and two border patrolmen two hours to catch up to the vehicle near Marfa. The Border Patrol there had already been alerted and was waiting.

Pablo's heart jumped when he saw the red lights flashing behind him. His mind started racing. Just stay cool. Just stay calm. Act like a dumb wetback. You don't know nothing. You're going to Odessa. You just visited your sister in Ojinaga. They're stupid pendejos. They won't find it. They can't find it.

The feds ordered him out of the car. They made him lean against the hood, both hands forward. Pablo felt them pat him down, first his legs, then his crotch, then move up his torso and down his arms. They found the ounce of heroin inside a balloon secured to his upper arm by a rubber band. Before removing the heroin, they lifted his arm up and snapped a photograph.

He was tried in the federal district court in Pecos and was sentenced to eight years in the federal penitentiary. In an appeal, his attorney argued that the authorities did not have probable cause to search him without a warrant. The appeal was denied. Pablo was thirty-one years old.

For a beginner, he wasn't having much luck.

Chapter Four

THE UNITED STATES
v. PABLO ACOSTA

Pablo got out of the federal penitentiary three years early for good behavior. The first four and a half years of the eight-year sentence he spent at Fort Leavenworth, Kansas, making brooms in prison shops by day and taking advantage of the adult education program at night. He enjoyed studying but later boasted that he learned more just talking to the attorneys, accountants and other professionals he had shared jail space with. The final six months he spent at La Tuna, the federal penitentiary near El Paso.

The prisons provided another type of education. When he was released in 1973, Pablo Acosta had all the connections he needed south of the border to pick up where he had left off. Even better, he could now also tap into numerous Anglo and Chicano crime networks north of the Rio Grande through friendships he had formed in prison. With those networks, someone who had done five years in the federal pen on a heroin conviction carried a respectable calling card.

One of his most important friends was Martin "Shorty" Lopez, a heroin dealer from Odessa whom Pablo met in the penitentiary. Shorty, who took his nickname from his jockey build, was a self-proclaimed third-generation wetback. Born near Corpus Christi and raised in the Odessa area, he had picked cotton and worked in the cotton gins. Shorty arrived at Fort Leavenworth nine months after Pablo had started his sentence. But they were both released about the same time and continued their friendship.

Pablo's first task when he got out of jail was simply to get ahead. He was thirty-six years old and had nothing. His wife Olivia and their daughter Karen had stayed with close friends in Ojinaga while he was behind bars. He brought his family back up to Odessa, moving into a gray two-bedroom rental house in the lower-middle-class neighborhood where his mother and some of his brothers and sisters lived.

Following his release, he got work repairing roofs and soon after began subcontracting jobs from former employers. Even though the money was good, Pablo had made a decision while still in jail to get into the drug business. He knew there was plenty of money to be made. Why be discouraged by a setback? Why not learn from the experience and be wiser the next time? Why not let other people take the risks smuggling drugs from Mexico? It was safer to set up a distribution business in the United States. In his spare time Pablo started going back and forth to Ojinaga to establish his drug connections.

By the time Pablo was released from jail, Domingo Aranda had already been burned to death on the riverbank outside of Ojinaga. Manuel Carrasco was now the drug lord of the border town and the principal connection for anyone dealing in heroin or marijuana in Odessa and Midland. Pablo began obtaining drugs either directly from Manuel, or through Shorty Lopez, who went to work for Carrasco.

Odessa police informants soon identified Pablo, the roofing subcontractor, as an up-and-coming heroin and marijuana dealer. The informants rode with undercover police around town to point out Pablo's gray bungalow and the homes of his drug contacts. Soon, Odessa police officers began stopping Pablo on any pretext to check his driver's license and look him over.

Whenever these stops occurred, Pablo had a way of politely straining his ear, as if to try to understand the police officers better. "I sorry, I no speak English" was a refrain he found useful at those moments, even though he understood English as well as anyone else.

Pablo got in trouble with the law again in November 1974,

not for narcotics but for beating up a former Ector County commissioner over an unpaid debt for a roofing job. The ex-politician was a partner in a roofing company that had subcontracted a job to Pablo and a dispute had arisen over money. As security, Pablo took one of the roofing company's dump trucks and a gas-fired tarpot, hiding the equipment behind an automobile upholstery shop that Shorty had set up as a front for dealing heroin. Pablo called the ex-county official, telling him to come to the upholstery shop so they could work out the problem. But when the former commissioner entered the shop, Pablo, his brother Hector Manuel and a third man jumped him, beating him with riding whips and rubber hoses. Pablo was arrested, photographed and then released on a $1,500 bond.

Pablo soon realized it was time to move away from Odessa. His home was under constant surveillance, as was Shorty's upholstery shop and other residences and businesses from which Odessa heroin dealers operated. After considering his options, Pablo moved his family across the state line to Eunice, a one-stoplight farm-and-oil town in southeastern New Mexico. For the following two years, he lived quietly with his family in a two-bedroom house on 19th Street next to the playground of a Baptist church.

In Eunice, Pablo set up another roofing company and invested in heavy equipment. He bought a dump truck for hauling away old shingles and debris from job sites, a gas-fired tarpot for melting blocks of tar and other roofing equipment. He was a good organizer and did not mind getting his hands dirty. The business brought in money and was an ideal front. Rooftops were secure places for working out deals. Dressed in work clothes, buyers would climb up to the roof with him and talk business. They were out of earshot and it was easy to keep an eye on the neighborhood from the top of a building.

Though he had moved from Odessa, a two-hour drive from Eunice, narcotics investigators had not lost track of him. Word quickly spread to the New Mexico State Police about a heroin dealer named Pablo in southeastern New Mexico who could move a pound of heroin at a time.

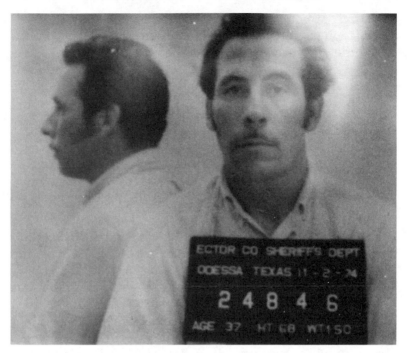

This mugshot was taken on November 2, 1974, after Pablo Acosta and one of his younger brothers beat up a former Ector County commissioner for allegedly failing to pay Acosta, then a roof-repair subcontractor, for a job in Odessa. (Photo courtesy of the Ector County Sheriff's Department)

Cunning and careful, Pablo might have continued dealing from Eunice indefinitely if it had not been for a chance drug bust at John F. Kennedy International Airport in New York, 2,000 miles away from rural Eunice. New York narcotics officers arrested a dope dealer named Julio with several ounces of cocaine. The dealer was from southeastern New Mexico. He owned a private security firm in Hobbs, an hour away from Eunice, and had a host of drug connections throughout the United States.

In the treachery of the drug world, Julio worked out a light sentence in exchange for his help in busting one of his big-time heroin contacts in southeastern New Mexico, Delfino Rendon. A Hobbs barber in his early thirties, Rendon had dark skin, a baby face, pure-white teeth, curly hair and a pleasant personality. He had worked as a barber in downtown Hobbs until getting hooked on heroin. To support his own habit, he started developing his own string of addicts and was believed to be capable of distributing a pound of heroin per week. The American agents believed that, directly or indirectly, he was getting the heroin from Manuel Carrasco, the drug lord of Ojinaga.

The DEA flew Julio to New Mexico to set up a deal with Rendon. Julio convinced Rendon that he had a couple of important buyers from New York who needed a kilogram of black-tar heroin. Meanwhile, New Mexico narcotics officers began following the curly-headed heroin dealer to see who he would contact to fill such a significant order. They were stunned when they followed him to Eunice and watched him walk into a white two-bedroom home on 19th Street, the home of Pablo Acosta.

The surveillance officers were ecstatic when Rendon left Acosta's residence a half-hour later. They followed ex-barber back to Hobbs. Pablo, they believed, was a bigger dealer than Rendon. The preceding year, an undercover agent had come close to buying three pounds of heroin from Pablo, but the deal fell through when Acosta became suspicious.

Later that day the narcotics agents were certain that Pablo Acosta was going to be the source of the heroin. Shortly after returning from his visit to Pablo, Rendon called the client Julio had set him up with—a DEA agent posing as one of the New York buyers. "My people can put a pound together right away. Can you come down tomorrow?" Rendon asked the undercover agent.

The next morning the two undercover agents arrived in Hobbs in an orange sedan. Lester Tuell, the DEA agent posing as the buyer, was a tall, lanky Midwesterner with curly brown hair. Tony Riccio, a state narcotics officer, was dark-haired and lean with a Brooklyn accent. They met Rendon at a restaurant for lunch. Following lunch, Riccio went to the men's room. Rendon followed.

"Lemme see whatcha got," Riccio grunted, exaggerating his New York accent. Rendon showed him a sample of the heroin. Riccio looked at it closely and grunted his approval. He showed Rendon some cash.

The undercover agents followed the curly haired ex-barber to Eunice. They could see Pablo's dump truck parked outside. The agents watched Rendon walk up to the front door and knock. The door opened and Rendon disappeared inside.

Five minutes later the agents saw the door open again and Rendon came out. He walked up their orange sedan and stuck his curly head through the window. "It's on. We'll meet you a couple miles outside of town," Rendon told the undercover officers. He gave them instructions on how to get to a deep pit that had once been mined for caliche, the hard white clay used to surface the oilfield roads outside Eunice. Next to the pit were low sand hills covered with desert scrub, and oilfields with pumps and small storage tanks.

"Wait for us on the highway. We'll be by about four o'clock," Rendon said.

The surveillance officers had thought the heroin transaction would take place at some home or building in either Eunice or Hobbs, or at a bar. They had prepared meticulous diagrams of each likely site showing the location of the doors, windows, and other details that would be important information in case someone started shooting. But those preparations were now useless. Instead, they called for a DEA Cessna from Albuquerque to monitor the operation and coordinate the action from the air. A signal was agreed upon. Riccio or Tuell would open the trunk of the car as soon as the deal was done. The aircraft would then radio to the half-dozen backup agents, both federal and state, to move in.

After going back into Pablo's house after talking with the undercover agents, Rendon was jumpy. Pablo knew what it meant. He gave him a gram and waited until the curly-headed dealer rolled his sleeve back down. As they drove out the highway past the cemetery, Rendon was super-relaxed. Pablo pulled a glass jar from under his coat and put it on the seat between them. Inside the jar was a pound of "black tar" heroin. It was dark brown and looked as inoffensive as modeling clay. A few weeks earlier, it had been gummy opium in a laboratory somewhere in the mountains of Chihuahua or Sinaloa. Refined into crude heroin, it had been transported through Parral to Manuel Carrasco's territory along the Rio Grande and finally smuggled into the United States hidden in the underside of some vehicle and delivered to Pablo. Since it was Rendon's deal, it was now his responsibility to hand the heroin to the buyers and collect the money while Pablo stayed at a distance.

They spotted Tuell and Riccio sitting in the orange sedan next to the entrance to the caliche pit. Rendon turned onto the dirt road and the orange sedan followed close behind. They parked near the caliche pit and everyone got out.

It was late November 1976, and a cold breeze was blowing across the desert. As Rendon walked up to the two buyers, Pablo pulled his straw cowboy hat low to cover his eyes. He leaned against the cab of Rendon's pickup and watched over the hood. He was nervous. Usually he was extremely careful about customers, dealing only with people he had known for a long time. He knew Julio, he knew Rendon, he knew other local dealers. But this was the first time he had laid eyes on the two Anglos.

Was this a mistake, Pablo wondered?

Rendon and the two men were standing at the rear of the orange sedan. Rendon flashed a smile as he handed the jar to Riccio. The other undercover agent opened a vial to perform a quick field test—standard procedure among buyers who want to make sure they are getting what they are paying for. Tuell dropped a pinch of the heroin into the liquid and shook it. All three men watched the vial intently and smiled when the solution turned deep violet.

"The shit looks okay to me," Tuell said.

Rendon was always nervous at such moments but also exquisitely happy. Brokering a deal meant a ten percent cut for him, and money meant a continuation of the opiate-induced serenity he craved so badly. He wanted to get the cash and get the hell out of there.

That is when Riccio popped open the trunk. A mile up, the spotter in the DEA Cessna saw Riccio's signal through binoculars and radioed for the backup vehicles to move in. Rendon and the two undercover agents, meanwhile, bent down as if to pull the money out of the trunk. Just as Rendon bent to get a look at the cash, Riccio shoved a police badge in his face and pointed a revolver at him.

"New Mexico State Police. You're under arrest, Delfino. Get your fucking face to the ground."

Pablo was ten yards away. Rendon's pickup truck separated him and the other men. He could not hear clearly what the Anglos were saying, but he realized something was wrong when he saw Rendon abruptly straighten up. He saw a gun in the hand of the dark-haired man with the New York accent. It was all happening so fast, Pablo did not know what to think. Was it a rip off? Was it a bust? Pablo pulled a .38-caliber revolver from his belt when he saw the men shoving Rendon to the ground behind the orange sedan.

Riccio yelled, "Police! Get your hands up!"

If Pablo even thought about shooting, he quickly changed his mind when he saw a van barreling up the dirt road from the main highway. He turned around and sprinted into the sand hills, running in and out of the low mesquite and greasewood bushes. His cowboy hat flew off as he ran. He heard Riccio shout, "Stop, or I'll shoot!" He kept running. A gun sang out and Pablo heard the bullet whing into the sand just in front of him. He kept running. Another heroin conviction and he knew he would be in jail for twenty years.

One of the officers in the van was a New Mexico State Police narcotics officer, Richard Paz. Paz had been the lead officer during the surveillance and had followed Rendon to Pablo's house in Eunice. He had wanted to arrest Pablo for a long time, and now the bastard was running off through the desert. Paz had been born in a village upriver from Ojinaga and was half-Tarahumara Indian, a tribe from the mountains of Chihuahua famous for their speed and running endurance over harsh terrain. He threw down his walkie-talkie and sprinted after Pablo. He could see Pablo's head bobbing up and down in the distance and began closing the distance between them. Pablo was in good physical condition, but he was thirty-nine years old, fourteen years older than the Mexican-born narcotics officer now closing in on him.

When they had run nearly a mile through the low brush-studded sand hills, the New Mexico narcotics officer saw Pablo turn and take aim from a distance of only fifty yards. Paz swiftly dropped to his knees and shot first. Pablo took off again, but the state narc lost him in the brush and sand hills.

The rapidly approaching darkness and Pablo's cunning saved him from capture. The heroin deal at the caliche pit took place about five in the afternoon, when the sun had already set. While the DEA airplane droned overhead, the police combed the area until it was too dark to see. They were sure he was still somewhere in the sand hills, but any further searching would be reckless: He had a revolver and it was clear he was willing to use it. An hour after Pablo ran from the caliche pit, the police called off the hunt.

A month later a federal grand jury in Albuquerque delivered an indictment charging Pablo Acosta, Delfino Rendon, Delfino's brother and a fourth person with possession of heroin with the intention of distributing and for aiding and abetting. Everybody but Pablo went to jail.

Later Richard Paz learned that Pablo had made inquiries about him. Pablo wanted to know if that "young Mexican boy" was *chota*—a cop—or just someone who had been trying to rip him off.

"He's *chota*," a horse trainer familiar with both sides of the border told Pablo. "I've seen him around before in Hobbs."

"Then you go and tell him something for me," Pablo said. "You tell that fucker I could have had him if I wanted. The son of a bitch almost stepped on me, that's how close he came to me. And tell him I'm thankful he was Mexican. If I had to get screwed, at least it was by a Mexican."

Paz learned from the horse trainer just how Pablo had escaped. A few minutes after Paz shot at him, Pablo crawled backward into a narrow corrugated pipe that had been put under one of the caliche roads for drainage. He pulled a tumbleweed in front of it to hide his face. Moments later Paz stepped close enough for Pablo to reach out and grab his ankle. Later that night, after his pursuers abandoned the search, Pablo walked to the highway and thumbed a ride to Odessa. From there one of his cousins drove him to Ojinaga.

Years later, Pablo would cast the incident in a different light, giving associates and visitors a self-serving version of the incident. He just happened to be along for the ride with Rendon, and it was Rendon doing a deal without telling his friend what was going on that caused him to get caught in the middle. As an ex-con with a prior heroin conviction, he had no choice but to flee.

"The only black tar I ever dealt with was the kind you use to waterproof roofs," he would claim to a visitor.

The close call with the law forced Pablo to flee to Mexico. The federal indictment made it a good idea for him to stay there.

It turned out to be a good business move. In 1976 the Ojinaga underworld, until then under the control of Manuel Carrasco, was in turmoil and full of opportunities for an enterprising, hard-working and sometimes ruthless drug dealer with loads of connections in the United States and an understanding of how things worked in both countries.

Over the next few years, Pablo set about creating a narcotics empire of enormous reach, one that would place him in the ranks of the top drug lords of Mexico.

Chapter Five

LA PLAZA

"¿Quién está manejando la plaza?"

In Mexico this question is generally understood to mean "Who's in charge?" or "Who's running the show?"

In its most literal sense, the word *"la plaza"* refers to a place of gathering—a town square, a marketplace, a bullring. Thus *"la plaza de armas"* is a parade ground, *"la plaza de toros"* is a bullring, and so forth. Colloquially, however, *la plaza* refers to a police authority and a police commander's jurisdiction. And so the inquiry "Who's in charge here?' would bring the answer, *"Comandante* So-and-So."

To the Mexican drug underworld, however, the question has another meaning, a very precise and well understood meaning. When someone in the drug trafficking world asks who has the *plaza*, it is interpreted to mean, "Who has the concession to run the narcotics racket?"

For decades Mexican informants tried to explain the idea to their law enforcement contacts in the United States. When somebody had the *plaza*, it meant that he was paying an authority or authorities with sufficient power to ensure that he would not be bothered by state or federal police or by the military. The protection money went up the ladder, with percentages shaved off at each level up the chain of command until reaching the Grand Protector or the Grand Protectors in the scheme.

To stay in the good graces of his patrons in power, the *plaza* holder had a dual obligation: to generate money for his protectors and to lend his intelligence gathering abilities by fingering the independent operators—those narcotics traffickers and drug growers who tried to avoid paying the necessary tribute. The independents were the ones who got busted by the Mexican Federal Judicial Police, the Mexican equivalent of the FBI, or by the army, providing Mexico with statistics to show it was involved in authentic drug enforcement. That most of the seized narcotics were then recycled—sold to favored trafficking groups or outrightly smuggled by police groups—was irrelevant. The seizures were in fact made and there were headlines and photos to prove it.

Usually, the authorities would protect their man from rivals; other times they would not, preferring a variety of natural selection to determine who should run the *plaza*. If the authorities arrested or killed the *plaza* holder, it was usually because he had stopped making payments, or because his name had started to appear in the press too frequently and the trafficker had become a liability. Sometimes international pressure became so strong that the government was forced to take action against a specific individual—regardless of how much money he was generating.

It was a system that enabled the Mexican political and police structures to keep a lid on drugs and profit handsomely from it at the same time.

When Pablo Acosta fled New Mexico for Ojinaga in late 1976 the Ojinaga underworld was in a state of flux.

Manuel Carrasco, Pablo's source of marijuana and heroin and the drug trafficker who had converted Ojinaga into an important hub for narcotics, was on the run. The Ojinaga *plaza* was up for grabs.

These changes came as a result of a relatively insignificant accidental shooting that later flared up into a full-scale gun battle, bringing Carrasco's career to an end, at least in Ojinaga. The shooting took place one evening in March 1976, in the town's outlying *zona de tolerancia,* the red light district, eight months before Pablo Acosta fled to Mexico. Carrasco and several drug associates had been getting drunk and shooting their pistols in the air in revelry with several bar girls. One of the rounds ricocheted, hitting one of the girls in the foot.

According to informed accounts given of this pivotal incident, Carrasco was in the bar in the company of Heraclio Rodriguez Avilez, nephew of a powerful drug kingpin in Parral some 150 miles south of Ojinaga and one of Carrasco's chief suppliers. Heraclio had flown into town in a light airplane earlier that week with three gunmen to discuss money that Carrasco owed the Parral drug boss. Heraclio was a trusted member of the Parral clan who evidently knew how to take care of situations. Only two weeks earlier, he and his men had disarmed the entire municipal police force of Parral to show who was truly in charge of the agricultural community. The traffickers marched the city cops at gunpoint to a hill outside town where they left them tied up.

Heraclio's visit to Ojinaga, it is believed, was tied to a financial crisis Carrasco was experiencing due to a string of serious losses—major drug shipments that had been fronted to him by the Parral drug lord but that had been seized in the United States. During the previous nine months, thirty pounds of Carrasco's heroin and a ton of his marijuana had been confiscated in drug busts in California, Illinois and Texas. An airplane he had borrowed from the Avilezes had crashed. In all, the dope busts represented multimillion-dollar losses for Carrasco. The Ojinaga drug *don* still had to pay for these loads, and that was the purpose of Heraclio's visit. How—and when—was he going to make good on those debts? Carrasco had apparently satisfied the nephew of his source, for they were having a grand time partying together in the *zona* until the bullet hit the girl.

The drunken group drove the wounded girl to the home of Dr. Artemio Gallegos, a retired military surgeon who ran a private practice out of his book-lined home near the town square, not far from the police station and the army garrison. While Carrasco, Heraclio and his men sat in the waiting room, the doctor set about fixing up the wounded woman. Just as he finished cleansing the wound, however, a carload of municipal policemen led by the chief of police pulled up in front to investigate.

Heraclio had been sober when he marched the Parral

municipal police force out of town at gunpoint. But when the police chief accompanied by other municipal cops walked into the waiting room, a drunken Heraclio pointed his semi-automatic pistol at the police chief and began to squeeze the trigger. The police chief had only time enough to grab Heraclio by the arm and shove him; Heraclio pushed the policeman backward to free his gun hand. Then everyone started shooting. Drunken dopers and terrified cops ran in confusion from book-lined room to book-lined room or out into the street, shooting back and forth. The doctor, the nurse and the wounded bar girl ducked behind the examination table just as one of the *pistoleros* fired a machine gun at them.

The incident would have had a Keystone Cops quality to it if no one had been hurt. But during this gun battle, Heraclio was shot through the heart and died instantly. One of the policemen was shot in the arm. Manuel Carrasco was hit in the lower back. The gunfire ended when someone in the street shouted that soldiers were coming. The remaining gunmen fled.

Troops from the nearby garrison arrived moments later, but Heraclio's men were able to escape the dragnet. Manuel Carrasco was taken to a hospital in Chihuahua City. The wound was not serious and he was soon released.

In the meantime, rumors began circulating that the gunfight was the result of a power struggle for control of the Ojinaga *plaza*. Someone had wanted Manuel Carrasco out of the way, a logical assumption due to Ojinaga's growing importance as a transit point for narcotics.

State police in New Mexico, however, later picked up a scenario that American narcotics officers thought was more likely: Manuel Carrasco took advantage of the unexpected confusion to shoot Heraclio to clear the drug debt. Manuel could then claim that he had already paid off the big debt he owed in Parral and did not know what Heraclio or his men had done with the money.

But then Manuel got shot too.

According to accounts later picked up by the New Mexico State Police, the older Avilez, then in his seventies, called the hospital in Chihuahua City where Manuel was getting patched up and asked him what happened to Heraclio. Manuel reportedly said in a saddened voice, "There's been a problem, *Señor* Avilez. Heraclio has been killed."

After Manuel gave an edited account of the shooting, the older Avilez asked "And what about the money?"

"I don't know, I gave it to him earlier that day. I don't know what he did with it."

But Heraclio's *pistoleros* had a different story to tell. They had eluded the army and made it back to Parral about five days later. One of them, a pilot named Huitaro, supposedly said, "That's bullshit. I *saw* Manuel shoot Heraclio." None of the survivors could remember any money being handed over to Heraclio.

Old man Avilez not only put a price on Manuel Carrasco's head, he also put out a contract for every one of the municipal cops in Ojinaga. They were *all* to be killed.

Rumors flashed around town that two airplanes full of Avilez men armed with machetes and machine guns were on the way with orders to butcher the policemen. To the last man, the Ojinaga police force fled to the United States. Some of them went to towns in New Mexico, others to communities in Oklahoma where they had relatives. U.S. Immigration and Customs authorities in Presidio proved very understanding. They obtained special permits for the police chief and the deputy police chief and their families. And they looked the other way as the remainder of the Ojinaga police force came to the United States, bringing their families with them.

Manuel Carrasco disappeared too, and his vanishing act left the Ojinaga underworld in disarray. Treacherous himself, he suspected everyone else of sinister intent and did not say a word of his whereabouts even to his closest associates. He simply abandoned a lucrative *plaza*. It was as if the proprietor of a multimillion-dollar firm walked out the door one day without saying goodbye to any of his employees and never came back.

Rumors later circulated that "higher-ups" had decided to promote Carrasco to a bigger, more challenging *plaza* in the state of Sinaloa. Other stories circulated that he was able to buy his way into the military and was now the general of an army unit in the state of Durango. Other rumors had him hiding out from old man Avilez's vengeance in the port city of Veracruz.

For a short time one of Manuel Carrasco's cousins was thought to be running the *plaza*, but he was soon arrested in the United States.

The Ojinaga *plaza* fell by default to Shorty Lopez, Pablo Acosta's pal from Fort Leavenworth. Like Pablo, Shorty had distributed heroin and marijuana in West Texas for Manuel Carrasco. But while Pablo was content to base his operation in Odessa and later in Eunice, Shorty preferred to work out of Ojinaga. He had married a woman from the town and gradually started spending more time there than in the United States. He would run drug loads to American clients, then head back to Mexico with suitcases full of money.

Shorty's star in the Carrasco organization began to rise after he evaded American police in a high-speed chase through the mountains on Highway 67 between Marfa and Presidio. He was returning to Ojinaga late one night with money for a marijuana load he had smuggled to Fort Stockton across the dirt ranch roads of the Big Bend. With the money in a satchel, he took the two-lane highway to Presidio for the easy return trip. But ten miles from the border, a police car pulled up behind him, red lights flashing. Shorty didn't know if he was being pulled over for speeding or if someone had informed on him. As soon as he saw lights, he gunned his souped-up pickup and tried to outrun the law. It *would* have been awfully hard explaining how an ex-con came by the tens of thousands of dollars in that leather bag. And Ojinaga was only ten miles away. All he had to do was make a mad dash for the border. The high-speed chase ended at a sharp bend near Presidio. Shorty lost control, skidding off the highway. His truck rolled down the slope. The policemen thought they were going to find a mangled body at the bottom of the ravine. All they found was a wrecked pickup truck, broken mesquite bushes, crushed cactuses, flattened greasewood and a few traces of blood heading off into the desert.

Shorty broke his leg as he was thrown from the truck. His face and chest were cut and bleeding. The way he later told the story, he managed to elude the police and drag himself to the Rio Grande just west of Ojinaga. He swam across with the satchel firmly gripped in his mouth, then hobbled up to an adobe shack near the river's edge. He banged on the door to wake up an elderly widower who lived there alone. "Listen, old man," Shorty said, gritting his teeth in pain. "I'll make it worth your while. Go find Manuel Carrasco and tell him to come and get me. I'm hurt, and I'm hurt bad."

The accident left him with a permanent limp, but his resourcefulness and daring earned him Manuel Carrasco's esteem—and a promotion: Manuel put him in charge of a big desert ranch southeast of Ojinaga where Carrasco raised cattle and goats. The animals were a front. The ranch's real purpose lay in a long dirt runway and the bulk cargo that arrived constantly from distant parts and in the underground warehouses where the merchandise was kept from prying eyes.

As his importance to Manuel grew, Shorty began dealing directly with more of the drug lord's buyers and with his drug suppliers in the mountains of Chihuahua, Oaxaca and Sinaloa. Shorty soon came to see the drug business in its broad outlines rather than just in its parts. Eventually he was handling the movement of drugs all along the border from Pilares, a village 100 miles upstream from Ojinaga, to Boquillas, 150 miles downstream near the Chihuahua-Coahuila state line—the stretch of the Rio Grande that roughly defined Manuel Carrasco's Ojinaga *plaza*. But it was always Manuel Carrasco who dealt with the authorities, jealously guarding his official contacts.

That changed after Manuel disappeared.

When Carrasco could not be located for the *plaza* money, his protectors began investigating who was left in charge.

Manuel Carrasco reputedly had been paying $100,000 on the tenth of every month. The unpaid balance began climbing as the months went by. Several months after Manuel vanished, Shorty started getting official visits from Chihuahua City. Manuel was not making his payments and was falling behind, Shorty was informed. *Someone* named Shorty Lopez had better come up with the money.

Shorty protested the amount. He had been privy to much of Manuel's dealings, sure, but not *all* of his dealings. A hundred thousand dollars a month was predicated upon the total volume of Manuel's drug movement. For Shorty, just starting to pick up the pieces of an organization abandoned by its chief, the sum would be ruinous. Ultimately, Shorty struck a deal and was left in peace to work the *plaza*.

Former underworld associates of Shorty Lopez said that Shorty at first made the payments in Manuel's name, but as the months went by he began to consider the *plaza* his own. After all, he was the one generating the money for the *plaza* payments now, not Manuel. Manuel had left him in an ambiguous situation and had not tried to contact him, not the other way around.

Adding to his self-importance, Shorty quickly got big in his own right. He soon had all the trappings of a drug lord—his own ranch equipped with a runway, a warehouse for marijuana storage and his own pilots and runners. The focal point of the smuggling operations shifted away from Manuel's property to his own.

"So what am I supposed to do?" Shorty once asked an American friend. "If Manuel's not here to pay the *plaza* fee and they make me pay instead, that means I have the *plaza* and not Manuel. I don't owe him nothing."

By the time Pablo Acosta reached Ojinaga—the day after his close call with the police outside of Eunice—Shorty had been making the *plaza* payments for five or six months. Their meeting in Ojinaga was like a slaphappy reunion of boyhood chums.

Shorty handed Pablo a machine gun and a semiautomatic

pistol and put him to work. At first Pablo did duty as Shorty's chauffeur and bodyguard and escorted his friend and boss here and there in the dusty border town or to Shorty's desert ranch east of San Carlos, *La Hacienda Oriental*. It was barely forty miles from Ojinaga, but it took six hours to get there along a bumpy and frequently washed-out dirt road.

Pablo, meanwhile, worked his own drug deals, supplying the American networks he had left behind from his Mexican sanctuary. When the indictment against him for the heroin deal in Eunice was handed down in January 1977, Pablo knew there was no going back. He hired his own runners to take loads for him and had his brothers and others collect. Occasionally, he drove to the narrow international bridge, half a mile from his brick house on Calle Sexta, and watched the activity at the port of entry on the American side.

He was untouchable in Mexico so long as he remained under Shorty's wing. Shorty guaranteed his protection in exchange for a percentage of each deal Pablo cut. If Manuel Carrasco had still been in charge of the *plaza*, Pablo would have paid Carrasco instead. There *were* laws to be obeyed, but they were not the ones written down in the code books.

As he became settled, Pablo opened a small clothing boutique on Avenida Trasviña y Retes for his wife Olivia. They called it Karen's, after their daughter. He also opened a hole-in-the-wall restaurant in downtown Ojinaga in one of the adobe buildings near the town square. The restaurant specialized in *cabrito*, roast baby goat, and was a favorite rendezvous in the early afternoon for local hoodlums. He also did a lot of business there with Americans who came down with stolen automobiles or other goods they wanted to exchange for drugs.

In the United States, Pablo had rarely gone around armed. In Mexico, it was a necessity. A clean, well-lubricated .45 semiautomatic was just as much an article of clothing as were cowboy boots and oval belt buckles. Pablo believed he was going to have to defend himself sooner or later, and he wanted to be prepared. He kept his pistol stuffed in his belt at the hollow of his back. He never failed to take advantage of opportunities to practice shooting. Driving Shorty to his ranch or while with friends out in the desert, he would suddenly slam on the brakes if he saw a rabbit or a quail, leap out with his gun already drawn, and Bam! Bam! Bam! let off round after round until he had either killed the scurrying animal or run out of ammunition. He got to the point where he could hit a quail at forty yards with his .45 semiautomatic.

He and Shorty liked to draw on each other for practice, but Pablo took the roughhousing even further. Many of the drug *mafiosos* gathered in the morning or afternoons to water, feed and exercise their quarter horses at stables owned by Fermin Arevalo, one of Manuel Carrasco's former associates. Like the other dopers, Pablo had acquired horses and went about his chores at the stables just like everyone else. But he had a habit of drawing on everybody, a quirk that made his victims nervous. He would appear out of nowhere, his chrome-plated semiautomatic flashing into his hands. Or he would spin around to aim at someone behind him, or draw face-to-face like an old-time gunslinger.

Some just waved him off as a trigger-happy punk. "Ah, go stick it up your ass" they would tell him.

Pablo just shrugged.

One day, he was certain, a fast draw would make the crucial difference between his life and someone else's.

Like many of the *campesino*-traffickers, Shorty was detached from the effects of the substances he dealt. He could sell a pound of black-tar heroin, his mind whizzing and clicking as he tallied up the profit, yet perhaps never once give any thought to the thousands of doses of chemical enslavement his profits represented. Then he could turn around and give much of the money to the poor in the Ojinaga area.

It was the tradition of a drug lord to take care of people in need, of course. For one thing, it was good for business. Give a peasant food for his malnourished children, he will become a loyal pair of eyes and ears in the sinister desert. A lot of small-time welfare added up to a big-time intelligence network.

But with Shorty, generosity was not mere pragmatism.

He enjoyed helping the underfed *campesinos* who scrounged for a marginal living on the harsh land. Stories were told of how Shorty would fill his pickup truck with groceries in Ojinaga before making a trip to his ranch. On the way he would stop at this adobe hovel and that, distributing the food and supplies, having nothing left by the time he got to his ranch. One of the beneficiaries of Shorty's generosity was a one-legged invalid everyone called Pegleg. He had a big family and lived in a village outside Ojinaga. One of Shorty's former associates recalled how Shorty drove up to Pegleg's primitive adobe one day and tooted his horn to rouse the man from the shack.

"Goddammit, you lazy old fart, I'm going to put you to work," Shorty said, slapping the astonished man on the back.

He took Pegleg around the ranches and *ejidos*, bought him a couple hundred hogs, a truckload of feed and started the man and his family raising pigs. With similar directness he got other people to raise goats, sheep, chickens, turkeys.

Many ranchers in the area of San Carlos, a *pueblo* of two thousand people near Shorty's *La Hacienda Oriental*, owed their well pumps, tractors and fencing to Shorty's impulsive altruism. During his short reign as drug lord of Ojinaga, Shorty came to be known as the benefactor of San Carlos.

Shorty could afford to be generous. Business boomed the moment he took over from Manuel Carrasco. With the marijuana and opium-poppy harvest that fall of 1976, trucks streamed from the interior of Mexico with a dual cargo: carrots, apples, woolen Oaxacan blankets and an endless variety of goods for Ojinaga merchants. Under some of those loads were secret cargoes for Shorty.

It was so easy to sell marijuana! A bonanza for drug sellers like Shorty was assured from the hippies and ranchers, campers and hunters, Hispanics and Anglos, Blacks and Indians, from as far away as California, Montana or North Carolina who drove up to low spots in the river looking to score. They knew where to go. Once they spotted someone on the other side who could only be there for one reason, all they had to do was holler something like "Hey, you a Messkin?"

The man on the other side of the muddy river would cup his hands to his mouth and yell back "Yeah, gringo. Whaddya want?"

"Twenty kilos."

"I can get it for you."

"How much?"

"Come across, let's talk."

And the deal was on.

Such small-time river deals along the sparsely inhabited and poorly patrolled Big Bend could dispose of an entire truckload of marijuana in no time.

Shorty also sent trusted runners up to Fort Stockton across the dirt backroads of the desert with 1,500-pound loads stashed in campers. Light airplanes also flew directly to Shorty's ranch, loaded up, and left at night, returning undetected to the United States through the mountain passes of the Big Bend with 400 or 700 or 1,000 pounds of marijuana per trip.

The money was rolling in. Shorty was making his monthly *plaza* payments. Everybody was happy.

Everybody except Manuel Carrasco.

Toward the end of 1976 word began spreading in Ojinaga and in the surrounding *ejidos* and towns that Manuel Carrasco, still in hiding from Avilez, was planning to kill Shorty. The rumors became so strong that finally Pablo and some of the other drug dealers began urging Shorty to leave town for a while.

Manuel Carrasco considered Shorty a traitor. Shorty had taken advantage of his self-imposed exile to grab what was rightfully Manuel's. It didn't matter that Manuel had not trusted Shorty enough to contact him and clarify the situation. It only mattered that Shorty now considered himself master of the *plaza*, that he was boasting about it and making money Manuel thought was his. Shorty was going to pay for it with his blood.

Shorty kept a pistol and an American assault rifle on the floor of his truck, but he did not walk about town armed and he did not always have a bodyguard with him.

In the early spring of 1977, Shorty accidentally ran into Manuel Carrasco in Chihuahua City. He and a couple of his men had taken some Ojinaga girls to the state capital for an outing, spending several days shopping and partying. One afternoon they turned a corner in one of the quieter downtown side streets near the state government buildings. There was Manuel Carrasco, arm-in-arm with his wife, walking toward them! It was like finding the proverbial needle in the haystack, only they had not even been looking.

Manuel Carrasco was tall in his cowboy boots, with a look of stolid dignity in his ranchero suit and hat.

"You little son of a bitch," Carrasco sneered when he recognized Shorty. "If I don't kill you right now, it's out of respect for my wife."

It didn't take much to throw the 110-pound Shorty Lopez into a bantam-rooster flutter. He marched up to Manuel, who towered over him by about ten inches. "I'll fight you any time you want," Shorty yelled. "You name the time and place."

Manuel's wife nervously tugged on her husband's arm. Shorty's men pulled him away. Without another word, Manuel and his wife brushed past the small group and disappeared around a corner.

During the three-hour drive back, Shorty's men tried to reason with him. If Shorty hadn't been so goddamn cocky, he could have settled it with Manuel right then and there in Chihuahua City. All it would have taken was a few words explaining how Manuel had left him in the lurch.

"Why don't you make a deal with him? You could still work it out with him," one of the men said.

"Oh, the hell with him!" Shorty said.

Manuel Carrasco caught up with Shorty on May 1, 1977, outside the river village of Santa Elena. Shorty had a load of marijuana to ship north that day and had sent his runners to take it across the Rio Grande somewhere downstream from the tiny village. Following the smuggling operation, he returned to Santa Elena with his driver to party with the locals.

Manuel Valdez, the driver, was a young, eager *campesino*

who worked on Shorty's ranch with two older brothers. The young Valdez occasionally chauffeured the drug lord around the desert, doubling as bodyguard.

A week earlier Manuel Carrasco had spread the word from Chihuahua City that Shorty's end was imminent—the kind of psychological terrorism Manuel seemed to relish. Shorty kept on about his business.

Shorty was convinced he could come out on top in a shoot-out with Manuel Carrasco. Manuel could choose the time and the place, but Shorty's intelligence network, the fruit of his generosity, would alert him ahead of time to the danger.

And he was right.

Late that afternoon, Shorty and Valdez left Santa Elena to drive back to the ranch in the desert highlands. They had to drive ten miles downriver, then cut south into the mountains. The bumpy road was tough even on the sturdiest four-wheel drive. The road followed the foothills below the mammoth limestone wall of the Sierra Ponce, going in and out of broad arroyos, sometimes following the floor of dry washes for a mile before turning again onto higher ground.

Several miles from the fork, Shorty saw a pickup approaching, the driver waving frantically. They stopped next to one another in a swirl of dust. The pickup's driver had benefited from Shorty's largesse at one time. "Be careful," he said. "They're waiting up ahead to kill you—Manuel Carrasco's gunmen."

The rancher had learned of the ambush by driving into it. A man with mouthful of steel-capped teeth had stepped out in front of his truck and yelled *"Judicial!"* Other men brandishing machine guns who also passed themselves off as *judiciales* searched his truck. They were up by the fork, on the other side of an arroyo. The rancher did not know if Manuel Carrasco was there himself, but he had seen plenty of men.

Shorty's blood began to boil. He wasn't about to run. He was going to show them what kind of stuff he was made of. He grabbed an assault rifle from the floor and slapped an ammunition clip into it. "You drive on. I'm getting in the back," he shouted to Manuel Valdez.

A village situated on the Rio Grande, Santa Elena had a population of 300. Pablo Acosta was born here amid the poverty that still marks much of rural Mexico. Later, he used the isolated river village to smuggle narcotics into the United States. He also came here in times of trouble because of Santa Elena's apparent impregnability and the loyalty he commanded among the villagers. (Photo courtesy of Carolyn Cole)

Grabbing some extra clips, Shorty shoved one of the semiautomatic pistols into his belt and jumped into the back of the truck. Valdez checked his own handguns and placed them—chambered and cocked—next to him on the seat. He put the truck in gear and moved on up the bumpy road. Shorty lay flat in the bed of the pickup, ready to spring up at the right moment.

The ambush site was several miles away. The road dropped nearly ten feet into a wide, flat-bottom arroyo. One had to drive across the arroyo bed and climb the steep slope on the opposite side to get back onto the road. Carrasco's gunmen were waiting on both sides, on the top of the rises. As soon as they knew it was Shorty in the middle of the arroyo they were going to gun him down.

But the advance warning had allowed Shorty to prepare. When Valdez drove down into the wash, the gunmen could see only one man—and it wasn't Shorty. They let Valdez drive through and up the other side. Once the truck had bounced up to the top of the wash, the man with steel-capped teeth walked into its path and shouted *"Judicial!"*

What happened next took place in the space of time it takes for about a dozen men firing simultaneously to shoot several hundred rounds of ammunition.

Shorty jumped up from the bed of the truck, firing a burst from his AR-15 at Steel-Tooth, then turning his fire on the group of men that had started to emerge from the mesquite brush the moment Steel-Tooth halted the truck. Several of those men fell. Valdez leaped from the pickup cab at the same moment, firing toward the other side of the road. The hammering of machine guns became thunderous. Bullets coming from three directions tore into the pickup. Manuel Valdez was hit and fell to the ground. Shorty jumped down from the truck and ran up the road shooting backwards.

Steel-Tooth was hugging the ground to keep out of the line of fire. He had been grazed by Shorty's initial spray of bullets. When he saw Shorty running, he got to his knees and aimed. A .45-caliber bullet tore into Shorty's spine. He fell face-forward to the ground.

The marks people later saw in the dirt showed that Shorty had crawled a short distance, scratching and clawing the ground, then writhed in the scorching sand. Tire tracks showed that a heavy vehicle had driven again and again over his frail body before finally driving over his head. Shorty was probably already dead when someone stood over him, lifted a heavy machete high and then brought it down with savage force that cut off the top of his skull at the hairline.

Only the bodies of Shorty Lopez and Manuel Valdez were found later. The assailants fled with their own dead and wounded. Reports later reached San Carlos that several men had checked into clinics in towns across the state line in Coahuila. One of the men had steel-capped teeth and claimed to be a *judicial*.

Several days after the shooting, the town of San Carlos was full of the grim festivity of a rural funeral. The small stone church at one end of the town square was festooned in black. People who had come from all over for Shorty's funeral jammed the square. A priest celebrated a requiem mass in the belief that Shorty's charity absolved at least some of his sins. Then the pallbearers, mafiosos wearing Western clothes and cowboy boots, emerged from the church with the coffin on their shoulders and carried it through the thick crowd to the hearse. The funeral procession ended at Shorty's ranch where he was buried to the music of a *norteño* group that sang ballads about his exploits.

Shorty's memory lived on in song—and in irregularly shaped bone fragments about the size of a quarter said to have been cut from the portion of Shorty's skull severed by the machete. Holes had been drilled through the fragments allowing thin gold chains to be inserted. The skull-fragment pendants started showing up around the necks of Ojinaga traffickers, giving grounds for rumor that Manuel Carrasco remained in charge even though he was rarely seen again in Ojinaga.

The skull fragments were emblems of loyalty—and were grim warnings against betrayal.

Chapter Six

INTERREGNUM

The murder of Shorty Lopez left the drug movement without a *capo* all along the Texas Big Bend. Raids by civil and military authorities from Chihuahua City, though not unusual even when someone had the *plaza*, became more frequent and indiscriminate.

The raids were the government's way of asserting authority in the isolated, nearly lawless border town following some sensational murder played up by the newspapers in the state capital, or complaints by local authorities or citizens with influential connections that the local gangsters were really getting out of hand. People caught up in the sweeps were chained together by the neck and herded into the back of confiscated pickup trucks, then taken to jail in Chihuahua City or Ciudad Juarez.

With Shorty gone, those who would normally have been alerted directly from Chihuahua City about the coming of troops now somehow did not get the message and wound up in chains in the back of pickup trucks. Pablo himself was picked up several times "for questioning," he later told friends, once spending several weeks in the medieval-looking penitentiary in the state capital.

After Shorty's death, the Ojinaga underworld expected some arrangement to be worked out quickly. Whenever the traffickers gathered at Pablo's downtown restaurant or at the stables where they kept their racehorses, they all asked the same question: "Who is going to take over the *plaza*?"

They speculated that someone would be sent from another part of the country to take over, or the authorities involved in protection rackets in the federal police or the army would tap one of the Ojinaga traffickers for the job. And if someone *did* get the nod, the word would spread quickly and the other traffickers would then make arrangements to come under the wing of the new *padrino*. But six months went by and nothing of the sort happened.

Pablo Acosta knew how dangerous it was to operate without some sort of patronage. Get caught with drugs and you could expect an excruciatingly painful interrogation and a longer sentence than in the United States—unless, of course, you had enough cash on hand to extricate yourself.

At the same time, the market was literally knocking down the door. Small-time American buyers swarmed the riverside or prowled Ojinaga's rowdy *zona* trying to score. Compared to the days of Shorty Lopez, however, not that much dope was being made available. The people with drugs to sell were being cautious. As the months dragged on, longtime wholesale buyers both in Texas and New Mexico and as far away as Alabama and California began to make "Hey what's going on?" telephone calls to their Ojinaga connections. Important customers threatened to take their business elsewhere.

Like the other dealers, Pablo moved just enough heroin and marijuana to pay his bills and to string his clients along. Like everyone else, he realized that someone was going to have to take over the *plaza* if business was to flourish once again.

In early 1978, some of the most important members of the Ojinaga drug world met at the stables to decide what to do. Pablo Acosta was present, as were two other up-and-coming traffickers, Victor Sierra and Rogelio Gonzalez. About a dozen other people involved to one degree or another in drug smuggling were also there.

Victor Sierra, a nephew of bar owners in the notorious *zona*, had worked as a runner for Manuel Carrasco and then for Shorty Lopez after Manuel disappeared. Like Pablo, Victor had become big enough to make deals on his own—after paying a percentage to Shorty for protection.

Rogelio Gonzalez, meanwhile, was a flying ace who piloted loads for anybody who needed his services and was willing to pay.

The smugglers chatted as they went about their chores—almost all of them had quarter horses that needed feeding and exercising every day. Someone started talking about several tons of marijuana that had just arrived in town from the interior, *mota* that was already stashed in caves or in underground storage tanks on ranches east of Ojinaga. The owners needed to start selling to pay off their suppliers, but they were afraid of the fickle Mexican law.

"Someone has to go and make arrangements with the authorities," one of the men said.

They had talked before of the need to send someone "down there" to talk to the federal *comandante* in Chihuahua City, the ornate state capital surrounded by pleasant mountains, prosperous cattle ranches, thriving Mennonite farms and impoverished government *ejidos*. Ojinaga came under the jurisdiction of the same federal police *comandante* who was in charge of the periodic raids.

Victor Sierra knew that Shorty had been making monthly payments at the *comandancia*, the federal police headquarters in Chihuahua City. If they wanted to work out some arrangements for protection, that's where they needed to start. Victor volunteered Pablo to go. "You'd be a good one," he said. Some of the other smugglers nodded in agreement.

Pablo could be boastful, liked being the center of attention and aspired to be number one. But he was also a realist. An ex-con and now a DEA fugitive, he was certain the American police knew he was operating out of Ojinaga. Legally a citizen of the United States, he worried the DEA could try to pressure Mexico into extraditing him were he to acquire a high profile.

And then, he really knew more about the American judicial system than the Mexican. He knew that in Mexico things were inverted. Cops were poorly paid, and were expected to supplement their income by fair means or foul. Politics and government service had become roads to riches, terrific rackets if you were on the inside. That system could be bent to work to the advantage of a narcotics trafficker if he knew how to cultivate the right authorities and become a member of the club. Shorty Lopez had learned some of the tricks and had operated, however briefly, with impunity. While in charge, Shorty had told his friend Pablo in general how things were arranged. But he had guarded the full extent of his contacts as jealously as Manuel Carrasco, and had taken most of his secrets to the grave. No, Pablo reasoned, it was better to operate under someone else's wing—at least for now.

Pablo was stooping over to give a bucket of oats to his palomino. He looked around and said, "Nah, I got all kinds of heat right now."

The field of candidates was pretty slim. Some of the men at the informal gathering were Americans. Others were Mexicans too young, too old, too inexperienced or too unreliable to be seriously considered. Other than Pablo, there were only two other possibilities: Victor Sierra and Rogelio Gonzalez.

Rogelio was a mystery to everyone. He had light skin and thin, fine features, in contrast to the swarthy, rough-hewn men around him. He could easily pass for a Frenchman from Marseilles. Most Mexican smugglers who flew were self-taught bush pilots, but Rogelio had been a flight instructor and mechanic in Mexico City before flying for traffickers in Sinaloa. He could land a Cessna 206 in a parking lot and then get it airborne again, or so it was said; he did make landings all the time at night on dirt runways with nothing but a signal fire at one end to guide him. At the same time, he was quiet, timid-seeming, and even prudish. The coarse talk about women that made up ninety percent of the talk among the dopers caused him to walk away in disgust. "If you didn't know him well you'd think he was gay," one Ojinaga smuggler commented later.

Among his close associates it was known that Rogelio and his wife, a beautiful Indian from southern Mexico, once killed several soldiers in a shootout in the state of Sinaloa, troops who had come to arrest him and take away his airplane even though he was "fixed" with the military commander. He and his wife were on the run when they came to Ojinaga. Rogelio never liked to talk about the shooting.

Flying drug loads was a way to make a living for Rogelio, and he made it clear he did not aspire to do anything beyond that. "Give me a plane and I'll fly it. That's all I want to do," he said.

That left Victor Sierra.

Victor was educationally a cut above the typical Ojinaga peasant smuggler. Originally from Ciudad Juarez, his mother had put him in a seminary after his father and an uncle were killed in an accident in Los Angeles. A pious woman who went to church every morning with her head covered with a black veil, she always knelt humbly in a back pew, her head bowed in prayer. She did chores around the church, such as laundering and ironing the altar cloths for the priest. She prayed fervently that her son would not succumb to worldly temptations and would serve the will of God. As young men, some of Victor's paternal uncles had gone to Los Angeles and made money any way they could. When they were older and better off, they moved to Ojinaga and bought some of the seedy adobe bars in the *zona* where some of the bawdiest, down-and-dirty strip shows in northern Mexico were put on. Victor's mother's prayers were as focused as a blowtorch, aimed at severing the bonds between Victor and his wayward uncles.

In the end the uncles won the battle for Victor's soul. He abandoned the cassock for a baggy pachuco outfit and a microphone and emceed midnight strip shows for his uncles. With the exception of prudish Rogelio, everyone hung around the *zona* and everyone had heard Victor's verbal wizardry. He was indeed a good talker.

"Why don't *you* go, Victor?" Pablo suggested.

"How do I know about all this? I've never done it before."

"You know what's going on," Pablo said. "You hung around with Manuel Carrasco. You hung around with Shorty Lopez. You've seen how it works up and down the ladder."

Someone else went through Victor's curriculum vitae: the facts that he had crossed truckloads of marijuana over Big Bend rangeland for Shorty, that he knew the ranch gates and back roads to Marathon and other Texas towns.

All his assets were tallied up: he was a smooth talker; he wasn't on anybody's wanted list in Mexico or the United States; he was young, but not too young; his vocabulary was polished when it needed to be; and he had never been in jail.

Pablo offered to back him with whatever money was necessary to make the *plaza* payments. "I'll contribute my part and a little bit more if I have to. I'm sure Rogelio here feels the same way." Pablo pointed around the stable to the various traffickers. Each nodded in agreement. But it took several more meetings before Victor agreed.

Only Rogelio raised any objections. He knew they were stymied without some sort of arrangement with the authorities. But from his Sinaloa experience he also knew that shifting alliances and intrigue within the Mexican government, international political pressures, changes in federal and state administrations and plain greed made protection costly and precarious. You had to pay everybody or nobody.

"I know that someone has to go, but I don't like it. Once you start paying, they'll bleed you for the rest of your life and you can never get out of it," he said.

Not long after that meeting in the horse stables, Victor Sierra was in Chihuahua City looking up the federal police commander.

The way Victor told about his experience later to his Ojinaga friends, he was forced to cool his heels for several days before being allowed in to see the commander. Not that the *comandante* refused to see him; he was never in. Victor sat around in a waiting area, suffering the suspicious stares of the tough-looking men walking in or out. After several days Victor was let in to the federal official's office, a small, unremarkable room except for the automatic machine guns stacked in a corner. The commander didn't get up. He just looked Victor up and down and motioned to a chair.

Before leaving Ojinaga, Victor had gone over and over

again with Pablo and Rogelio and anyone else with an interest in his success what he should say. They knew that the federal chief had his informants and probably already had at least a general idea of who was doing what in Ojinaga. So there wasn't any use hiding everything from him. On the other hand, there was no use telling him everything, either.

"Just convince him you know what's going on and you're willing to take over the *plaza*," Victor was told.

Victor chatted amiably with the federal official, punctuating his sentences with *Señor Comandante* to show respect. He finally got around to the real purpose of his visit. "We can't move anything because nobody has the *plaza* in Ojinaga, *Señor Comandante*. I want your permission to work the *plaza*," he said.

"How do you know that I'm the person to come to for this sort of thing?"

"Well, like I told you. I worked for Manuel Carrasco for a number of years. I worked for Shorty Lopez. I know what's going on."

The *comandante* kept pressing him about why he had come to the federal headquarters in Chihuahua City for his request. "How do you know to come to *me*?"

"I sometimes drove Manuel Carrasco here when he came to bring the *plaza* money."

They talked a while longer. The police official ended the interview by standing up and walking to the door. He motioned for someone to come, and soon two of the goons Victor had seen walking in and out of the federal police headquarters appeared in the doorway.

The *comandante* pointed at Victor and said, "Get him ready for me."

Victor soon wished he had stuck with the priesthood. According to his account later to his friends, the agents led him from the commander's office to a back room. They strapped him onto a chair and threw a hood over his head. They started pummeling him. Between the punches came the questions.

"I was a runner for Carrasco. I moved the loads. What more can I tell you?" he pleaded.

The beating was all the more terrifying because he never knew when or where the next blow would fall. The beatings lasted on and off for three days. At night, they threw him into a smelly holding chamber with a bare concrete slab for a bed.

The torture was a variation of three effective techniques employed by many Mexican police interrogators. They rammed Victor's head into a bucket of water until he thought he was going to drown; they strapped him naked to a bench and jabbed his thighs and testicles with a cattle prod, sending searing jolts of electricity through him; and then came the punches, the incessant punches to the rib cage, the abdomen, the kidneys, the head.

During the severest of the torture the *comandante* was absent. He came in during the respites, taking the role of friend and protector rather than tormentor, asking questions in an almost fatherly tone. Victor had gone to Chihuahua City to seek permission to work the *plaza* and instead had found the ultimate confessional. He finally told the federal policeman everything he wanted to know, about himself, about his entourage, about their activities.

Then on the third day, a miracle happened. The *comandante* offered him the *plaza*! Sure, Victor had talked, but he had put up resistance, and it took more than the usual to break him down. The *comandante* informed him he was satisfied that Victor had *huevos*, and it was apparent from the interrogation that he had contacts and a solid organization.

"You go ahead and work the Ojinaga area, but have $10,000 right here on this desk every month. And I want the first payment the day after tomorrow."

Bruised and shaking but relieved, Victor was back in Ojinaga the next day. When he saw Pablo, he embraced him. "Those people aren't human. I thought they were going to kill me. But we got the *plaza*."

It took a while for Victor to get over the torture. He was a healthy thirty-year-old with lots of girlfriends. He tried not to complain about the lingering pain from the electric shocks. But he did confide to close friends, in a voice strained

with fear, that he thought he had been permanently dam-
aged. For the next six months, he just couldn't get it up.

With the *plaza* arrangement in place, Victor Sierra slept
soundly at night, free of fear of arrest. But the arrangement
had its down side. Just as Rogelio had predicted in the meeting at the stables, the *comandante* soon got greedier and put
pressure on Victor for more money. The *comandante* began
showing up at Victor's house, leaving two men outside in a
car while he walked in without knocking.

"*Muchachos!*" the *comandante* would shout. "Everything
going all right?"

Victor and several of his men lived in a large brick house
with a waterbed in each of the four bedrooms, a stereo and
color television in the living room, and a well-stocked kitch-
en and bar. The house was an oasis of luxury in an
unremarkable dirt-street neighborhood near the runway of
the municipal airfield.

Pablo avoided Victor's house any time the *comandante*
was in town, and with good reason. The police official commandeered anything that wasn't nailed down. On one
occasion he strode into Victor's living room and spotted a
$600 semiautomatic pistol with pearl handles lying on an
end table. He let out an earsplitting A-i-e-e-e!" and picked it
up. "*Un regalito?*" he beamed, showing his "little gift" around
the room as if he had just unwrapped a Christmas present.
"What a little beauty!" He stuffed it into his waistband and
looked around for something else to take.

His attitude had changed remarkably since those first
days in Chihuahua City. Once grim inquisitor, he was now
Victor's *compadre*, a bosom buddy plopping down on the
sofa and asking for a drink. He would send one of Victor's
people to fetch his own men from outside. These agents,
sometimes the very ones who had participated in Victor's
torture, would make themselves comfortable on one of the
sofas and ask for drinks too. And food. And women from the
zona, the best-looking ones. And not tonight, but right now!
Victor had to send someone to fetch the girls, and the agents

sat around drinking his booze before stumbling to the back bedrooms.

One day the *comandante* showed up at the house with some bad news.

"It's going to cost you more to work," he announced after falling back into Victor's sofa. "Ten thousand was okay for starters, but I'm getting a lot of pressure from higher up. A lot of heat's coming down. They're putting higher fees on me to let you people work. I need twenty-five thousand a month from now on."

The *comandante's* informants told him how much Victor and his people were moving. Victor argued, but it did not matter. What the *comandante* wanted, the *comandante* got. After all, he had the federal police and the office of the attorney general behind him; and, if necessary, the army. Victor ended up over time paying $35,000 a month, he confided to one of his associates.

At every hike in the *plaza* fee, Victor passed the word on to Pablo, to Rogelio and to everyone else paying him in much the same language the *comandante* used. It was tough, but the raids by the soldiers had virtually come to a halt.

Victor's control of the Ojinaga *plaza* lasted until December 18, 1980, the day he and one of his lieutenants were arrested by DEA agents while en route to Las Vegas to oversee the shipment of a half-ton of marijuana. Victor rarely traveled in the United States, as a precaution. But this time he wanted to supervise the operation himself. It was the first time he was distributing that far west and he wanted to make sure nothing went wrong. In addition, he had always had an itch to see how the famed sin city of the desert measured up to his uncles' *zona de tolerancia* in Ojinaga.

It was a trip that Victor soon regretted. He and associate were waiting at the airport in Albuquerque to board a Las Vegas flight when federal agents nabbed them, telling Victor he was under arrest for drug trafficking, airplane theft and other charges. The feds had in hand an arrest warrant based on a secret nineteen-count indictment that had been handed down by a federal grand jury in Albuquerque six months earlier. Victor did not have an inkling of the indictment until the arrest at the airport.

He was tried in Albuquerque and sentenced to eight years in the federal pen.

During the two and a half years Victor was in charge, the Ojinaga *plaza* was relatively uneventful—a reflection of Victor's own character and the fact that business was booming. There was a share for everyone, so why fight? Enforcement was discreet. It usually consisted of throwing someone who hadn't paid debts into the canal with his hands tied behind his back and then fishing the miscreant out just before his lungs filled completely. One way or another, people who didn't pay their bills were made to cough up.

Ordinary citizens knew drugs were moving through their town, but it was a quiet, low-key activity and people went about their day-to-day lives without giving it much thought. Many people did not even bother to lock their doors at night; nor did mothers and fathers worry when their teenage children went out at night to cruise up and down Avenida Trasviña y Retes, the main boulevard. The underworld did its thing, the townspeople did theirs. Outside the Ojinaga Mafia, few people had even heard of Pablo Acosta. Or if they did know the name, he was that guy with the little restaurant uptown that served delicious *cabrito* and whose wife ran the clothing boutique on Trasviña y Retes with all those beautiful imported dresses in the store window.

Ojinaga was about to change.

Chapter Seven

LICENSE TO TRAFFIC

The U.S. Customs Service did not maintain an enforcement office in Presidio until 1976. What patrol officers there were in the Texas Big Bend lived ninety miles north in Alpine or were stationed at the Big Bend National Park headquarters at Panther Junction. The agents only went to Presidio on temporary duty.

Alpine was a pleasant town nestled among pretty hills and had civilized attractions such as a university campus. Presidio was a dull, two-motel border town without any paved residential streets, with dilapidated adobe neighborhoods near the center and mobile homes and cinderblock houses everywhere else. The midafternoon temperature hit 115 degrees Fahrenheit by the end of May and rarely dipped below 100 degrees until the end of October. Old-timers in Presidio joked that nobody who lived there had any reason to fear going to hell: Compared to Presidio, hell is gonna be a breeze.

Though difficult to get people to move to the border town voluntarily, it was impossible any longer for American federal authorities to ignore Ojinaga's importance as a drug conduit or Presidio as a front-line outpost. By 1976, Domingo Aranda, Manuel Carrasco, Shorty Lopez, Victor Sierra and other traffickers had transformed Ojinaga into a bigger narcotics hub than had ever before existed in the region. Large seizures of heroin and marijuana originating there were now being made in Texas, New Mexico and in other states as far away as Michigan and California. Intelligence from narcotics seizures showed that these drugs had been smuggled into the United States through the Texas Big Bend by land or by air. This information forced U.S. Customs to bite the bullet and open a patrol office in Presidio with a staff of ten officers. The agents worked out of a small prefab office behind the wooden, two-lane international bridge. One of the officers was responsible for intelligence while the others patrolled the river or, when tipped off, waited to "pop" drug smugglers as they waded or drove across low spots in the Rio Grande.

By 1978, Pablo Acosta's name had begun to figure more and more prominently in Customs intelligence reports generated by the Presidio office. During the years Victor Sierra had the *plaza*, Pablo worked hard to create a drug organization of his own. He had his own planes, his own runners and his own sources of marijuana and heroin in the interior of Mexico. Increasingly, narcotics smugglers picked up along the border frequently named Pablo as their source.

After Victor Sierra's arrest, Customs agents in Presidio were not surprised when informants began relating the new chain of command. Pablo Acosta, they were told, had taken over the *plaza*. Whoever had worked for Victor Sierra or had benefited from his protection arrangement with the authorities had switched loyalty to Pablo.

Exactly how Pablo took over Ojinaga is difficult to determine, but it is unlikely that he was subjected to the same gauntlet of interrogations that Victor Sierra had undergone in Chihuahua City. It is widely believed that during the nearly three years Victor Sierra was running the *plaza* Pablo very coolly and methodically cultivated the right people, placing himself in position to take over when the moment arrived.

Any lingering doubts among American authorities that Pablo was now in charge were dispelled one day in early 1981. Clayton McKinney, a Texas Ranger stationed in Alpine, had politely asked his police contacts in Ojinaga to pick up an American pilot who was known to make frequent flights between the Mexican border town and Albuquerque. The Mexican police were obliging; McKinney was a good sort who had done them favors in the past. The Mexicans

Former Culberson County Commissioner Ismael Espudo Venegas was an important member of Pablo Acosta's cocaine smuggling network. Though American, Espudo held the rank of federal security agent of the General Directorate of Political and Social Investigations, the political police of *Gobernación*–the Interior Government Ministry. The GDPSI was previously called the Directorate of Federal Security–the DFS. Such badges as the one above were carried by Pablo Acosta and other protected drug traffickers throughout Mexico, allowing them to operate with impunity. The *placa*, or badge, authorized them to carry weapons and instructed civil and military authorities, as well as private citizens, to cooperate "so that the bearer may carry out his legitimate duties." (Photo courtesy of Gary Epps, U.S. Customs Service)

collared the pilot, who went by the name Cristobal. They brought him to the office of the deputy director of Mexican immigration and left him alone with the ranger.

However, about twenty minutes into the private interview with the pilot, McKinney heard someone arguing outside the office, insisting loudly, "But Pablo said to let him go!" Pablo Acosta's name was repeated several times. A moment later one of the immigration officials came into the room and said, "I'm sorry, this meeting will have to end."

During the next two years, Customs informants provided further intelligence about the protection scheme Pablo had worked out. At first, Pablo made the federal police payments through intermediaries; then Mexico City created a federal police headquarters in Ojinaga and appointed the deputy director of Mexican immigration in Ojinaga as *comandante* of the federal police unit. Once appointed, the federal police commander collected directly from Pablo and passed the *plaza* fees on up.

Pablo made additional payments to the military through a former Ojinaga chief of police and radio station owner, Malaquias Flores, American intelligence learned. Police chief from 1977 to 1980, Flores was given an honorific rank of army *comandante* in 1980 that allowed him to walk around in a braided khaki uniform. Officially, Flores was a public relations official between the local military command and the civilian population. But informants told their American law enforcement contacts that his role was in fact to serve as the military's liaison with the drug traffickers. He collected the *plaza* payments from Pablo and took them to where they were supposed to go. As a go-between, Flores also conveyed the wishes of the military authorities to Pablo. In turn, Pablo transmitted his wishes and concerns by the same channel.

Pablo Acosta's role in Ojinaga was in many respects more sophisticated than that of any of his predecessors. Unlike Victor Sierra or Shorty Lopez, Pablo was able to obtain credentials from the agencies that protected his operations for himself and his lieutenants. The military and federal police badges gave him the authority to carry weapons and served as a shield for his activities. They made him untouchable wherever he went in Mexico. American agents in Presidio also learned that the commissioned officers working under the new federal police *comandante* were in fact thugs selected by Pablo from the ranks of his own gunmen and bodyguards. These men also were given federal badges.

The Mexican army, through the local garrison commander, provided Pablo with a different sort of protection. A Customs intelligence document dated September 14, 1982, summarized information from a "very reliable first-hand source" about the approaching harvest of a sixty to ninety-acre marijuana plantation on the Rio Conchos south of Ojinaga. The document stated that the plantation was surrounded by fences and was guarded by soldiers "under the command of Gen. Luis de la Soto Garcia Rivas, stationed in Ojinaga. The informant also states that there are six to eight soldiers armed with handguns and automatic rifles guarding the main gate at all times. Informant also states that Pablo Acosta, a confirmed narcotics dealer in Ojinaga, was at the farm recently."

That particular plantation was "raided" and burned a couple of weeks after the intelligence report was written. The raid was duly played up by the Mexican media which touted it as a "blow" against the *narcotraficantes* by the authorities. Mexican informants, however, drew for their American contacts in Presidio a different picture of the military action. The fields were of *sinsemilla*, a strain of marijuana grown mainly for the potent tops. Pablo was allowed to harvest the tops. Only then—in the presence of the media—did the military move in and slash and burn what was left.

In Ojinaga it was generally believed that Pablo obtained his military credential directly from Gen. Luis de la Soto Garcia Rivas, then army garrison commander in Ojinaga, as a gift from the commanding general of the Fifth Military Zone in Chihuahua City. At the time, the Fifth Military Zone was under the command of Gen. Juan Arevalo Gardoqui, who was later appointed minister of defense by the Miguel de la Madrid administration. The defense minister was implicated in the murder of a DEA agent, Enrique Camarena, in Guadalajara in February 1985. The American agent was kidnapped and tortured to death for exposing a vast marijuana complex in southeastern Chihuahua employing seven thousand farm workers, an operation that was protected by the Mexican military and federal police.

With his military and federal credentials, Pablo had become in essence a federal authority. Pablo showed his documents to people in Ojinaga on a "need to know" basis—people such as the chief of police, the mayor and the *comandante* of the state police. It was the equivalent of saying "This means you don't interfere."

As Pablo's reputation grew, American law enforcement agencies in West Texas and New Mexico began asking for a recent photograph of the new drug lord of Ojinaga to help in identifying him in the event the kingpin ever came across the border. The most recent photo anyone possessed of Pablo was the mug shot taken by the Ector County sheriff's department in 1974 when Acosta was arrested for assaulting the former Ector County commissioner.

In the spring of 1982, one of the more daring of the Presidio Customs patrolmen managed to photograph Pablo at a benefit rodeo at the bullring near downtown Ojinaga. The patrolman spotted the drug *padrino* sitting high in the stands of the small arena, surrounded by gunmen with M-1 carbines. The American agent was sitting about twenty yards away from the drug lord, below and to one side. When the next bull came bucking out of the chute with rider struggling to stay on, the American lawman breathed deeply, stood up and coolly snapped off two frames. Pablo and his men were none the wiser.

The prints were circulated for years among police agencies throughout West Texas and New Mexico. One of the photographs showed a group of six men staring down at the arena. Five of them were tough-looking *hombres* with steely eyes presumed by intelligence analysts to be Pablo's gunmen and bodyguards. The sixth man was Pablo's older brother, Juan Acosta.

The second shot presented a striking view of Pablo alone, also looking intently toward the arena, a cigarette in one hand. The photo was unflattering; it had been taken against the setting sun and Pablo's nose and chin were partly washed out by the intense light. He looked pensive. His eyes and his cheeks were obscured in shadows that gave him a cadaverous, cruel look. The distortion of light and shadow created an indelible image of ruthlessness.

The photograph itself inspired fear and helped determine law enforcement attitudes about Pablo—even before the bloody drug wars of Ojinaga began.

Chapter Eight

BLOOD FEUD

The killings started in the summer of 1982 and came to be known among American law enforcement as the Arevalo Wars, after Fermin Arevalo, the head of a rival drug clan who was passed over for the Ojinaga *plaza*.

Fermin was a gruff, unwashed *campesino* who had been famous in the region during the 1960s as a rodeo star, bank robber, cattle rustler and drug trafficker. Though only four years older than Pablo, Fermin was already a legend celebrated in northern Chihuahua ballads years before Pablo was out of Fort Leavenworth.

One ballad describes how Fermin robbed an Ojinaga bank with Wild-West daring and escaped even though surrounded and outgunned by the local police. The song goes on to recount how Fermin was finally captured on the highway after the *comandante's* men skidded their vehicles into a circle around his truck. The police chief jumped out, yelling triumphantly, "You won't get away from me this time, Fermin Arevalo!" The ballad predicted trouble for the police official once Fermin finally got out of jail.

Actually, the bank robbery was a much less daring exploit than the version celebrated in the folk ballad. With the connivance of a bank employee, Fermin had embezzled the equivalent of $24,000 dollars. He was arrested and sentenced to the notorious Islas Marias penitentiary, Mexico's Alcatraz, 100 miles off the Pacific coast from Mazatlan. He stayed in jail for a total of nine months.

While Pablo Acosta was making friends in Fort Leavenworth and La Tuna who would serve him well later, Fermin
was making connections of a different kind at Islas Marias.
Some of Fermin's jailmates were friends or relatives of important marijuana and opium-poppy growers in the west
coast state of Sinaloa. These jailhouse contacts arranged
introductions after he was released, and Fermin's craftiness
took care of the rest. Soon he was smuggling drugs heavily
out of Ojinaga, using his Sinaloa connections as his source.
Fermin's rise paralleled that of Manuel Carrasco, and he
was thought to have worked under Carrasco's protection
scheme. Fermin supplied heroin and marijuana to Odessa
and Hobbs, delivering it to some of his brothers who handled the distribution end of the business.

The drug profits began to show in big ways. Fermin
bought a twelve-thousand-acre cattle ranch in an isolated
region forty miles south of Ojinaga, about ten miles into the
mountains and accessible by a dirt road. He called the ranch
El Salto—The Jump—a hint about its use as a transit point
for narcotics. Near the ranch house was a long caliche runway. Fermin kept stolen airplanes there to fly drug loads
into the United States.

Narcotics agents in New Mexico investigating the distribution end of Fermin's organization were told by informants
of Fermin's ruthlessness. According to one source, someone
had once flown a load of marijuana into Fermin's ranch from
the interior of Mexico. Short of cash, Fermin killed the pilot
and bulldozed a hole somewhere on the ranch big enough to
bury the pilot *and* the plane. That way Fermin could claim
he never received the drug shipment and refuse to pay for it.
Later, the New Mexico State Police sent an informant to
attempt to penetrate Fermin's operation, but the agent never returned and was presumed killed.

Fermin's luck ran out one summer morning in 1976 when
a blue-and-white federal police helicopter landed outside his
ranch house. The raid happened six months after Manuel
Carrasco disappeared from Ojinaga. Fermin, his wife Antonia, their brood of daughters, and their son Lili and his wife,

Acosta and some of his gunmen in the spring of 1982 at a benefit rodeo in Ojinaga, shortly after Acosta took over the *plaza*. Top photo shows Acosta, cigarette in hand, watching the action. Below, Acosta's entourage includes his brother, Juan, second to the left.

Yolanda, had just sat down to breakfast when they heard the deafening whirr of helicopter rotors. With his family in the line of fire, Fermin had no intention of putting up a fight. Hands in the air, he strode out the front door, Lili right behind him. They were taken by helicopter to Ojinaga, to the stables Fermin owned. While the *judiciales* were making the raid on his El Salto ranch, soldiers had surrounded the stables and arrested just about everybody they found there. All of the captives were unceremoniously chained together by the neck.

Usually stoic and self-controlled, Fermin cursed bitterly when the soldiers began giving away his racehorses, saddles, saddle blankets, bridles, bags of oats and miscellaneous stable equipment to bystanders. A soldier led Fermin's favorite quarter horse into the crowd and handed the reins to a man standing there. "Take it," the soldier said.

Altogether, the authorities picked up nineteen people on that raid. They were taken on a bumpy 400-mile ride to Ciudad Juarez in the back of the pickup trucks the authorities had confiscated. Most of the men, including Lili, were released from the jail in Ciudad Juarez within a few weeks. Once back in Ojinaga they quickly got all their horses and equipment back. Fermin, however, was charged with possession of a kilogram of heroin and more than a ton of marijuana that had been found somewhere in town. He stayed in jail for the next three years, first in Ciudad Juarez and then in Chihuahua City where friends arranged monthly weekend furloughs for him.

Fermin's first furlough was barely a month away when Pablo Acosta was brought in to the Chihuahua City penitentiary, chained by the neck to other prisoners. Pablo had been picked up in a raid in December 1977, a year after Fermin was arrested, and would very likely have languished in jail if it had not been for Fermin's help. Outside his own circle of relatives and friends, Fermin was not known for his generosity. But in jail he began helping indigent *campesinos* he thought had been arrested unjustly. He arranged for legal help or paid their bails, bonds and fines.

Fermin took a liking to Pablo. They knew each other already, having met on several occasions involving Manuel Carrasco's drug deals. They also had some distant ties of kinship and a wealth of mutual acquaintances in Ojinaga, Odessa, Hobbs, Fort Stockton and other towns in Texas and New Mexico. To assist Pablo in his case, Fermin invited a Chihuahua City attorney to the jail. He also talked to his acquaintances in the jail administration about Pablo. Finally, he loaned Pablo enough money to take care of the expenses entailed in securing a release.

Pablo was out of jail before Fermin got out on his first furlough, and showed his gratitude by helping organize a fiesta at Fermin's desert ranch to welcome him home. Pablo brought his wife and daughter to the fiesta. "He offered to supply all the beer," one of Fermin's in-laws later recalled.

Pablo and Olivia began to socialize with Fermin's son Lili and his American wife Yolanda. They went to dances together at Los Arcos or to the monthly Lions Club dances. Whenever horse races were held, they were certain to be seen together. Pablo was also a frequent visitor to Lili's home in Ojinaga and came to know Arevalo in-laws who lived across the river in Presidio. Since Pablo could not cross safely into Presidio, he frequently sent his new friends on such errands as buying money orders at the post office in Presidio to mail to his mother in Odessa or to his wife when she stayed up there.

From 1976 to 1979 Fermin ran his drug business from the jail in Chihuahua City, using his sons Lili and Lupe to carry out the deals. As they got older, the sons began working their own deals as well.

The brothers, Pablo soon found out, preferred to operate independently on the fringes of the Ojinaga movement. When the small group of traffickers held a meeting at the stables in early 1978 about sending someone to Chihuahua City, Lili and Lupe were not there. After Victor Sierra got the *plaza*, the word was that the Arevalos were not paying into it. That did not change when Fermin got out of jail in 1979. The Arevalos apparently had some kind of an arrangement of their own that allowed them to work, other traffickers believed. Occasionally the Arevalos were seen in the company of Chihuahua state policemen, meaning possibly that Fermin had worked out an arrangement with the governor's office. Pablo drew his own conclusions and kept his mouth shut.

After getting control of the *plaza* from the federal system in early 1981, Pablo continued to socialize with Fermin Arevalo's sons Lili and Lupe. But before the year was out, rumors were flying in the Ojinaga underworld that the Acosta and Arevalo factions were on a collision course.

Jealousy and mutual suspicions were at the root of the conflict. As one of the pioneers of the drug business in the Ojinaga area, Fermin had always hoped eventually to work out an arrangement with the federal authorities to take over the Ojinaga *plaza*. But Pablo, an upstart, had gotten it instead.

Except for Fermin, not too many other people were surprised by the selection of Pablo. Fermin was sullen and taciturn, a loner who did not get along easily with people. Pablo, on the other hand, had a winning personality and liked being around others—particularly people in positions of power and authority. And more successful than Fermin in the narcotics business, Pablo also had more money to spread around.

The most serious problems for Pablo centered on Lili Arevalo, Fermin's youngest son. Pablo suspected Lili of having snitched off a planeload of marijuana to the American police. Not only did the loss of the drug load result in a serious financial setback, but the ground crew was arrested and Rogelio Gonzalez, the pilot, lost his life when he panicked and ran into his own propeller blade.

That bust took place on January 22, 1981, only a month after Victor Sierra's arrest in Albuquerque, and made headlines all across the United States. Though Rogelio generally flew for the Arevalos, Pablo for this deal needed three loads of marijuana flown to the United States in a single night and asked Rogelio to do it for him. The loads were to be flown to an isolated farm road near Orla, Texas. The pilot had to land on the narrow road and taxi up to a ground crew who would guide him in with the light of a bonfire and then quickly

unload the marijuana. To transport the loads, the pilot would
have to make three round trips in quick succession of about
400 miles each, a feat requiring the stamina and flying skill
that Rogelio was known for.

The Orla landing site was a paved two-lane farm road
that had been used by Victor, Pablo and other Ojinaga smugglers since 1978. It was west of Orla, a tiny farming
community near the Pecos River—among the most isolated
regions of an already desolate West Texas. One of Victor
Sierra's runners "discovered" it one day in 1978 when he
took a wrong road on the way to Pecos from Carlsbad, New
Mexico. Impressed by the isolation, the runner spent the next
three nights parked along the side of the road to count the
number of vehicles driving by from dusk to dawn. In three
nights, exactly three vehicles drove by. The site had a built-
in beacon, the huge Duval sulfur mine that shone at night
like a brilliant star. All Rogelio needed to do was zero his
plane in on the sulfur plant, then veer toward the highway.

About 9:30 on the evening of January 22, 1981, Rogelio
took off with the first of Pablo's loads. Waiting for him on
the stretch of road near Orla was a ground crew that included one of Pablo's brothers, Hector Manuel.

Rogelio never came back for the second marijuana load.
Back in Mexico, Pablo kept waiting, straining his ears for
the hint of an airplane motor. Several hours after the pilot
was due back, Pablo understood that *something* had gone
wrong and drove to Ojinaga to make phone calls.

Yes, there had been a bust, he soon found out, and only
one member of the ground crew had managed to escape.
Slowly the details began coming in. Texas state narcotics
officers had been hiding next to the farm road, waiting for
the plane to land. As soon as Rogelio landed and taxied up,
the ground crew began unloading the bales of marijuana and
putting them into a van. The police moved in, catching the pilot
and ground crew by surprise. Contrary to his usual practice
of remaining in the plane, Rogelio had jumped out to help
transfer the marijuana to the van. When one of the American
cops shouted "Police!" Rogelio panicked and backed up along

the cowling. As he did so, he stepped into the propeller blade. The propeller sliced through his head all the way down to his chest. He was not the only casualty. One of the ground crew was shot when he aimed a machine gun at one of the policemen. In all, six men were arrested, including Pablo's brother.

The bust was a serious setback for Pablo. In one night he lost a pilot, his ground crew, a plane, a load of marijuana, a first-rate landing site and one of his brothers. The bust *was* sensational, and it got a lot of media coverage in the United States. Texas authorities said it was the first time an entire ground crew had been caught along the border with pilot, plane and load. One of the men was found with Mexican federal police identification. Wire reports that dwelt on the gore were published as far away as Anchorage.

Pablo was furious. The American police must have had advance notice that the airplane was coming. Pablo's suspicions that Lili was the snitch were aroused by a casual remark Fermin's son had made the very morning of the bust. Lili had owed the pilot some money for a drug deal and had not paid him back. As security Rogelio had taken Lili's souped-up pickup and told him he would only give it back when Lili paid up. The morning of the Orla bust, before Rogelio's mangled body had even reached a morgue and before news of the bust had gotten around, Lili went to Rogelio's house to take back the pickup. Someone heard Lili say, "He's not going to be needing this any more" and reported the remark to Pablo.

How could Lili have known so soon that anything had happened to Rogelio? An off-the-cuff remark was not evidence that Lili was behind the loss, Pablo realized, but he began to suspect that the Arevalos were going to be a problem.

Over the next year, several of Pablo's loads coming from the interior of Mexico to Ojinaga were hijacked. Again without proof, Pablo suspected the Arevalos.

A year later Pablo and Lili had a dispute over a load of marijuana Pablo had given to Lili on credit. The way the complex deal was explained later to American authorities, Lili had fronted—sold on credit—a load of marijuana worth $54,000 to one of Pablo's cousins in Odessa. But when he struck the deal with the Acosta cousin Lili did not have the marijuana on hand and had to go to Pablo for it. As it turned out, Pablo did not have the necessary amount of pot on hand either and had to borrow the balance from one of his lieutenants, a tall, balding, up-and-coming trafficker who went by the name Marco DeHaro. It was a chain of debt in a convoluted deal typical of border drug transactions. Somewhere in the loop, the money vanished and never got to Pablo or his underling.

Pablo confronted Lili about it. Fermin's son claimed he was never paid. To confirm, Pablo called his cousin in Odessa but was told Lili was "lying through his teeth." He *did* send Lili the money, the cousin insisted, and Pablo should have been paid by now.

To get to the truth, Pablo arranged for his own cousin to be kidnapped at gunpoint from Odessa. Taken to Ojinaga in the trunk of a car and kept under guard for several days, the cousin stuck to his story, that he had sent Lili the money. In fact, he had sent his two sons with the cash and they had personally turned it over to Lili.

The sons agreed to come down to Ojinaga from Odessa if it meant Pablo would free their father. Neither of the sons had ever seen Lili Arevalo before the dope deal. "All I want is for you to point out to us who you gave the money to," Pablo told them when they got to Ojinaga. Pablo shoved the brothers into the back seat of a Bronco with tinted windows. The Bronco was driven by Marco DeHaro and another Acosta *pistolero* named Damaso Martinez Prieto. "As soon as you see the guys you paid, you point them out to Marco and Damaso," Pablo said.

It was August 29, 1982, a significant day in the history of Ojinaga. That morning and afternoon Lili and his brother Lupe were at their father's stables feeding, watering, and exercising racehorses. In the evening, they drove to town to get something to eat and stopped at a popular ice-cream parlor, the Neveria Alegria.

The two boys from Odessa spotted the Arevalo brothers in the ice-cream parlor and pointed Lili out to Marco. "That's him there! He's the one we gave the money to!"

The Bronco sped around the block. When it came back there were only two men in it—Marco with an AR-15 and Damaso with an M-1. The Bronco slowed to a stop in front of the ice-cream parlor just as the Arevalo brothers stepped into the street, ice cream cones in hand. One of the gunmen fired through the open window, the other over the hood of the Bronco. Lili was hit twenty-one times and fell backward onto the sidewalk. Lupe was hit twice, once through the liver, and fell headfirst into the gutter. A ricocheting bullet grazed the forehead of a teenager standing nearby. In one account of the killing, Lili struggled to get to his feet but then fell back and started to crawl. Marco ran up to him and shot him in the head with a .45-caliber pistol. The gunmen jumped back into the Bronco and sped away.

Relatives of the Arevalos were at a drive-in restaurant on the Chihuahua highway. It was two miles away from the center of town, but they said they could hear the clatter of machine-gun fire even from there. They claimed later they saw Marco driving south in a Bronco, followed by Pablo in another vehicle.

The gunfire was heard all across town. It did not take long for word to spread that Lili Arevalo was dead and Lupe seriously wounded, or for speculation to surface that a gang war had started between the two drug families

An American friend of the Arevalo family had been driving down the main street when the shooting happened. Like everybody else, he heard the gunfire and quickly found out what it was about. A little later, the American saw Fermin driving into town with a freshly slaughtered steer in the back of his pickup. The American flagged Fermin down. It was obvious from the amiable greeting that Fermin had not heard about the shooting yet.

"I hate to be the one to break the news to you," the American began somberly, "but Lili's been shot to death and Lupe's in pretty bad shape."

They drove together to the doctor's office where Lili's body had been taken. Other than a tightening of the jaw and a narrowing of his eyes, Fermin did not display any emotion as he viewed the shredded body of his son. The American had known the Arevalo boys since their birth. He shook his head and said, "Who in the hell could have done this?"

Fermin said coldly, "I know who did it."

The trafficker did not elaborate and his American friend did not press him.

Chihuahua state police were quoted in newspaper stories saying that roadblocks had been set up between all the major towns in northeastern Chihuahua in the hope of apprehending the murderers. An Ojinaga newspaper identified Marco as one of the killers.

Lili's funeral came quickly, as funerals must in the scorching desert. Lili's body lay in an open casket in a little chapel in one of the Ojinaga funeral homes.

Pablo's wife Olivia visited the funeral parlor with her young daughter Karen. Olivia had heard rumors that it was Pablo who was behind Lili's murder, but she did not believe it. Pablo had called her from out of town to assure her it was not so and to ask her to visit the funeral home.

It took a lot of courage for Olivia to go the chapel. When she and her young daughter entered, Karen tugged at her elbow and said, "Mama, Mama, look at Lili! What's the matter with Lili?"

Olivia, plump and expensively dressed, broke into tears when she saw Lili's widow. "I don't know why anybody would have killed him and done it so awfully," Olivia said, dabbing her eyes. "Who did it? Do you know who did it?"

"We already kind of know who did it," Yolanda Arevalo said frigidly.

"It wasn't Pablo," Olivia assured her. "Pablo was out of town. He's still out of town. He called me to tell me how sad he was about Lili. He asked me to come and visit you. You must believe me."

"There's no use you crying now," Yolanda said. "Whoever did it, his turn will come some day. He left my kids without a father and I hope the one who killed Lili has kids too, because that is going to leave them without a father too, just like he left my children."

The Acosta and Arevalo children had always played together and it had always been the hope among the parents that Pablo's daughter one day would marry Jaime, Lili's son, or Marco, Lupe's son.

Head bowed, Olivia left the funeral home. The womenfolk, at any rate, never again met face to face.

Chapter Nine

GUNSLINGERS

If there was an official investigation into the shooting of the Arevalo brothers, the results were never made public. What is certain is that no one was ever charged with the murders.

Pablo sent messages to the Arevalo family insisting that he did not send anybody to kill Lili. He never mentioned Marco or the other gunman by name, only that the murderers had acted on their own and that he was not responsible for their independent actions.

The messages did not placate the Arevalos. Not long after Lili's funeral, Fermin's stocky wife Antonia visited friends in Presidio and asked for some boxes of ammunition for a 12-gauge shotgun. The friends did not believe the ammunition was for target practice.

Fermin was disconsolate over the death of his son and brooded for long periods at the El Salto ranch. Everyone in Ojinaga and across the river in Presidio expected a showdown. People with an interest in the outcome or with family ties to either clan closed ranks behind Pablo or Fermin.

Given Fermin Arevalo's reputation for ruthlessness, quite a few people in Ojinaga and Presidio figured Fermin Arevalo would finish Pablo off in short order.

The feuding heated up two months after Lili's death when three would-be hitmen ambushed Pablo and Marco DeHaro in broad daylight in front of Samborn's Restaurant. On this day Pablo and Marco, the balding gunman who was thought to have killed Lili, were inspecting a house under construction on a dirt side street half a block from the Chihuahua highway. Marco was carrying a German-made semiautomatic rifle, while Pablo had his ever-present .45 pistol stuffed in his belt. It was three in the afternoon on a windy, overcast day. The house belonged to an acquaintance of Pablo's in the Mexican Department of Motor Vehicles. Having worked in construction in the United States, Pablo had an interest in building techniques and was pointing out construction shortcomings and details to Marco, explaining to him how he would have done the job.

As they were leaving the worksite Marco saw a car with darkened windows slow down and drive by, as if for a close look at them. Then Marco saw the car back up abruptly and stop in the dirt street next to the cement-block wall of the restaurant.

"We better get out of here," Pablo said.

They had driven to the house in Pablo's truck. Pablo jumped behind the wheel as Marco readied his rifle. Out the back window Marco saw a man with a machine gun jump out of the car, crouch down, and take aim. "He's going to shoot," Marco yelled. "Gun it, Pablo!"

Pablo swore as he pressed on the accelerator. The two-lane asphalt highway was three inches higher than the dirt road. The truck bounced onto the asphalt just as the gunman opened fire. Bullets tore through the back window. Another pickup with a man, a woman and a small girl was coming up the highway. Pablo smashed into the side of it. Pablo's truck spun around to the opposite side of the road, throwing him out onto the pavement. Blood was streaming down his face. Marco thought he was dead.

Marco was not hurt. He slid out of the pickup on the driver's side and crawled up to Pablo. The truck was between them and the shooters and Marco could see from under the truck that one of the gunmen was running toward them. The gunman was barely twenty yards away, evidently intending to run across the highway and finish them off at close range. Marco leaned against the truck and visualized where the man would be. Then he popped up and let off several bursts over the hood of the truck. The gunman spun around as the bullets tore into his chest. He fell on his back next to the highway.

By then two other assailants had scurried from the car and were shooting automatic rifles from across the road.

Marco dragged Pablo behind the front wheel and straddled his body as he fired over the hood.

One of the ambushers had ducked behind a heavy cargo truck parked in front of the restaurant. With a well-placed burst, Marco shot him down and ducked back down behind the pickup. Marco could hear bullets from the third gunman slapping against the other side of his truck. He looked to his left and saw the man, woman and little girl who had been in the truck Pablo had collided with. They were hugging the ground and the man was covering the girl with his own body. Marco looked in the other direction and saw a school bus coming. It was the bus from the agricultural high school near the village of Tecolote on the Chihuahua highway.

The bus always made a stop in front of Samborn's to let students off. As it did so the bus drove between Marco and the remaining gunman. The driver slowed when he saw the wrecked vehicles, then slammed on the brakes when he realized he had driven into the middle of a gun battle. Marco could hear the driver screaming at the students to hit the floor. "Get your heads down," the driver yelled when several students peered with curiosity out of the window from the back of the bus.

The remaining gunman took advantage of the shield provided by the school bus to drag his wounded comrade into their sedan and jump behind the wheel. He slammed the car into gear and bounced onto the highway. With a screech of tires he sped up the highway, but Marco was ready for them. The moment the bus came to a stop Marco had sprinted a few yards to the bus and dropped to the ground behind one of the huge tires. As soon as the fleeing sedan bounced onto the pavement and began to speed away, Marco ran out and opened fire. The bullets hit their mark: the car began to zigzag down the highway and crashed into a ditch.

Marco ran back to where Pablo was sprawled out and felt for a pulse. Pablo was still alive. Marco flagged down a passing pickup truck, driven by a teacher from one of the federal schools. The teacher, a pudgy middle-aged man with dark circles around his eyes, had been on his way home, not far behind the school bus. He was feeling sleepy and longed for a nap. Thinking the bus was stalled from a collision, the teacher stopped to offer to help push it to the side of the road. He heard Marco calling him over.

Marco was straddling Pablo's body, nervously looking around for other gunmen. He recognized the teacher. In a tone that was more an order than a request, Marco said, "*Profe*, help me get this man to a doctor."

Like everyone else in Ojinaga, the schoolteacher knew the name Pablo Acosta, but he did not know what Pablo Acosta looked like and did not ask the identity of the injured man. Marco lifted Pablo up from under the shoulders while the teacher lifted the drug *padrino*'s legs. Pablo was bleeding badly from the scalp and eyebrow and the teacher suggested putting him in the bed of the pickup rather than in the cab. "Too much blood," he said to Marco.

The teacher began to realize that he had gotten himself involved in more than a traffic accident when he saw Marco retrieve several machine-gun clips from Pablo's wrecked truck and pick up the drug lord's .45 from the road. As he got back behind the wheel of his truck, the teacher for the first time noticed the body on the other side of the road with round blotches of red on the chest.

"Step on it," Marco ordered after getting into the passenger seat. "There may be more of them around here."

"What happened?" the teacher ventured.

"A bunch of jerks tried to kill us."

The teacher suddenly felt a chill up and down his spine. He raced into town, swerving through intersections with his horn blasting, eager to get these people where they had to go as quickly as possible. Marco was looking to the right, to the left and out the back window, as if expecting more carloads of assailants to drive out at any second.

Marco pointed to a side street. They pulled up in front of a brick house on Calle Sexta with a high wrought-iron fence. The two men lifted Pablo from the bed of the truck. Pablo seemed to be coming around. Olivia let out a cry when she opened the front door, and they half-carried Pablo into a back bedroom and laid him on a bed. Olivia rushed to get a towel and wiped the blood from Pablo's face.

The teacher realized who the wounded man was when he heard Marco tell Olivia what had happened to "Pablo." Over the years the teacher had observed in dismay how *los narcotraficantes* were becoming heroes in the eyes of many of the students. He had scolded some of his students for imitating them in their dress and speech, but the upbraidings had little effect. The students ended up petitioning to have one of the drug traffickers sponsor a graduation celebration, an idea vetoed by the school administration. Now he was in the home of the *padrino* of them all. The teacher's eyes went from Marco to Pablo to the imported French furniture, then to Olivia. He realized he had no business there any longer.

"I'm off," he said, heading for the door.

"Thanks, *Profe*," Marco said.

The kindly teacher made it home to his family a little later, too agitated for the longed-for nap.

Pablo soon regained consciousness. As he lifted himself up on his elbows, he said groggily "Is it over?"

Most of the blood was coming from above his eyebrow where his head had hit the steering wheel in the crash. A bullet had also creased the top of his skull, and Olivia feared his skull was fractured. His head ached terribly. He needed medical attention.

Olivia was angry. She blamed Marco for the gunfight. She was certain it was the result of the murder of Lili Arevalo. And now Marco had gotten Pablo "into another shootout." She yelled at him to get the hell out of her house.

But Pablo would not hear of it. He decided it would not be a good idea to seek medical help in Ojinaga. He was sure the ambush could only have been the work of the Arevalos, and they could be waiting for him to be taken to one of the clinics in Ojinaga. He had the protection of the authorities to run his business but was on his own when it came to fending off rivals. He wanted Marco to fly him to Torreon, an industrial town in Coahuila, for medical treatment. Though self-taught, Marco was an expert pilot. But the wind had started to whip up, a rainstorm was about to break out at any minute, and it would be dangerous to take off in a light plane.

Instead, they decided to drive to Torreon taking the dirt back roads. It was slow and bumpy, but it would be safer than the main highway. It took more than a day of rough driving through the desert to reach the industrial town. They went to a discreet private clinic where Pablo's skull was X-rayed. There were no fractures. The doctor cleaned and sutured the scalp wound and the gash above Pablo's eye.

When they stepped out of the clinic, Pablo's ruthless side emerged. He had learned even before leaving Ojinaga that the two men in the fleeing sedan had been taken to a hospital, badly shot up but alive. One of them died later that day. The other had been hit eight times, but none of his wounds appeared mortal.

His teeth clenched, Pablo said to Marco, "Let's go back. I want to get that motherfucker." He snapped his finger loudly, suggesting what he wanted to do with him. Marco did not like the idea. There was still the chance of another ambush.

"Let's go to Mexico City," he suggested.

Pablo was adamant. He suspected who was behind it, but he wanted to find out for sure from the remaining gunman. The survivor was in a small two-story hospital in downtown Ojinaga under police guard.

At three o'clock the following morning, they got back to the ranch outside San Carlos. Pablo quickly roused his brother Juan from bed and rounded up several other men. "We have to hurry. We have to be there by five a.m." Pablo and his entourage bounced in a frenzied rush along the dirt road to Ojinaga. Once in town, Pablo banged on the door of a female friend and asked her to pose as the wounded man's sister.

"You tell them you just got into town and ask for your brother. See how many people they got watching the guy."

The small army of traffickers pulled up near the hospital. The woman walked up to the emergency entrance and was let in after knocking repeatedly on the door. She came out a few minutes later. "They said nobody with gunshot wounds was brought to the hospital." But she had seen two city cops in the building.

Half an hour later, Pablo rang the emergency bell and pounded the door. A young, slender nurse opened the door slightly. Pablo slid his hand and foot in the opening and shouted "*Judicial federal*, open up!" The nurse swung the door open and eyed him suspiciously. He was as bandaged as a mummy. Marco, Juan Acosta, and several more of Pablo's men, all of them armed with assault rifles, poured into the corridor.

"We want the man you have in here. The one with gunshot wounds," Pablo said. "He's got a lot of enemies out to get him, and the only way to save him is to get him out of here *right now*."

The nurse said, "Wait a minute" and went into a room. She tried to lock the door, but Pablo forced it open. Another nurse was inside.

"Where is he?" Pablo demanded.

One of the women pointed upstairs.

Pablo waved his .45. "You walk in front. Walk!" When they got to the room, Pablo pushed the two nurses in front of him and shouted to the policemen to drop their weapons. The wounded man, who was hooked up to an oxygen mask and a variety of wires and tubes, woke up. His eyes filled with terror when he saw Pablo and his men.

The nurse protested. "If you unhook that man, he'll die."

"He's going to die anyway," one of Pablo's men replied.

At the sight of all the machine guns, the policemen had gingerly pulled their Mexican-revolutionary-war .38-caliber revolvers out of their holsters and placed them on the floor. A retired policeman in Ojinaga later said the two guards had received a visit from the *comandantes* of the state and federal police just before Pablo and his men arrived. The *comandantes* instructed them not to offer any resistance if someone came by for the patient they were guarding.

Pablo's men grabbed the wounded man under the arms and dragged him screaming from the building. They punched him to quiet him down and shoved him into Pablo's pickup truck. On the way out of town they stopped along the highway and Marco hooked the two confiscated police revolvers onto a telephone pole for the policemen to recover.

They headed back to San Carlos. Marco was driving and the wounded man was sitting between him and Pablo. He was a young man with a dark complexion and a thick black mustache. Only the darkness masked his terror. On the way he told Pablo what he wanted to know. It was "the Arevalos" who hired him for the hit. They gave him and his companions 250,000 pesos each, about $500 at the time, to kill Pablo. All three of the the hitmen were from Cuauhtemoc, a town in the apple-growing region of southern Chihuahua.

"You are a *pendejo*," Pablo snarled. "If you had *asked* me for that money, I would have given it to you. Now you're not going to get to spend that money and neither is your family."

Their truck bounced in and out of arroyos. Juan Acosta followed in their tracks in another truck, and then came a third vehicle with more *pistoleros*.

The wounded man kept groaning from the pain of his wounds and kept pleading for mercy. "Please, spare me. I have children."

"You think I don't have children?" Pablo roared, feeling the pain in his skull. "You should have thought about that before. Now it's too late."

Pablo had hardly slept for three days. He shoved his pistol under his right buttock so the wounded man could not make a grab for it and leaned against the passenger door to try to sleep. But his injured head kept banging against the window at every bump in the road. Finally he said to Marco. "We have to stop. I have to get some sleep."

They put the doomed man into Juan's truck. Pablo ordered his brother to take the man to the ranch.

As Marco stood guard, Pablo stretched out on the desert floor next to the truck and slept for a few hours. When he woke up the sun had already come up. They drove on to the ranch. When they got there Pablo found his men had already had some sport with the wounded gunman. His end could not have been very pleasant. Juan told Pablo they had already dumped the body way out in the desert for the buzzards to finish off.

Pablo was furious. He had been too tired to interrogate the man thoroughly the night before. "I wanted to question him more and I wanted to kill him myself, you stupid motherfucker," Pablo yelled.

"*Hermano*," Juan began apologetically. "I thought you had already asked him everything you needed to ask him last night."

Following the Samborn's shooting, as the incident came to be known from the nearby restaurant, Pablo began taking more precautions. At the horseraces on Sunday he surrounded himself with more gunmen than ever before. He began traveling around town with carloads of *pistoleros*.

Both sides seemed to be recruiting for a showdown. One of Pablo's nephews, Pedro Ramirez Acosta, abandoned life in Odessa to enlist in Pablo's cause; Pablo gave him a machine gun. A sullen, acne-scarred man, Pedro told relatives in Odessa as he prepared to leave for Mexico, "I don't like it in this country and I'm leaving for good. We may never see one another again. I'm going to join my uncle."

Pablo had always been interested in trading weapons for drugs, but now acquiring a huge arsenal had become a necessity: he needed lots of weapons, preferably Colt AR-15s, and .45-caliber pistols, to arm all of the newcomers.

The shooting in front of Samborn's Restaurant was just the first round. One Sunday afternoon, about a month after that ambush, two of the Arevalo clan were machine gunned in a ferocious battle on the main street near downtown Ojinaga. They were parked in a Bronco in front of a taco stand on Avenida Trasviña y Retes. The state *comandante* was in the back seat after having attended a rodeo with the Arevalo men. As they were preparing to get out, a pickup truck suddenly raced up and seven men—three in the cab and four in the back—opened fire with Uzis, AR-15s, Kalashnikovs. Three of the attackers were leaning over the top of the cab and the rifles jerked in their hands from the recoil as they pumped rounds into the Bronco. The other gunmen were firing from behind the opened doors of the pickup. The combined gunfire created a tremendous roar and sent a thick cloud of gunsmoke into the sky.

All that saved the two Arevalo men was the arrival of an Arevalo cousin who bushwhacked the bushwhackers from a nearby street corner with a 9mm pistol. He fired at them from behind while the Acosta men were machine-gunning the Bronco. Four of the Acosta faction fell before they even realized they were being shot at. Panicking, the remaining gunmen piled their casualties into the back of the pickup and sped away, taking a few last shots at the Bronco before their vehicle skidded around a corner. Authorities found an AR-15 and more than two hundred shells in the street and counted seventy-eight holes in the sheet metal of the Arevalo Bronco. The two Arevalo men had been hit half a dozen times each and were taken to a hospital in Alpine in serious condition. Both survived.

The state police *comandante*, who ducked to the floor-boards when the shooting started, miraculously survived without a scratch. He reportedly tried the next day to arrest some of the people involved. Witnesses had seen Lili's killer, Marco DeHaro, and Pablo's older brother Juan among the attackers. But the arrests were blocked by the federal police *comandante*. As with all the other killings, officials publicly promised an investigation. No results were ever made known and no one was ever arrested.

Pablo was said to be upset about the shooting, particularly with his brother Juan. Again, Pablo denied ordering the shooting and claimed the men acted on their own. He scolded Juan by saying, "The problem is between me and Fermin. Why should they pay for something that is between me and another man?" After the wounded men recovered, he sent word to them on three occasions that he was sorry about the shooting.

The Arevalos were unmoved. Five months later, at a

dancehall in San Carlos, Pablo's brother and his bodyguard were murdered. The dance took place at a downtown civic building. By three in the morning, almost everybody except for the diehard revelers like Juan had gone home. Suddenly the lights went out. Gunshots rang out. When the lights were turned back on, Juan was crawling to the entrance on all fours with blood streaming from his chest. He died before reaching the door. His bodyguard, an Acosta cousin, was killed outside as he ran to Juan's truck for a rifle.

Arevalo clansmen later boasted they were behind those slayings.

The slaughter continued. In March 1983 two bodies were found by the edge of the Rio Grande. Each had been shot twice in the back of the head. One of the dead men was a distant cousin of Pablo's and a former Ojinaga police chief. The other victim was the former police chief's seventy-one-year-old stepfather.

There were further killings that many attributed to the Arevalo War. During a three-year period that started with the death of Lili Arevalo, the American intelligence officers across the river compiled a list of twenty-six murders that were somehow connected with Pablo's organization and the feud with the Arevalo clan. The list was considered incomplete.

"Those were only the ones we found out about," a former agent noted later.

Chapter Ten

DEATH IN THE DESERT

W e can't do shit, Pablo! He's a thorn in the side. You need to either talk to him or scare him, or ..."

Hector Manuel Acosta, Pablo's younger brother, listed the options one day in late August 1983 just after Pablo returned from a trip to Mexico City, echoing the opinion of everyone else in the Acosta faction. The killings were making everybody uneasy. Fermin seemed hell-bent on vengeance until either Pablo was dead or Fermin himself was killed. And a lot of people could die—were already dying—in the process.

Pablo favored a deal. As far as he was concerned, it was time to bury the dead and go on. All the more so because the shootouts were causing pressure to be brought by local authorities. A relatively discreet disappearance like the kidnapping and murder of the sole surviving Samborn's hitman was easy to hush up. Not even the usually well-informed drug intelligence officers in Presidio picked up on that one. But shootouts in broad daylight? It was costing Pablo money to keep things quiet, even though he said he had not ordered any of those shootings. Perhaps wanting to please the boss, his men had acted on their own. But he was held responsible.

Pablo later said he had extended an olive branch to Fermin through intermediaries to try to settle their differences after Juan was killed.

"Let's talk about this. I'll meet you anywhere you want, but we leave the weapons behind," Pablo said.

Fermin refused.

By the time he came back from a trip to Mexico City that August, Pablo had decided it was time for a showdown. Either he and Fermin work out their differences once and for all or they shoot it out and get it over with.

"I'll kill him myself if it comes to that," said Pedro, Pablo's nephew from Odessa.

Pablo said, "No, let's go over and talk and see what happens."

But Pablo did not want to leave anything to chance. He later told Fermin's wife that he went himself to scout out the El Salto ranch with binoculars. He lay in the mesquite with his men on a low hill at a distance from the ranch house. Below their position was Fermin's modest brick ranch house with several dusty pickup trucks parked in front. To one side were the rough-board corrals with several horses. Everywhere else was parched, blinding desert and deep arroyos that carved up the terrain here and there into miniature Grand Canyons.

Pablo surveyed the roads through his binoculars. In one direction, a well-graded caliche road wound off into the distance and joined the two-lane Camargo highway. A second, uneven road connected the ranch with the Camargo highway farther south.

The Arevalos later believed Pablo hid out on the hill for two days, waiting for Yolanda Arevalo, Lili's widow and Pablo's erstwhile friend, to leave before making a move.

At the time, Fermin was in the process of selling the twelve thousand-acre ranch, but the property was registered in the names of his sons. After Lili's death, Yolanda had moved ninety miles north of the border to Fort Davis. Fermin, who needed her signature to consummate the sale, invited her down to the ranch. She made the trip with her children on August 23, 1983, and they departed the next morning under the gaze of Pablo's binoculars.

That left only Fermin, his wife Antonia, a maid and a handful of workers at the big cattle ranch, so far as Pablo could tell.

Following Yolanda's departure, Pablo and his men abandoned their surveillance post and went back to Ojinaga to prepare for a showdown. Pablo carefully selected people to go with him: his brother, Hector Manuel; his nephew, Pedro; Zacarias Guzman Gutierrez, the half-brother of the slain former chief of police; and a fifth person, described by the Arevalos later as a short, stocky, dark-complexioned man with a receding hairline. More carloads of gunmen would have been perceived as a provocation, as would the presence of Marco DeHaro. Pablo made a point of leaving him out of it.

Before heading out to Fermin's ranch, Pablo took his men out to the desert where they fired hundreds of rounds of ammunition for practice.

Hector Manuel was not a very good shot, so Pablo had him drive. Before leaving, all of them donned bulky bulletproof vests despite the desert heat. They reached the dirt road leading to Fermin's ranch half an hour later. Hector Manuel guided the red-and-white Bronco along the bumpy road while everyone else kept a tense eye out for an ambush in one of the frequent dips where the road dropped into an arroyo. They reached the cattle guard that marked the entrance to the ranch, a couple of pylons and metal pipes laid closely together across the road to keep the livestock from wandering out of the grazing land. In either direction an irregular barbed-wire fence followed the desert rangeland as far as the eye could see.

Half a mile farther up the road they saw Fermin's brick ranch house. As they approached it Pablo said, "Drive around the corral first. I want to make sure no one is hiding there." Once around the corral, they stopped ten yards in front of the house.

Pablo and Hector Manuel jumped out. Their muscles tensed. Pablo saw Antonia, Fermin's wife, peer out the door.

"What do you want?" she scowled.

Antonia, a stout, strong-willed woman who had borne and raised eight children, stepped out alone and stood in front of the half-opened door. "What are you going to do, kill me too?" she said.

"I want to talk to Fermin."

"He's not here. He's in town."

Pablo could see that she was nervous and was convinced Fermin was inside. The same horses were in the corral as in

the morning, when he had observed the ranch through binoculars. The two trucks were still parked in front of the house.
If Fermin had been at home when Yolanda was there, surely he was home now.

The drug lord walked up the house alone, his semiautomatic pistol in hand. His men were covering him from behind.
He knew Fermin would not shoot with Antonia standing
there. She would be dead just a few seconds after Pablo.

Pablo pointed to the hills. "I know Fermin is here. I've
been watching you. I saw Yolanda leave before noon with
the two children. I know your husband is here at the ranch
with some of his men. If that motherfucker wants to fight,
tell him let's do it now and get it over with."

Pablo spoke loudly, thinking that Fermin was within earshot. "If you don't want to fight any more, tell Fermin let's
quit and make peace."

"Fermin is not here," Antonia said once more. "He hasn't
come out here today. God up above knows that I am telling
you the truth."

There were a couple of chairs. Pablo shoved his pistol
into his belt and sat down. He motioned to the other chair.
"Sit down. We have to talk."

She shook her head and folded her arms defiantly.

"We have to put an end to this," he said. "I know that you
think I had something to do with killing Lili, but I didn't.
And neither did my brother Juan." He went on, almost pleading, explaining that it was Marco and Damaso who did it,
not him. "Sure they were my people, but I wasn't there when
they did it and they did it without my permission. I got mad
with those two guys too, you know. But they already did it.
It was too late."

Antonia had heard this before and did not believe it. If
Pablo had been sincere, he would have done something about
those two men right away. If nothing else, he would not have
created any obstacles with the law. Instead, he went around
town with Marco just as before, buddy-buddy. All the anger
and hatred she felt suddenly began to spill out. "You may
not have done it with your own hand, but you paid them to

do it," she spat out. "Compared to you and the ones who killed him, he was just a boy. He was just a defenseless boy and he didn't owe you any money."

Pablo could feel the sun beating down. Underneath the bulletproof vest it was like an oven and sweat was rolling down his spine and back and his still-firm stomach. It must have been 110 degrees and he wished he had brought his hat. Horseflies from the corral were buzzing around them, attracted by the sweat and the fear. He noted the determination in Antonia's dark eyes.

"You are wrong and there has been a lot of blood because you are wrong," he said.

He enumerated the people who had died on both sides because she was wrong. There was Juan, Juan's bodyguard, Sergio Gonzalez; Jose Luis Gutierrez, the former police chief, and his stepfather, Agapito Mendoza. Two Arevalo men had been seriously wounded on Avenida Trasviña y Retes. There was already much more Acosta blood in the balance, even if the tally included the three failed hitmen in front of Samborn's Restaurant and the four men shot by the Arevalo cousin during one of the downtown ambushes.

"Why don't we quit? You're still ahead," Pablo said.

Fermin's wife shook her head.

"Do you think you would break even if you kill me?"

"Yes."

Tears had begun to stream down Pablo's face. Antonia later remembered thinking, when she saw the tears, that Pablo had suddenly understood the enormity of what he had started, that excuses and apologies were of no use, that there was no turning back. It was just too damn late.

Pablo reached around behind his back and in a flash pulled his silvery .45 from his belt. He chambered a round and cocked it. He grabbed the pistol by the barrel and handed it to her. She took the weapon by the pearly handle, but held the pistol limply.

"If you think that will bring Lili back, then kill me. All you gotta do is ..." he said, crooking his trigger finger.

Antonia looked at the heavy semiautomatic. Here was

the opportunity she had longed for to avenge her son's death. The slightest pressure on the trigger now would fire the weapon. Then she looked up over Pablo's shoulder. She could see his men in the Bronco barely ten yards away. The vehicle was bristling with machine guns. Pablo's men had jerked to attention when he handed Antonia his pistol and all of them were staring at her. Quite possibly for a brief moment Pablo had forgotten about his men, but Antonia knew she would have only seconds to live herself if she took him up on his offer.

She handed the automatic back.

"This is not how I'm going to kill you, Pablo," she said, quivering with hatred.

The young maid came out of the door and whispered something to Antonia. Antonia went into the house, returning moments later. Her expression had changed. She seemed as inflexible as ever, but more willing to talk. Pablo suspected later that Fermin had already gone out the back door and that the maid told Antonia to stall Pablo for time.

They continued the futile dialogue a short while longer. Pablo began to grow angry at her intransigence. An hour had gone by in the blistering afternoon sun and he was getting nowhere. He started swearing. Then he strode back to the Bronco. As he climbed in the passenger side, he shouted:

"If Fermin doesn't want to put an end to this, you tell that son of a bitch we're gonna screw him over, and screw him over good."

Pablo told Hector Manuel to take the rougher of the two roads out. He figured that if Fermin had managed to organize his men for an ambush while he was talking with Antonia, it would be along the other road. Though better graded, it offered numerous potential ambush sites.

The Bronco kicked up a thick cloud of white caliche dust as it bounced down the uneven road. A half-mile from the ranch house was the cattle guard, then the open desert up to the Camargo highway.

As they approached the cattle guard, they saw a large white pickup truck coming towards them barely a hundred yards away. "We gotta stop that motherfucking truck. Maybe it's Fermin," Pablo said.

They were thirty or forty yards away from the fence when Hector Manuel slowed down. What happened next confirmed Pablo's belief in his own privileged destiny and elevated him to the status of living legend.

According to Pablo's account, Fermin had ducked out the back door of the ranch house with one of the hired hands while Pablo was pleading with Antonia to put an end to the fighting. An arroyo ran behind the ranch house. Bent over and carrying machine guns, Fermin and the ranch hand had scurried along the arroyo bed and positioned themselves on both sides of the road near the cattle guard. They waited to ambush Pablo and his men if they drove out that way.

As the Bronco approached, Fermin and the ranch hand jumped up from their hiding places and opened fire. Pablo and Hector saw it happening as if in slow motion: Fermin scrambling to his feet, Fermin standing straight up on the mound of earth next to the ditch, naked from the waist up; Fermin jamming the rifle stock into his shoulder and squeezing the rifle grip with the other hand; and then Fermin cutting loose with a stream of bullets that at first hit the Bronco low and then moved up.

Bullets first blew one of the Bronco's front tires, then slammed into the radiator, then pelted the hood, and then ripped across the window, spraying glass and bullets and bullet fragments everywhere. Inside the crowded Bronco five men groaned, screamed and cursed as the terror of imminent death gripped them. Pablo and Hector had instinctively ducked toward the center, banging heads as they tried to get under the shelter of the dashboard.

Pablo's forehead was peppered with broken glass and a bullet had creased his right eyebrow and another his skull. He could feel the warm blood trickling down his face. In the back seat, several bullets slammed into Pedro's bulletproof vest and knocked him backward. Zacarias dived for the floorboards while the other gunman in the far back clawed in panic at the carpet. Zacarias slid one arm up to the handle of Pablo's door and shoved the door open. He stuck his machine gun under the door and shot wildly to keep anyone from running up to the Bronco and finishing them off.

Pedro was stunned by the impacts to his bulletproof vest but quickly recovered his senses. Seeing no alternative, he swung his machine gun over Pablo's head and started shooting with a deafening roar right through the windshield, showering Pablo with a stream of hot cartridge shells. The weapon was on fully automatic. Pedro took aim first at Fermin, then at the ranch hand, then at the truck that had stopped on the other side of the cattle guard. The truck's driver was Fermin's ranch foreman who was returning from Ojinaga. When he saw the shooting, the foreman jumped out with a rifle and took aim.

Fermin made a fatal mistake. Once he pulled the trigger, he did not let up until he had expended the entire forty-round clip. That's when Pedro stuck his machine gun over the front seat. Pedro had steady nerves and a deadly aim.

They heard someone scream "A-h-h-h! I've been hit."

Fermin dropped into the ditch. Then the ranch foreman fell to the ground next to the truck.

Suddenly, the desert was silent. They got out of the shot-up Bronco cautiously. Pablo's face was covered in blood.

Hector Manuel was trembling. "*Hermano*," he said to Pablo, "there's another one but I can't see where he went."

Pablo sent them to look for the third gunman, but they only found a machine gun lying in the dirt and footprints indicating the man had run off into the brush. Later they found out what happened to him. A bullet had hit him in the middle of his large oval belt buckle and the impact had knocked him to the ground, the wind kicked out of him. As he got back to his feet he saw Fermin get shot and fall into the ditch. Then he saw the ranch foreman drop into a heap. Throwing his rifle to the ground, the ranch hand ran for his life.

The drug lord and his men were in a savage frenzy. It was later believed that Zacarias ran up to Fermin and sliced him open with a knife from the belly to the sternum in revenge for killing his half-brother, Jose Luis Gutierrez, the former police chief. Someone else fired more rounds into Fermin's body. The ranch foreman had fallen in the road near the truck. He had been hit once in the hip and once in the head. The bullet tore a gaping, triangular chunk from his cranium. Pablo's men dragged his body by the legs off to the side of the road and left it lying behind a mesquite bush.

Pablo at the wheel, they commandeered the foreman's truck and headed back to the ranch. Pablo believed Fermin had set up another ambush at the other ranch entrance, sending two pickup trucks with three men each. He feared these men would now attempt to intercept them at the Camargo highway. For their own protection, they needed to go back to the ranch to take hostages.

"We have to get the women. They won't ambush us if we have the women," he told his men.

Halfway back to the ranch they spotted Antonia and the maid, walking in the direction of the cattle guard. When the women saw the white ranch truck approaching, their faces broke into broad smiles. They did not recognize Pablo's bloodied face until he screeched to a halt and jumped out.

Pablo was bleeding profusely. He wiped the blood from his eyes and grabbed Antonia by the arm. He shook her and said sarcastically, "Going somewhere?"

Antonia's lips were trembling. "I'm going to pick up my kids."

"On foot? To Ojinaga? Then let me give you a ride."

"I don't need your help," she said.

He slapped her furiously and shoved her and the maid into the cab of the pickup between him and Pedro. The other men were in the bed of the pickup. They drove to the ranch to look for a tire for the Bronco, but could not find one that would fit. They ransacked the house looking for ammunition. They drove back toward the cattle guard.

They drove around the shot-up Bronco. The men in the back of the pickup jumped out and got into the Bronco, starting it up despite the flattened tire. They fell in behind Pablo's truck.

Pablo had never come so close before to the reality of death. He was both nauseated by his bloody wounds and ferociously elated that he had survived. "You thought I was the one that died. I saw that in your face," he said with sinister glee. "But I wasn't the one who died. Do you want to know who was the one who died? I'm going to show you."

Pablo slowed the truck at the cattle guard. All that was visible of Fermin were his boots. With a bloodstained finger, Pablo pointed to the side of the road.

"Fermin wasn't at the ranch?"

"No."

"Then who is that?"

"I don't know."

"You know who it is. You sent him to kill me. And you are responsible for his death."

Antonia put her face in her hands and began to weep.

"We opened him up like a goat," Pablo said with a low, guttural, unnatural laugh.

A little farther up the road, they passed the body of the ranch foreman, a burly man of thirty-five, the maid's cousin, lying face down in the dirt. It was the maid's turn to weep.

The two women assured Pablo's security until they could get to Ojinaga and he could alert his people. He was convinced six men were still on the lookout for him and would try to ambush him, but he knew they would not try anything as long as Antonia was his hostage.

The vehicles made it as far as El Chapo, an out-of-the-way train station and village where the road to San Carlos begins. Both of the vehicles had leaked all their coolant through bullet holes in the radiator. The motors were beginning to give out. Pablo borrowed a truck from one of the villagers. They waited until dark before setting out again.

They stopped at a motel in Ojinaga where Pablo made some telephone calls, ordering more gunmen to meet him in front of Antonia's house. On the way to her home, he warned, "If somebody tries to shoot me between here and there, I'm gonna to shoot you first. You're gonna die before I do."

He swerved the truck around in front of her corner house.

"You get in that house and don't leave it," he said. "If anything happens to you, they're gonna blame me for it. So you stay in that goddamn house."

One of Fermin's sisters called the state police. Afraid of being ambushed themselves, the police waited until late the next afternoon before going out to El Salto for the bodies. When they arrived the bodies were already starting to bloat from the hot sun. The police scoured the area and picked up a total of ninety-five shells of different caliber. They brought the bodies in the back of a pickup to a funeral home in Ojinaga.

Fermin's widow and one of his sisters, Victoria, visited the state prosecutor's office in Ojinaga and demanded justice. But the prosecutor gave them the brushoff.

"These kinds of cases are taken care of at a higher level," he told the women. "And frankly, I'm afraid to do anything about it," he confessed.

Nevertheless, Fermin's widow did what no one else had dared to do up to that time. She filed a criminal complaint against Pablo and the case managed to reach a judge.

In Mexico there are no grand juries and no trials by jury. For homicides, state police investigators write up an incident report, certify the death occurred, order an autopsy and take statements from witnesses. Then the *expediente*—the file—is sent to a state judge to rule whether the evidence is sufficient for criminal charges. If he decides there is, he issues an arrest warrant. The warrant is turned over to the prosecutor, who in turn gives it to the state police *comandante* to execute. The state and federal police are essentially agents of the judicial system, as opposed to the executive branch in Anglo countries, hence the term *judicial* to describe these agencies and their agents.

Three weeks after Fermin's death, a judge issued arrest warrants for Pablo, Hector Manuel, Pedro, Zacarias and the unknown fifth man. They were charged with murder, kidnapping and burglary.

Pablo later told a close friend that he had to pay a total of 200,000,000 pesos, then worth about a million dollars, to quash the warrants.

He ended up frequently parking in front of Antonia's home in Ojinaga, or having one of his men do so, in order to intimidate her.

A tough and defiant woman, Antonia never left town, but much of the Arevalo clan did. Some moved to Presidio. Many more moved on to Houston.

Chapter Eleven

PADRINO

With Fermin Arevalo finally out of the way, Pablo could sit back and revel in his fame as *padrino*, a role that required displays of generosity.

It actually felt good to give things to people. Frequently, he started the day by spreading 1,000-peso notes around to the grimy *chicleros* and shoeshine boys in the town square or at the hotels. If he didn't go himself, he sent someone in his name.

People, most frequently destitute older women, rang the bell on the high wrought-iron gate in front of his home on Calle Sexta. If he was at home, he never failed to allow them in and hold audience in the manner befitting a *padrino*. He listened to them in respectful silence and spoke to them kindly. He was moved by the desperation in their eyes. It reminded him of his mother's eyes, and the eyes of his aunt Hermenegilda when they lived in those miserable hovels down by Santa Elena at *Ejido Providencia*, when the money and food had run short and there were so many hungry bellies.

Pablo also understood what it took for proud people to come to him and beg. He never "gave" them what they asked for; he "loaned" it, knowing that the semantic white lie allowed the petitioner to save face.

"*No tenga cuidado, señora.* Don't worry about it. You can pay me back when you have the money."

Someone once reminded him that loans are meant to be paid back.

"Forget it," he answered. "They are poor people. How do you expect them to pay me back?"

Pharmacists in Ojinaga became familiar with the sight of elderly women and men coming in with a note from Pablo saying, "Go ahead and fill out the prescription. Someone will come by later with the money." Then one of his men, quite often his nephew Pedro, would drop into the pharmacy later in the day and peel off what was owed from a fat wad of money.

Sometimes Pablo picked up the cost of transporting sick people to the general hospital in Chihuahua City or paid for the entire cost of their surgery or medical treatment. On other occasions he had some of his men go out and round up a cow, usually from one of his own ranches, but he wasn't always a stickler about where the animal came from. He would have the animal slaughtered and would give the meat to hungry families.

Recalled a close friend of Pablo's who witnessed some of the informal audiences at the drug lord's home: "He often talked about their poverty. He would ask me, 'Why doesn't the government do more for them? Why are they paid so little? In the United States, people are always paid more or less well, enough at least to get by on. Here they are paid a salary of misery.'"

For Pablo, giving was not as compulsive as it had been for Shorty Lopez. He gave with the idea of getting something back, even if only a sliver of useful intelligence from some toothless old peasant up the river. What was a crisp $20 bill for a tip that American police were patrolling the river, say down by Lajitas? Or that a truck carrying 600 pounds of marijuana had come through his *plaza* and the owner hadn't sought his permission or paid him tribute?

Over the years, Pablo had a fortune in water pumps, fencing, plastic irrigation piping, and other equipment trucked in from the United States. The materials got distributed to a lot of ranches, gratis. Those ranchers would look the other way when Pablo's men drove through or landed an airplane late at night. He had purchased their silent complicity.

There were times when the petitioners were not welcome.

A former friend of Pablo's recalled the day he and the drug lord of Ojinaga were in the Los Alamos Bar across the street from the ranch-style home of the garrison commander. Next to the general's residence was an apartment building reserved for garrison officers, and they frequented the bar. On this particular occasion, a lieutenant in civilian clothes walked up to Pablo and without beating around the bush asked for some money. The soldier explained that he had vacation time coming and he wanted to visit his family in Michoacan. Pablo pulled some money out of his shirt pocket and gave the officer the equivalent of $100 in pesos. The officer looked at the money with an air of dissatisfaction and said, "Couldn't you make it more?"

Pablo took out the wad of money again and gave him another hundred. He watched the officer stuff the money in his pocket and walk out.

Pablo was the beneficiary of the arrangement with the military. Without it, there was no way he could do what he was doing. Soldiers protected his fields, soldiers protected his shipments. Yet even he was disgusted by the behavior of the army lieutenant. "It's really a disgrace that a man with such a position could lower himself so shamefully," he told his friend.

Everybody was hitting Pablo up for money, and he had to work hard to make money for himself. It was almost like a system of taxation. He built a bridge over an arroyo on the road to El Mulato; he built an old people's home in downtown Ojinaga; he added rooms to the agricultural high school and paid for furnishings; he clothed and equipped soccer and baseball teams; he had Ojinaga schools painted and repaired. To officialdom he gave away scores of the automobiles and trucks stolen in the United States and taken to him in Ojinaga to be traded for drugs. It was easy to get them registered in Mexico, stolen or not, and they made terrific gifts to the authorities.

Few mature adults in Ojinaga were fooled by Pablo's run of the town. The alliance of crime and authority was scarcely disguised, and many citizens understood it for what it was: a form of contempt for the people. When a new garrison commander came to town, he sent troops to block off the street in front of Pablo's house on Calle Sexta—not to arrest Pablo but to prepare the way for a courtesy visit by the new general. The soldiers were not posted outside to stop the crooks but to detain and question citizens who inadvertently turned down the street while the general was with Pablo, possibly working out the *plaza* payment with him.

The young were the most taken by Pablo, and gauging his influence among them was as simple as asking questions in the street. Said a young road worker one blistering afternoon in Ojinaga about a year after it was all over: "If anyone ran this town, it was Pablo. The guy had balls to spare. He was the one who told the military and the police what to do. If someone stole some grass from him, all he had to do was to call the military and the police and they would keep looking until they found it. He knew how to spread the money around."

The road worker, covered from head to foot with sweat and dust, continued: "Yeah, he got a lot of respect, he and his men. If they'd said to me 'Hey, grab this machine gun and pistol and come join us,' I would have grabbed the machine gun and pistol and joined them. That's the way to make money. And that's the way to get a lot of …"

He thrust out his skinny hips to show what he meant and smiled through the dust on his face. "Pablo had a lot of girlfriends, *mano*. And he had something *big* to love them with too."

He spread his callused hands widely to show how big he thought Pablo's was.

"That guy had it all!"

The shootout with Fermin both helped Pablo by enhancing his aura of invincibility and hurt him by giving him a high profile on both sides of the border.

A newspaper story appeared in one of the Ojinaga weeklies a few days later giving the bare facts and simply noted that Fermin Arevalo and Adalberto Hinojosa, the ranch foreman, had been "ruthlessly murdered" around five in the afternoon the previous Wednesday at Fermin's El Salto ranch. The article omitted Pablo's name, even though his role in the death duel had been the talk of the town for days.

Embellishments to the stories about the showdown quickly began to circulate. In one, Pablo sliced off Fermin's penis and testicles and then went back to the ranch to present them to the widow with a question: "Which part of Fermin would you prefer?" Another version had Pablo filling Fermin's abdomen with stones and then dragging the body behind the perforated Bronco until there was nothing left of Fermin but a shredded torso.

Dr. Artemio Gallegos, whose office had been the scene of a shootout that brought Manuel Carrasco's Ojinaga career to an end, performed the autopsy at the funeral home. He counted fourteen bullet holes in all and sewed up the long abdominal incision Zacarias had prepared for him. The doctor certified that the dead trafficker was not missing genitalia or limbs.

The embellishments made Pablo appear formidable, unbeatable, ferocious—a warning to would-be rivals for the Ojinaga *plaza*. Only Pablo and the four men with him at El Salto knew how close they had come to being the losers that day.

Pablo nurtured the image of his invincibility with a deft gesture. He had the shot-up red-and-white Bronco towed to Ojinaga and placed on blocks right next to the main highway barely a city block away from his home on Calle Sexta. The vehicle remained enthroned there for years, a warning to anyone who would challenge him.

The high profile also had disadvantages. To the Americans, Pablo had become one of the best-known drug traffickers in northern Chihuahua. His notoriety helped other big dealers maintain their own anonymity, an asset in the drug business. Drug bosses in the interior of Mexico instructed their runners to claim, if they were caught, that the load belonged to Pablo. Rightly or wrongly, much of the narcotics seized in West Texas was assumed to belong to Pablo. It was one of the prices a drug lord paid for fame.

Another price Pablo paid was that of bearing responsibility for violent acts of which he had no part. As with the loads of narcotics, any shooting was automatically attributed to him. And with murder and mayhem seemingly breaking out all over, Pablo was beginning to look very bloodthirsty indeed.

For authorities across the river, the problem was that violence was beginning to spill into Presidio and the Texas borderlands to the east and west.

Just two months before Fermin's death a couple of men shot each other to death inside a pickup truck in downtown Presidio in what was presumed to be a drug-related altercation. They had been driving down the main drag with a third man sitting in between when they started blasting away at one another with pistols. The pickup crashed into the wall of a Texaco gas station. When onlookers opened the door on the driver's side, the driver fell out dead. The same when they opened the other door—the passenger tumbled dead to the ground. The man in the middle was in a state of shock. Crisscrossing his chest were graze wounds from the gunfight between his companions.

It later turned out the two dead men had begun a drinking spree at Pablo's house. The conclusion was that the shooting was drug-related and Pablo was behind it.

Then, several months after Fermin's death, someone drove up behind a pickup truck on the highway to Redford and opened fire on some kids in the back. A twelve-year-old boy was killed. Texas authorities didn't have a clue to the murder, but word spread that it was Pablo Acosta's doing, just like all the other shootings.

And more than ever before, American lawmen were getting shot or were being fired upon. The year before Fermin's death, someone from El Mulato, a village downriver across from Redford, seriously wounded a border patrolman. Shortly after that, several Texas narcotics officers waiting to nab drug smugglers down by Redford were greeted by a spray of machine-gun fire from *across* the Rio Grande.

These and other incidents caused authorities in Presidio

and Brewster counties to worry that it was just a matter of time before their jurisdictions would become uncontrollable battlegrounds. What happened in Mexico was not their business; what happened on the Texas side of the river was. Not long after the death of Fermin the sheriff of Presidio County, Rick Thompson, sent an "envoy" to Pablo to relay a simple request in the hope of forestalling such a development: "I asked one thing of Pablo," Thompson recalled. "I asked him that anything explosive, the killings and things, remain outside of my county. I didn't want any bodies scattered on this side of the river with no explanations."

Pablo never sent a reply to the sheriff but in November 1983 he invited one of the Texas Rangers stationed in Alpine, Clayton McKinney, to meet him in Mexico. McKinney and a Texas Department of Public Safety narcotics officer met Pablo on a hill outside Ojinaga. In an arrogant display of his power, the drug lord posted eighteen well-armed men around the hill. Pablo never said exactly *why* he wanted to meet the American lawman, neither when he extended the invitation nor when McKinney showed up. But it became apparent as they talked amid the greasewood bushes and brown desert grass that the Ojinaga drug lord wanted to set the record straight about all of the shootings. He was not behind the killings that had occurred lately, he insisted; and even the death of Fermin Arevalo was overblown by the border rumor mill; he and his men had gone to the El Salto ranch to try to work things out and Fermin had ambushed them. What is a man to do in such a situation but defend himself, Pablo asked the Texas lawman?

Pablo and Clayton McKinney held further secret meetings.

Pablo evidently wanted to appease the Americans. He had authorities on his side of the river under control. Now it was to his advantage to work out some sort of mutual back-scratching arrangement with the *gringo* law. Being in charge in Ojinaga, Pablo was in a position to provide cooperation in some investigations when it wasn't forthcoming from the Mexican authorities, a frequent complaint among American law enforcement.

The shootings and killings in Presidio didn't completely come to an end as a result of these unusual contacts. Just after the first meeting a Mexican game warden shot another man to death just outside Presidio. But Pablo did bring about some changes. Following the meetings with the Texas Ranger, no more American officers were getting shot at. The Border Patrol later picked up reports that the drug lord had spread the word. Anyone shooting at an American officer was going to have to answer to Pablo. "If it looks like you're going to get caught with a load," Pablo reportedly told all of his people, "drop everything and run. If you can't run, surrender. I can always get you out on bond. I don't want any U.S. lawmen getting killed."

According to McKinney, Pablo later was also helpful at times in recovering stolen cattle or vehicles and in providing help in other investigations when assistance could not be obtained from Mexican authorities. On one occasion he sent somebody across the river on an "errand" for him late one night. The errand boy was someone the Americans wanted for jailbreak and was someone Pablo evidently considered dispensable. When the man got to the other side of the river, Pablo, parked on the opposite riverbank, flashed his high beams and the fugitive was caught.

There were other instances of "cooperation." But years later, reflecting on that first meeting with Pablo Acosta, McKinney said he never could really understand what had been in it for the drug lord. As long as Pablo stayed in Mexico, he could not be arrested by American policemen anyway; and in light of all of the criminal activity his organization was involved in, the help he gave U.S. law enforcement in certain instances did not amount to much. McKinney speculated that Pablo had another motive, one stemming from a very logical assumption: Pablo knew that, sooner or later, his power in Mexico would come to an end. The moment could come when he might actually *want* to surrender to the Americans. Pablo wanted to have some contacts in place to help smooth the way.

Part Two

The
Organization

*T*his report focuses on the Pablo Acosta Organization, believed to be responsible for most of the narcotics flowing into Texas from the Ojinaga, Chihuahua, area. The Acosta organization accomplishes its smuggling operations mostly by land and sometimes by private aircraft. Acosta's heroin is noted for its high purity, known to be as high as 93 percent, which is known as black tar due to its appearance. His marijuana has improved, with most of the recent seizures traced to the organization being of high quality tops.

This organization is also responsible for approximately 70 percent of all 4x4 and pickup thefts reported in the Texas Panhandle, West Texas and eastern New Mexico areas. Thefts usually involve new and used Ford Broncos, GMC Jimmies, Chevrolet Suburbans, Blazers, four-wheel drive vehicles, etc. These vehicles are then driven directly to Mexico and traded for drugs.

The Acosta organization is also a reported major receiver of stolen weapons traded for drugs. There are over 500 known members and associates of the Acosta organization with factions in Amarillo, Dallas, Fort Worth, Hereford, Lubbock, Big Spring, Odessa, Midland, Kermit, Pecos, Monahans, Fort Stockton, Presidio, El Paso and Big Bend, Texas, and Hobbs, Portales, Artesia and Roswell, New Mexico. Associates in other Texas and New Mexico cities, as well as in Kansas, Oklahoma, Missouri, Nevada, Idaho, North Carolina and Michigan, have also been identified.

He pays high level protection for this freedom from the federal to the local level of Mexican government, and spends close to $100,000 per month for this protection.

Acosta's organization is very fluid and many of the members know only the person with whom they deal directly. Because of this, Acosta is very well insulated. Being a blood relation or having a long-time family or business relationship is the exclusive qualification for membership. The organization is extremely difficult to penetrate because of this criterion for membership.

From the introduction to a confidential 223-page U.S. Drug Enforcement Administration report, *The Pablo Acosta Organization*, April 1986

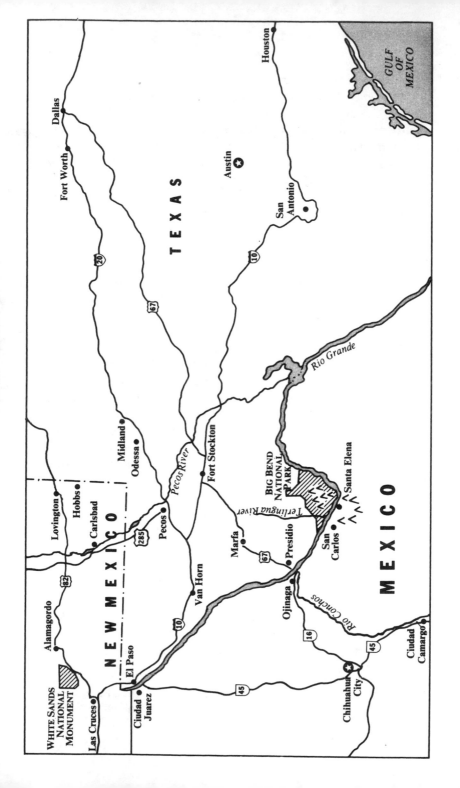

Chapter Twelve

SMUGGLERS

Pablo's organization was growing fast even before the showdown with Fermin Arevalo. Branches of the Acosta organization were springing up throughout Texas and New Mexico. Narcotics dealers from as far away as California, North Carolina and Michigan came to Ojinaga to deal directly with Pablo. Buyers sometimes sent their own people to pick up the purchase and smuggle it into the United States, but more frequently they paid extra to have Pablo send it to them using one of his own couriers. Those runners were often trusted acquaintances from Pablo's roofing days in Odessa and Eunice.

Sammy Garcia was in many respects typical of the smugglers working for Pablo. The son of a cowboy who had worked all his life on the open range of the million-acre King Ranch in southeast Texas, Sammy knew what cowboy life was really like and wanted to do something else. He worked at a variety of jobs in central Texas until one day in 1973 he ran afoul of the law for the first time. He and a cowboy friend named Billy got the wild idea of rounding up someone else's steers and selling them at an auction. But the rustlers were arrested that same night while feasting at an Abilene steakhouse.

When he got out of jail, Sammy started hauling hay from New Mexico to east Texas, then worked on roofing jobs wherever he could find them. On the side, Sammy and his second wife Becky started selling marijuana out of their home near Fort Hood, Texas.

In 1975, Sammy met Pablo during a roofing job in Hobbs. Pablo Acosta was the subcontractor for the work and needed some additional help. With a round, rubbery face, Sammy was friendly, cheerful and amusing. People tended to like him immediately. After doing several roofing jobs together, Pablo invited his new hand out for a few beers. It didn't take either long to understand the other's *secret* occupation. Pablo, the Eunice roofing subcontractor, soon became Sammy's main marijuana connection.

After Pablo fled to Mexico in late 1976, Sammy began going to Ojinaga to buy marijuana from him there or at times drove to Fort Stockton to buy from Acosta cousins. By that time, Sammy had moved to New Mexico and was working full time in the oilfields hauling drilling equipment for a trucking company. Selling marijuana was still part-time work.

As Pablo formed his organization from his border sanctuary, Sammy remained a faithful, steady buyer—a hundred pounds of pot here, a hundred there. Then he started doing odd jobs for Pablo in Ojinaga. But when the blood feud started in 1982, Sammy insisted on defining the limits of their relationship.

"I'll do anything you want me to do, with one exception," he told Pablo. "Don't ask me to kill anybody. I don't want any part of it."

The good-natured ex-cowboy became a runner for Pablo in 1982, about the time Pablo's gunmen murdered Lili Arevalo and seriously wounded his brother, Lupe. Thereafter Sammy smuggled two or three loads of marijuana a week out of Mexico. His job consisted of driving the pot to its destination, collecting the money and bringing it back to Pablo. Frequently, with marijuana hidden in the propane tank of his truck, he used the international bridge between Ojinaga and Presidio. When the Rio Grande was low, he would sometimes drive his 4x4 across the river at fords downstream.

Despite his aversion to violence, he could not avoid becoming the object of it. On more than one occasion, while midstream in his truck or before descending a slope to cross the muddy waters of the Rio Grande, he got shot at by someone hoping to steal his load. However, Sammy had some protection. Whenever the plan was to cross a load on the river, Pablo would always send a gunman in another vehicle to escort him. Thanks to the armed security, the several hijacking attempts were foiled.

Pablo's parting words to many of his drug runners when they prepared to leave Ojinaga could be vaguely menacing, veiled hints at what he might do to them if they let him down in any way. For Sammy it was always a sincere *"Vaya con Dios*—God be with you."

If Sammy happened to be going through Odessa, Pablo would ask him to drop by and see his mother and leave some money with her.

Friendship and Sammy's personality accounted in part for the courtesy. But there was also a pragmatic business reason, one of employer to keen employee who has found a way to give a substantial boost to company profits. During the course of his involvement with the Pablo Acosta organization, Sammy perfected a difficult-to-detect smuggling technique that eventually allowed Pablo to cross millions of dollars worth of narcotics—perhaps billions if measured in street value—into the United States. That method involved a clever conversion of propane tanks on the back of pickup trucks into hard-to-detect stash sites.

In earlier years, enforcement in the Texas Big Bend had been so sporadic that couriers working for Manuel Carrasco or Shorty Lopez did not take great pain to hide the load. They simply threw flour sacks full of pot into the back of a pickup, covered the cargo with a tarpaulin, then drove across the river at some shallow spot.

With the passage of time policing efforts became much less casual. When enforcement got turned up in the Big Bend with the introduction of a Customs patrol unit at the international bridge in Presidio, someone within the ranks of the Ojinaga smugglers got the bright idea of running loads of narcotics inside empty propane tanks.

Propane-powered pickup trucks were becoming popular on both sides of the border as a result of the Arab oil embargo and soaring gasoline prices. Truck owners began to install

110-gallon tanks in the bed of their trucks and convert the vehicles to propane; or they rigged them up to run on both gasoline and propane. Liquefied natural gas was much less expensive than gasoline, and a driver could go a long way on a tankful.

Ever looking for new ways to smuggle drugs, the Ojinaga dealers were quick to adapt. At first, the method was crude but effective. The smugglers installed tanks on trucks that still ran on gasoline. They cut a square hole in the tank and stuffed it full of marijuana bricks, frequently not even bothering to seal the hole back up. After every nook and cranny was filled with up to 120 pounds of marijuana, the tank was bolted snugly to the bed of the pickup right up against the cab wall so that the hole could not be seen. Metal tubes and whatnot were jerry-rigged to look like they were going to the motor, which in fact ran on good old gasoline. It was easy for smugglers to drive across the international bridge with such loads as it took a few years for the American authorities to catch on.

However, after a series of drug arrests in the United States involving propane tanks, many of the smugglers abandoned the method and searched for other places in vehicles to hide narcotics. Some installed false gas tanks or compartments under the floorboards.

As far as Sammy was concerned, those methods were okay—except for the limited payload. He believed that more could still be done with propane tanks. With the dedication of a gifted engineer, Sammy set about conjuring up new and improved propane tanks

The ex-cowboy began experimenting in the body and fender shop of an Ojinaga acquaintance. At first, he cut a rectangular opening at the base or back of the tank just like everyone else, but he reinserted the metal plate after introducing the marijuana. Then he sealed the edges into place with Bondo, a body and fender putty that dries as hard as rock. Once the putty dried, he smoothed the seams with an electric sander until there was not a trace of a joint. He spray-painted the result and then ground in caliche dust. His finished tanks looked like they had been sitting in the back of his pickup for years, touched only by the wind, the rain and the blistering desert sun.

That innovation was useful until the day when an American officer opened the pressure-release valve on a modified tank and got a faceful of marijuana fumes. That driver went to jail and the smugglers went back to the drawing board. It was an ongoing technological race—how to keep one step ahead of lawmen who were always looking for clues that would give cause to seize a propane tank and open it up.

After that bust, federal, state and local police were being instructed at seminars how to spot phony cylinders, even the ones that had been sealed tightly and expertly repainted. Touch the stem of the pressure valve; if it's not cold, there's no propane; open the pressure-release valve, let it bleed a little, and then take a whiff—you'll know the difference. American customs and immigration inspectors at the rickety fifty-year-old wooden international bridge started checking a lot of tanks, especially in vehicles driven by a solitary Mexican male wearing a straw cowboy hat, oval belt buckle and cowboy boots. Then it was all tapping, touching, banging and auscultating until the authorities were convinced the tank really did have propane in it.

Sammy discussed the technical problem with Pablo. If the tank trick was going to continue to work, the 110-gallon propane tank had to have the look and feel of an operating tank. In fact, it had to *be* an operating tank and a stash site simultaneously.

In a flash of inspiration, Sammy thought of adding a smaller tank *within* the standard propane tank and rigging the truck to run on both gasoline and propane. In a series of tests, he hooked up a one-gallon or two-gallon capacity propane tank to all the valves and gauges of the main tank. That way, there was indeed propane inside in case anyone thought about opening the pressure release valve or checking the gauges. The gauges would register pressure and the truck would be running on propane. In case the propane ran low, Sammy also reversed the wires on the dashboard fuel meter. When it read propane, the truck would actually be running on gasoline and vice versa. The bag of tricks fooled American policemen for several more years.

Until Sammy came up with this new and improved version, no one in Ojinaga who valued his freedom dared to cross the international bridge any longer with narcotics stashed in a tank for fear of some clever inspector discovering a fatal flaw in the apparatus.

The day he finished tinkering, Sammy invited Pablo to the body and fender shop. Sammy's face broke into a broad smile as he pointed to the tank mounted in the bed of his pickup. He challenged Pablo to find a way to detect that it was not authentic. Pablo looked it over and over again, and was impressed. He had to admit he could not tell the difference from a regular propane tank—yet he knew there was more than a hundred pounds of marijuana inside. He had seen Sammy load it up earlier at one of the drug warehouses. Sammy was so certain it could not be detected that he told Pablo he was going to cross the international bridge with the load.

"You're crazy," Pablo said.

"I'll bet you a thousand dollars I can call you at your house from the other side in fifteen minutes," Sammy replied.

"You're out of your mind. Don't do it," Pablo said.

"Is it a bet?"

Pablo shrugged his shoulders, as if to say it was going to be Sammy's fault, not his, if he got caught.

"It's a bet," Pablo replied.

Sammy jammed his pickup into gear and drove toward the international bridge. Pablo and his *pistolero* entourage followed, stopping at the international bridge. Pablo watched as Sammy was waived through the outbound inspection lanes on the Mexican side and drove across the wooden bridge to American side. Then Pablo drove back to his brick home on Calle Sexta and waited.

Exactly twenty-two minutes later, Sammy called to collect his bet. Just as he had expected, the American inspectors had gone over his truck from top to bottom. Just as he had predicted, they let him go after they couldn't find anything.

"They went over that tank like a bunch of monkeys trying to rape a football," he boasted from the pay phone in front of the Balia Restaurant in Presidio. "Have my money ready for me when I come back."

Sammy later modified his invention even further by cutting the plate out at the top, around all of the gauges. He secured the plate with a three-foot-long bolt that screwed into a nut welded to the bottom of the interior. The head of the yard-long bolt was hidden underneath one of the gauges. Then Sammy Bondoed around the seam of the plate, sanded it smooth and restored the tank to its former dullness with some spray paint and street dirt.

That particular improvement came about after American authorities caught someone using Bondoed plates. Then they started feeling underneath every suspicious tank for tell-tale bumps or grooves. Even on good jobs it was sometimes possible to kick the plate in, once the location of the plate was suspected. But the authorities never even dreamed of looking for Bondo where Sammy had cut the plates. Who would think of cutting into the *top* of the tank around all the gauges? And with the three-foot bolt that anchored it to the bottom of the tank, the plate couldn't be budged even with a sledgehammer.

Sammy continued to use the bridge to cross loads until an unexpected occurrence gave him a case of the jitters and forced him back to the river crossings. Not long after showing off his clever audacity to Pablo, he drove across the international bridge with yet another well-concealed load. He went across just as one shift on the American side was getting off duty and another was coming on. One of the Border Patrol officers whose shift had just ended recognized him. The patrolman waved him down after he had passed through the Customs inspection station.

Sammy could shoe a horse just about as well as any of the best in Texas, and the patrolman knew it. Sammy had made the mistake of showing him a certificate for a professional horse-shoeing course he had completed and ended up promising to shoe a horse for the federal officer the next time he was in town.

A promise was a promise, the patrolman reminded him. A glum Sammy followed him in the 115-degree midsummer heat to a ranch outside Presidio. The patrolman leaned against Sammy's truck the whole time, watching in polite silence as Sammy lifted up the front hoof and went to work trimming and cleaning the hooves and fitting new horseshoes.

The sweat pouring from Sammy's face was not simply a product of the fierce heat. As each minute went by, he knew, pressure was building up inside the tank from the decomposing marijuana, a natural process accelerated by the heat. If the pressure built up enough some of the Bondo could pop loose and send a blast of that unmistakable aroma smack into the border patrolman's face.

The federal officer was still in uniform. His badge glimmered in the sun, and so did his pistol. By the time he finished with the horse, Sammy's rubbery face looked as if it had suffered a meltdown.

"You okay?" the border patrolman said.

Sammy wiped his face with a drenched handkerchief. "Yeah, yeah," he said, putting his tools away hastily in the cab of the truck. "It's just this heat. I've got to get out of this heat. You can pay me later, okay?"

Flooring it, he drove off with the load.

Ojinaga during marijuana-harvesting season was a city with a shortage of motel rooms. People flocked to town to cut deals with Pablo or with other traffickers under his wing. The drug lord had his clients stay at the Motel Ojinaga or the Hotel Rohana and put a guard on them to control their movements. He did not want them to meet one another. That could be bad for business. When he took them to one of his drug emporiums to select marijuana, he brought them one at a time for the same reason. The Americans were not usually very adventurous in Ojinaga, in any event. In fact, it sometimes took coaxing just to get them to come *out* of their rooms—particularly the first-timers unnerved by all the armed men floating around. And the soldiers! Even lowly privates frequently accosted Americans they knew were there for drugs and demanded money. A $20 bill would send the nervy soldier away.

Pablo liked to add to the fear because it increased his control. He would go to the buyer's motel room with a half-dozen of his *pistoleros*. As soon as the motel door opened, the gunmen would rush in like commandos and take positions around the room—after checking the bathroom, the closet and anywhere else someone with sinister intent could hide. Then Pablo walked into the room looking like a Mexican bandit who would sooner shoot you than talk to you. He would stride past the buyers, who were by then dizzy with fear, and would plop down on one of the beds.

Pillow against his back and dirty ostrich-skin cowboy boots stretched out on the bedspread, Pablo would snarl, "Let's talk."

Inspire fear. It was a lesson he had learned at the knees of his candelilla-smuggling father and uncles. The people who came to him in Mexico for drugs would remember the fear they had felt, that icy terror that gripped them in the chest and throat. It was a first step in creating a docile clientele. Pablo knew that when he sent his people to them with loads later on the clients would pay up, cheerfully, gratefully, because they *believed* that if they did not that awful apparition they had seen in the Ojinaga motel room could himself come to collect—in pounds of bleeding, quivering flesh.

That is where runners like Sammy came in. The good, docile clients would call Pablo from distant cities in the United States, like retailers to a wholesale distributor, and place an order—in coded language just in case the phones were tapped. Pablo would write down a telephone number and give it to Sammy. "Take the load to so-and-so in such-and-such city. When you get there, call this number. If you got any problems, call me and I'll work them out."

When Sammy came back from a run, it was usually with $40,000, $50,000 or $60,000 in cash in a suitcase. Pablo expected the money to be stacked neatly by denomination in bundles of $5,000 or $10,000 tied with rubber bands. He got upset if there were any $1, $5, or even $10 bills. On some nights, two or three runners would come in at the same time, and it would turn into an all-night marathon counting all the lush greenbacks. The following morning Pablo would trundle the money to a thick steel vault in a bank that did business out of one of the wings of the Hotel Rohana.

Although his inventiveness kept him ahead of the law, Sammy knew that sooner or later he was going to get arrested. He kept telling Pablo he wanted to start a roofing business and get out of drug trafficking entirely. Pablo, who sometimes talked about getting out himself and opening a restaurant in Tijuana or buying a huge cattle ranch somewhere in northern Mexico, encouraged him and promised to help him set up the roofing business.

But invariably, after the harvests in the spring and fall had begun and there was a lot of marijuana to be moved, Pablo would call Sammy at his home in Hobbs and say, "We're ready. Do you think you can come down?"

And, as was his habit, Sammy went right back down to Ojinaga. It was so much easier making money this way, though Sammy had to recognize that all the violence and killing was beginning to scare him, even more than the thought of getting arrested. He had known Lili and Fermín and had been welcome in their homes. After Lili and Fermín were killed, he saw that he was getting caught in the middle of a deadly, unending blood feud. Just after Fermín died, one of the Arevalo brothers who lived in New Mexico offered him $20,000 to kill Pablo; Pablo, not knowing about the Arevalo offer, promised him $100,000 to kidnap that same Arevalo brother and bring him to Ojinaga. That is when Sammy made it clear to Pablo he did not want any part in the violence.

It was getting crazy. Little by little, many other people he knew were getting murdered while others would just disappear. Images of buzzards circling in the sky and bleached bones littering the desert came to mind when he imagined what had happened to them. Sammy thought it ironic. He had managed to avoid the draft and Vietnam only to enlist in another war. If the drug "soldiers" were not being blown away in ambushes or gunfights, they were getting hopelessly addicted. He had seen both of Pablo's younger brothers, Hector Manuel and Armando, succumb to heroin.

One of the events that persuaded Sammy it was time to start considering other options was the time Hector Manuel was brought to him shot up with heroin *and* bullets. Hector and Pedro had gotten themselves into a gunfight with some marijuana growers up in the mountains. The way it was explained to Sammy, Pablo's brother and nephew had gone to the field to harvest some of the crop and were going to truck it back to Ojinaga. However, the growers, mountain Indians Pablo had contracted for marijuana, claimed they were cutting into a field they had not paid for. That is when the shooting started. Sammy was just getting ready to bring a load across when Hector showed up clutching his belly and begging for a ride to his sister's house in Odessa.

"I'll give you a ride," Sammy said. "But I'm not bringing any of your goddamn syringes, or your heroin, or any of your guns. You can get your wife to cross that shit for you."

Obligingly, Hector jammed a needle into his arm *before* getting into Sammy's truck. By the time they were across the river, Pablo's younger brother had vomited all over the floor of the truck.

Then Sammy himself began abusing drugs, particularly crack cocaine. His second marriage had already become shaky when his wife, Becky, caught him in bed with another woman at a motel in Ruidoso. She gave him one more chance. He lost even that when he arrived home stoned from a week-long party in Ojinaga and got into a spat with her. He slugged her so hard the back of her head left an indentation in the wall. He blamed it on the cocaine. She said it did not matter, their marriage was over.

When he was arrested while on a marijuana run in January 1985, Sammy was actually relieved.

That final trip had started out just like the hundreds of others he had made, though with a couple of differences that later led him to understand *how* he got arrested. A few days before the arrest, the wife of one of Pablo's uncles started pestering him to run a load of marijuana for her to Odessa in one of his propane tanks. *La Tía*—Auntie—as everyone called her, was the second wife of Manuel Acosta, who had been arrested in 1984 by Customs investigators for marijuana trafficking through Big Bend National Park. Manuel had masterminded a smuggling network that was supplied by Pablo that delivered primarily to Dallas in recreational vehicles.

After Manuel's arrest, *La Tía* continued to live in Ojinaga. She was a squat, flat-nosed woman with stringy hair. Sammy had suspected for a long time that she was supplying Hector Manuel and Armando with heroin. The brothers were not able to get heroin from any other source in Ojinaga. Pablo had passed the word around that anybody selling heroin to his brothers was going to answer to him. On the sly, the brothers took small amounts of marijuana from one of Pablo's warehouses and brought it to *La Tía* to exchange for heroin.

The day before Sammy was arrested, *La Tía* dropped by his room at the Motel Ojinaga to ask for his help. She had close to 200 pounds of marijuana she needed to have smuggled to Odessa. "I'm counting on you because I know if you take it, it will get there safely and I won't get robbed," she explained.

He went with her to inspect the marijuana and shook his head when he saw it. Sammy had learned to tell the differences. This stuff was exactly like the pot Pablo had at the time in one of the Ojinaga warehouses. "I know where this is coming from," Sammy said. "I am not going against Pablo. You're going to have to get somebody else."

The old woman became angry and started swearing at him. Sammy calmed her down with a promise to find someone else to take it across for her and to keep their conversation to himself. "You're safe. I won't tell Pablo on you. What you do over here is your business, not mine."

The next day, Sammy readied a load at a ranch Pablo owned just east of Ojinaga on the road to El Mulato. This load, he decided, was to be crossed at the river. From there, Sammy planned on taking the river highway to Study Butte, then driving north on the state highway. But everything started to go wrong the moment he got to the Rio Grande. He got stuck in the middle and had to go find somebody with a tractor to pull him across. When he was finally on the other side, he drove on to Study Butte as planned, then headed north on Highway 118.

Just outside Alpine, Brewster County sheriff's deputies pulled him over and informed him he was under suspicion of transporting marijuana. The deputies evidently knew in advance he was coming but did not take him into custody. They told him not to leave town and followed him to a motel, where they waited until he got a room.

After sleepless hours wondering how the police could have found him out, he heard a pounding on the door. Outside, the parking lot was crawling with police and state and federal narcotics agents. A federal agent said they wanted to inspect the propane tank on his truck. After going over the tank for fifteen minutes, a DEA agent took out a knife and scraped away some of the paint at the top of the tank near the pressure gauge. He struck Bondo.

"Lock him up!" he shouted.

Sammy was questioned the next day by a DEA agent in a holding cell at the county jailhouse. Sammy later claimed the federal agent commenced the interrogation by kneeing him in the solar plexus.

While Sammy gasped for air, the agent sat down and said in a relaxed voice, "I need to talk to you about something. I just want you to know that tomorrow, by dinner, you can be out on the streets walking around free."

"How's that?" Sammy choked.

"You know Pablo Acosta, don't you?"

"I've heard of him, but I don't know him."

"Yeah, you know him. That's some of his stuff, isn't it?" the agent said, alluding to the marijuana they had found after breaking into Sammy's propane tank. "You've got to understand something. We're trying to end this trafficking shit, especially through little towns like Marfa and Alpine. I want you to help us."

"I can't help you on that, man," Sammy replied, still gasping for air. "This truck was left for me over at the park. All I did was to get in it and drive."

"Bullshit, you drove it across. What do you know about Pablo Acosta?"

"Nothing."

"Listen, you give me five names and the location of a couple of river crossings, and I swear you'll be a free man by tomorrow."

Sammy thought about it. Those five people the DEA wanted to know about were friends. And then, if he *were* to be released the next day, it would look awfully suspicious to a class of people prone to paranoia. He would have to live with the fear of someone *suspecting* that he had snitched, and with the terror of anticipating what those suspicions could do to his health. Besides, Pablo was a good friend. He might be a desperado, but he had always treated Sammy with respect.

"I'm sorry. I can't help you," Sammy repeated.

The next day Sammy was taken to Pecos, where he was arraigned before a magistrate at the federal courthouse.

Later, Sammy understood who had fingered him to the American authorities. The realization came even before he was in the penitentiary, but it was confirmed at El Reno, the federal pen in Oklahoma where both he and Pablo's uncle Manuel ended up serving their time. Just after he got to prison, Manuel came up to him to apologize for his wife's action. *"Dispénsame y a mí senora*—Forgive me and my wife," he said to Sammy.

Someone evidently had gone to *La Tía* with a proposition similar to the one made to Sammy while he was in the county jail in Alpine: "You give us five people and a couple of river crossings and we'll use our influence to get your husband out of jail early."

She evidently took them up on it. That was why she was selling heroin, Sammy realized—to exchange it for grass. *La Tía* was putting loads of marijuana together. Then she would hire someone like Sammy to take it across. When the runner got into the United States with it, the narcs were there waiting.

At least the sentence would be lighter than if she set them up with heroin. One day, she would go to collect from the American police.

Sammy had not fallen for the trick, but he was convinced *La Tía* had somehow found out when he was taking a load across. The Brewster County sheriff's deputies seemed to know exactly what kind of a vehicle to look for.

For *La Tía*, it was an act of devotion toward her husband, Pablo's uncle. For Pablo it was an act of treachery. If she had not been the wife of his uncle, Pablo would have made her pay for it with her life.

Instead, Pablo banished her from Ojinaga.

Chapter Thirteen

BONNIE

Sammy was convicted in May in the third-floor courtroom of the old federal building in Pecos. Pablo's mother and four of his sisters sat quietly in the back. It happened that Armando Acosta, one of Pablo's younger brothers, had been arrested about the same time as Sammy in a separate bust in the Big Bend National Park. Sammy's trial started the day after jurors found Armando guilty. The Acosta women continued to drive down from Odessa each morning for Sammy's trial.

Pablo had called his sisters from Ojinaga and told them that it was his wish for them to attend his drug runner's trial. After all, Sammy had always been loyal to him. And Sammy had always made it a point of stopping in to see Dolores, his mother, whenever he was in Odessa.

Becky, Sammy's wife, never forgave him for punching her. She had moved into an apartment in Carlsbad and taken their nine-year-old son with her. But after Sammy was arrested she promised she would wait until he was out of jail before filing for divorce. She even attended his trial. After the guilty verdict was read, Pablo's mother, then in her seventies, comforted Becky. One of Pablo's sisters translated as the old woman spoke in Spanish: "Don't worry, it's going to be all right. Pablo will take care of you," Pablo's mother said.

Several days after Sammy's trial, Becky got a telephone call from Ojinaga. The caller identified himself as Pablo. He was very polite and sounded concerned. He told her how much he cared for Sammy, how sorry he was that he had gotten busted.

"If you can come down and see me, I have some things to talk to you about. I want to help you," he said.

Pablo had used her on minor jobs in the United States before, such as picking people up at the river and transporting them to where they had to go; she had even acquired a driver's license and other documents for Marco DeHaro, Pablo's enforcer. She was even an occasional source of small quantities of cocaine for him when he had trouble getting it from other sources. She had spoken to him on the phone on several occasions when he needed to get in touch with Sammy.

But Pablo and Becky had never met.

A week after the telephone conversation, Becky borrowed money from one of Pablo's sisters and drove down to Ojinaga. It was four in the afternoon when she arrived and drove directly to Pablo's brick home on Calle Sexta. He was not in, so she left word with Pablo's wife that she was getting a room at the Motel Ojinaga.

Shortly after midnight, Becky heard a loud knock. She opened the door to see a rough-looking man with a scarred face wearing a dark blue cowboy shirt, black vest, large oval belt buckle, blue jeans and ostrich skin cowboy boots—Pablo's usual dress. Behind him were two equally tough looking men carrying assault rifles.

"Are you Sammy's wife?" he said.

"Yes."

"You and I need to talk," Pablo said.

Pablo proposed they talk in a downtown bar where they would be more comfortable.

By then Pablo had made it a habit of clearing out restaurants and bars anytime he wanted to go to one. It was for his own security and the safety of the patrons in case of another ambush. By the time they arrived downtown, the Bikini Bar, a popular watering hole at one end of the town square, was empty except for a bartender. The bar had cleared out quickly when Pablo's gunmen walked in and motioned with their rifles for everybody to get out. Pablo posted a couple of gunmen in front while another watched the back door. He and Becky sat down in the dim light of one of the booths with a bottle of El

Presidente brandy, Pablo's favorite, in front of them. They looked like an odd couple: a blond *gringa* with a look of sparkly-eyed innocence and a black-haired mafioso with a droopy mustache and a face full of sinister scars.

Pablo kept apologizing for Sammy's arrest. If it hadn't been for *La Tía*, Sammy would still be a free man. If he had known beforehand what *La Tía* had been up to, he would have been able to prevent it.

"You don't worry about it," Pablo said. "I will take care of it. When are you going to visit Sammy?"

"Maybe a month from now," Becky said.

"When you see him, tell him I'll take care of it and not to worry. That's all you need to tell him."

Becky wondered if Pablo intended to kill the old woman. "What are you going to do to her?" she asked.

"I'm going to run her out of Mexico and see to it that she has to make a living on her own. She won't ever get any help from my family, never," he said.

Pablo offered to help Becky pay her bills while Sammy was in jail, but he quickly realized that Becky did not want any help. She wanted to work and was ready to make a business proposition.

As the night wore on, she told the Ojinaga drug lord more about herself than she had ever told anyone except Sammy. She was the daughter of a Fort Hood soldier and had herself been a soldier for four years. She had fallen in love with Sammy not long after she got out of high school, attracted by his unpredictable lifestyle and his funny nature. Neither she nor Sammy had ever planned on making a career out of selling drugs, she told Pablo. They got involved in 1973 when once of Sammy's friends asked them to stash some marijuana overnight in their East Texas home and gave them $500 for their help. Becky could not *wait* for the friend to come around the next day and take the pot away—she had never even seen marijuana before and it was scary. But a year later, they were themselves dealing in one-ounce baggies of pot that they sold only to friends. The money helped pay the bills.

Casa Chavez was a warehouse Pablo used to store large quantities of marijuana and as a meeting place for gang members. Marijuana was cured in a large yard in the back with sheds and a high cement-block wall. Located across the street from a grammar school, the warehouse had once been a grocery store. (Photo by Terrence Poppa)

Becky was a hustler and her business grew. While Sammy was muling loads of marijuana for Pablo, she was running her own drug operation. She bought a pound or two pounds of cocaine at a time from a source in El Paso, catching a plane to Hobbs with it hidden underneath her clothing. Nobody was the wiser when the cheerful, well-dressed young woman stepped off the airplane with the self-confidence of an executive.

As she talked about her trafficking experience, Pablo realized that Becky was more deeply involved than he had ever realized. Through Sammy, Pablo had made use of some of her services, but Sammy had never really told him much about her other activities. She seemed to Pablo to be a lot more ambitious than Sammy had ever been. Whereas Sammy was content to mule loads and collect his $2,500 fee, Becky evidently had established a clientele of her own as far away as Alabama, Kansas, Oklahoma and Utah that she had been supplying through her own sources. She was dealing mainly in cocaine and marijuana.

Pablo could foresee doing business with her. But he wanted to start her off running loads just as Sammy had been doing. He wanted to see how she could handle it, and then they could talk about fronting her loads. He explained how things worked in Ojinaga: how much he would pay for each load she ran; how much he would charge for marijuana when she was in a position to buy it; what percentage she would have to pay him if she bought marijuana from some other source but brought it through his jurisdiction and so on. She already vaguely understood, but he explained the *plaza* arrangement: he was paying off the Mexican authorities for the right to run the zone, and anybody under him was protected too—provided, of course, they remained in good standing by paying him a percentage of their deals.

They started to drink and Pablo smoked some crack cocaine that his nephew had prepared. As the night wore on, Pablo told her a lot of stories about the good times he and Sammy had had together.

Pablo liked to spin yarns about himself, particularly after he had been drinking and smoking dope and had time on his hands. When Becky asked him if he ever went back to the United States, he said, no, they had framed him in Eunice and there was an arrest warrant out for him. He gave her a jazzed-up account of his escape from the American police: how he was shot a bunch of times as he ran from "bushel to bushel" —bush to bush—to get away; how some old Mexican in a truck with rattly sideboards found him lying on the side of a road and gave him a ride to Odessa. He went into elaborate detail describing how he made his way to Fort Stockton where one of his cousins wrapped him in a blanket and drove him to Ojinaga. The way Pablo told it, the blood from his many wounds had soaked in big blotches through the blanket during the trip to the border. When they drove through the inspection station on the Mexican side of the international bridge, an immigration official stuck his head through the window and saw the bloody blanket. He asked the cousin,

"What's the matter with him?" The cousin said, "Oh, nothing. He's sick. I'm taking him to see a doctor in Mexico."

Pablo even parted his hair and told her to feel the two long scars across the top of his scalp from the bullet wounds. He opened his shirt were there were some more scars. His face was full of them too. They were all authentic bullet wounds, although not a single one had come from his escape from the United States.

But Becky was impressed. Just from what Sammy told her about Pablo, she was already a true believer in Pablo's legendary invincibility.

When they finally left the Bikini Bar, it was nine o'clock in the morning and they were both very stoned.

Sammy had often told Becky about Pablo's drug emporium across the street from an elementary school in Ojinaga. Seeing was believing. The day after their marathon talk at the Bikini Bar, Pablo took her there to show her around and to get her first load of marijuana ready.

It was not actually a warehouse, though Pablo always referred to it as his *bodega*, the Mexican word for warehouse. It was an old adobe home across from a brightly painted cement-block elementary school in a working-class neighborhood a few blocks from the intersection of the Chihuahua and Camargo highways. Before Pablo bought the property in 1983 it had been a mom-and-pop grocery store. Pablo had never bothered removing the words Casa Chavez from the wall near the front door or the Pepsi-Cola advertisement. Those were the only traces of the earlier, licit use. The building had concrete floors, several small bedrooms, a filthy kitchen with a gas stove, a sparsely furnished living room and a bathroom with a grimy shower stall.

At the back was a smaller, whitewashed adobe building inside a one-third-acre lot surrounded by a high concrete-block wall. Pablo stored tons of marijuana at a time either in the smaller building or out in the yard. He would bring in freshly cut pot from plantations south of Ojinaga for processing. While still in the mountains, the marijuana plants were chopped

off at the base and piled high like Christmas trees into the
back of trucks. From there they were driven brazenly to
Pablo's Ojinaga "factory."

Inside the compound, Pablo had his workers prop the
freshly harvested plants against the walls for drying and
curing. Anybody driving up or down the unpaved street could
see the tops sticking out above the wall. When the week-
long curing process was over, a crew of one or two dozen
men, depending on how much *mota* needed to be processed,
would set about stripping the plants and grading the leaves.
In the whitewashed building were trash compactors for com-
pressing the marijuana into kilo bricks or into bales of thirty,
fifty or one hundred pounds. During the marijuana season it
was not unusual for his workers to be employed for months
on end, or for both buildings to be crammed full of marijuana bales and for trucks to be driving in and out at all hours
of the day and night.

Protecting the marijuana round the clock were Pablo's
heavily armed *pistoleros*.

The Ojinaga drug lord also had other stash sites. One was
a huge "fortress" on the road to El Mulato not far from the
river. U.S. Customs photographed it once from the air. The photo
showed an area of about two acres surrounded by twelve-
foot-high walls. In the middle of the property was a brick house;
to the sides were sheds and storage facilities, a huge propane
tank and a water tower. The only way in was through a huge
metal gate topped by a brick arch. It looked impregnable.

Because it was in town, Casa Chavez was more convenient for small deals, and it was used by a lot of Pablo's
friends to store their own marijuana, friends that included
people in positions of authority such as the federal police
commander. Several times in 1984, Sammy Garcia had seen
the commander bring truckloads of his own marijuana into
the compound. Once while Sammy was standing in the courtyard, the federal chief and some of his men drove in with
marijuana plants stacked high in the back of a truck. The
federal officer shouted at Sammy, "Hey, you! Come over here
and give us a hand unloading this stuff."

In Ojinaga, the drug warehouse was convenient for Pablo but much less so for the neighbors. The teachers at the grammar school directly across the street were distressed when they found out to whom the property belonged and for what it was being used. The old grocery store was barely thirty yards away from two of the cement-block classroom buildings. The windows looked out directly on Casa Chavez. During recess, children sometimes played in the dirt street right in front of the entrance to the block-wall compound.

When Pablo moved in, his notoriety had already spread due the killing of Lili Arevalo, not to mention his responsibility for the shootouts and ambushes in town and the murder of Fermin Arevalo at the El Salto ranch. Teachers broke into cold sweats at the thought of children caught in a crossfire. What if somebody drove by the compound and started shooting at people inside? Pablo and his men would then have to respond, and the school was right in the line of fire. School authorities erected a chain-link fence and had the children play on the opposite side of the school during recess. The teachers vainly prayed the traffickers would find some other place to do business.

Some of the classrooms facing Casa Chavez were also used for evening adult education classes. The teachers felt obligated to explain the situation to each new class—and to add, "If you hear any shooting, drop to the floor immediately!" The students usually turned to one another with furrowed-brow looks of apprehension but were never especially shocked by the news. Such was life in Ojinaga.

With Pablo's encouragement, Becky quickly created a small organization under the umbrella of his bigger one. He told her she had the run of the town. At first, she had only one helper, an oilfield worker from Hobbs who used to run marijuana with Sammy. Becky paid him $500 just to drive loads of marijuana across the river and to turn them over to her once in safer territory. Her theory was that the chance of getting caught was related to the distance from the river.

It was worth parting with twenty percent of her own profits for someone else to take the biggest risk.

Sammy had taught her how to prepare a propane tank. When she informed him during her first visit at the federal penitentiary that she was going to go work for Pablo, he cautioned her, "Do your own tank. The day you let someone else do your tank for you is the day you're going to get arrested."

Just as Sammy had done, Becky loaded up the tanks with kilo bricks of marijuana at one of Pablo's warehouses, then drove a few blocks away to an auto body shop owned by Armando, a friend of Sammy's. Armando was a short, pot-bellied smuggler with a greasy, pockmarked face. On occasions Armando actually did do some body and fender work and automobile repainting. But authorities on the American side of the river were aware of the real purpose of his little garage: Armando specialized in modifying vehicles to transport small amounts of heroin, cocaine and marijuana in hidden compartments.

Becky used Armando's electric sander and spray paint to prepare her tanks; mindful of Sammy's advice, she refused Armando's offers of help. She spent two hours, sometimes three, Bondoing and sanding and painting her own tanks. Eventually she got to be as good as Sammy had been at disguising a phony tank.

During the first month after Sammy's conviction, Becky was all business. She ran about three loads a week for Pablo, sometimes going without sleep for two or three days at a time. Then she would sleep for twenty-four hours at her apartment in Carlsbad before going back to Ojinaga for another run. A seventeen-year-old high school dropout and the girlfriend of one of her runners lived at the apartment and took care of her young son while she was gone or asleep.

Pablo was impressed with Becky's cool efficiency and nerve. She followed his instructions to the letter. He liked that she was tough and brassy with customers who thought they could withhold money from a woman. He even liked that she was tough and brassy with him.

After she built up some capital, he started selling loads to her outright for her to run to her own customers.

People in Ojinaga became accustomed to seeing her around town. It was not just the blond hair, fair skin and blue eyes that drew attention. Everywhere Becky went she carried an assault rifle or a semiautomatic pistol as brazenly as all Pablo's other henchmen and guards. Frequently she was escorted by another American who carried weaponry as well—one of her runners who doubled as a bodyguard while they were in Ojinaga.

Except for the most adventurous, tourists generally did not go out of their way to visit Ojinaga. When they did, it was to drive through on their way to or from Chihuahua City. Once Becky went shopping for blouses in a boutique on Avenida Trasviña y Retes, armed as usual with an assault rifle. When she came out of the shop she met some other machine-gun toting hoods. Just at that moment, a middle-aged American couple with cameras dangling from their necks drove up to the intersection and stopped for a red light. As they waited, they craned their necks at the crowd of *pistoleros*. Becky heard the man say as he pointed excitedly, "I told you! I told you it was like this!"

Becky already knew Marco DeHaro, the gunman who had started the feud with the Arevalo faction, from the half-dozen times she had seen him in the United States and had helped him take care of business for Pablo in Texas and New Mexico. After she began running loads for Pablo in May 1985, Becky started to bump into Marco practically everywhere she went in Ojinaga. If she drove to Pablo's drug *bodega* to pick up a load, there was Marco lounging around in the house; if she went to Armando's garage to fix up her propane tank, there was Marco leaning against the wall; if Pablo visited her in her room at the Motel Ojinaga, Marco frequently strode in right behind him, machine gun in hand.

Marco—tall, solidly built, balding—never said much. He always stared at her between half-closed eyes. At first she did not know what to make of it. He seemed bored when she talked. On one occasion when she spoke to him about business, she asked him bluntly "Are you even listening?"

One day in early June she came to town for another load of marijuana. Pablo, it turned out, did not have any on hand. He was waiting for a big marijuana shipment to come in and asked her to stay at the motel for a couple of days until it arrived. But she needed it fast. She asked Armando if he knew anybody with a hundred pounds. Before long Marco showed up. He sold it to her for less than Pablo would have charged her. On the return trip Marco suggested they work deals together. He had sources of marijuana and heroin, and customers of his own, he said, but not a good smuggling operation. She did.

Becky discussed Marco's proposal over with Pablo. He told her he did not have any objections, as long as he got his *plaza* fee.

The first deal Marco and Becky did together consisted of 200 pounds of marijuana. The load was split in half, and she sent two runners with the dope to a buyer named Rocky in Oklahoma City. She and Marco drove up together to Oklahoma City to collect.

Pablo had not lifted a finger during the entire deal. It was Marco's drug; Becky took care of the smuggling and collecting. But it was Pablo's *plaza*. When they got back from Oklahoma, therefore, they gave Pablo $11,000—payment for the privilege of bringing the marijuana through Pablo's stretch of northern Mexico and not running afoul of Mexican authority.

Their business relationship lasted about three weeks, then it became much more than purely business. Pablo never said anything about it. He loved Sammy like a brother; Marco was his friend; he respected Becky. What was going on between them was none of his business.

Chapter Fourteen

CLYDE

He came to be known as "*El Carnicero de Ojinaga*—the Butcher of Ojinaga."

Marco Antonio Haro Portillo, who preferred to go by the name Marco DeHaro, had aroused the curiosity of U.S. law enforcement ever since informants identified him as one of the triggermen who killed Fermin Arevalo's son, starting the bloody feud between the two factions. He was thought to be Pablo Acosta's chief enforcer, and drug-intelligence analysts labeled him the number two or number three man in Pablo's wide-reaching organization.

As Pablo's reputed enforcer, Marco was suspected by police in the United States of killing two men in New Mexico in September 1983. That double slaying occurred in a Hobbs shack one night when someone kicked in the door and killed two Mexican nationals with bullets to the head. The first man was shot in the forehead, and police later speculated he had been standing by the door when the killer burst into the room. The other man was found lying face down between the sofa and a coffee table, as if he had been scrambling for cover as the killer stood over him and fired at the back of the head. Another man was murdered in Odessa in March 1985, followed by another killing in Lubbock. The word on the streets picked up by American police was that these killings were on orders from Pablo Acosta. The dead men had not paid for large heroin purchases and had openly boasted about getting away with it. They were murdered to set an example.

In Ojinaga, Marco was widely believed to have killed a
number of people at Pablo's behest. The most brutal slayings
attributed to him occurred in February 1984, when three young
men were machine-gunned to death in a restaurant one block
from the town square. Two gunmen, one of them said by witnesses to be Marco, walked into the restaurant and shot the
men down before they had a chance to go for their weapons.

Marco came to Ojinaga in 1976 from the state of Sonora.
His father had been a police officer and his mother had smuggled narcotics. Before moving to Ojinaga, Marco worked as
bodyguard and chauffeur for a Mexican customs official in
the tiny border town of Sonoita, across from equally minus-
cule Lukeville, Arizona. When the official was transferred to
Ojinaga, Marco went with him.

Once in Ojinaga, it did not take Marco long to get involved
with Pablo's faction of the flourishing drug underworld. In
1979 Pablo first employed Marco as chauffeur, bodyguard and
gofer. Marco also took care of miscellaneous narcotics-re-
lated tasks such as escorting drug shipments and guarding
marijuana fields. After killing Lili, Marco became Pablo's
enforcer and began the spate of killings that earned Marco
his nickname. By the time Becky came to Ojinaga, Marco
owned a beautiful white Mediterranean-style home, splen-
didly furnished throughout, with a huge satellite antenna in
the backyard. It was the nicest house on the block.

Marco worked closely with Pablo until early 1984. Then
various reports indicated that he had been arrested and jailed
in Tampico on a weapons-possession charge or that he had
been sent out of Ojinaga because he was killing too many people, bringing too much pressure on the Ojinaga mafia from
Mexican authorities.

The balding trafficker later told Becky he spent a year with
the Mexican Federal Judicial Police, claiming he was attached
to the Mexican office of Interpol in Mexico City. She scoffed
until one day he showed her his police credential, a wallet-
sized Mexfed badge. On one of the brass plates was a
photograph of Marco, but the name on the credential was Juan
Barrera. The other brass plate contained the word Interpol

above a ribbon of red, white and green, the colors of the Mexican flag.

She doubted its authenticity until Marco started getting visits from a Mexico City friend who sometimes called him Juan. They talked animatedly about the "good old days" in Mexico City working for the Interpol division of the Mexican federal police.

Marco had a collection of other police credentials too. U.S. drug enforcement picked up a story of an instance in 1984 when Marco and a pilot flew into Torreon with a load of marijuana. The airport was swarming with soldiers and military vehicles and the pilot did not want to land: anyone peering into the cockpit could easily see the stash of marijuana. Marco, the story goes, told the pilot not to worry about it, they were covered. They landed, the pilot taxied to the avgas pumps. Marco then flashed a badge of the Directorate of Federal Security—DFS, the quasi-secret political police of Mexico's Interior Government Ministry. He asked for a specific document to sign, citing the document by name and number. After refueling, they took off again. It was either a display of Marco's remarkable chutzpah, or he simply did not have anything to worry about from the military. U.S. narcotics agents believed it was the latter.

Marco returned to Ojinaga from his stint with the federal police in Mexico City about six months before Sammy was convicted in Pecos. By that time, he had developed an organization of his own capable of bringing large amounts of drugs to the border, a new status that gave Marco leverage with Pablo. Pablo took him on as a business partner and they worked major drug deals together. Typical of the loose organization of the Mexican drug underworld, Marco was able to work deals independently of Pablo. He simply had to pay a percentage to Pablo for the right to operate in the established drug lord's *plaza*.

One of the first major investments Marco and Becky made together involved an acre of marijuana they planted and cultivated on a small ranch belonging to Marco in the mountains

Marco Antonio Haro Portillo, a.k.a Marco DeHaro, was Pablo Acosta's chief enforcer and was the gunman who started a drug war in Ojinaga by killing the son of Fermin Arevalo. This photo was taken shortly after DeHaro's arrest in Odessa, Texas, on November 20, 1985, on cocaine, marijuana and heroin trafficking charges. (Photo courtesy of the Ector County Sheriff's Department)

fifty miles south of Ojinaga. A fifteen-acre plot of land in the foothill of a mountain, the property had a couple of cement-block shacks, a shed, a makeshift greenhouse, a deep well, a pump for drawing ground water for irrigation and a gaso-line-powered generator for electricity. To get the project going, Marco and Becky flew to the mountains of Oaxaca in southern Mexico to purchase $25,000 worth of marijuana seeds from an acquaintance. Back in Ojinaga, they hired experienced field workers to prepare one acre for planting. Because of the sometimes freezing night temperatures, they had to let the plants germinate in pots inside a cement-block building that kept warm at night with heat lamps powered by the generator. When the seedlings were three inches tall, workers transferred them to the field under Marco's watchful eye.

Marco appointed an overseer and handed out assault rifles for defense against intruders. A few people had to remain there during the entire three-month growing period to keep the field clear of weeds and uproot male marijuana plants. As a result of the horticultural experimentation that went on in the 1960s and 1970s, pot growers learned that female plants contained the highest concentrations of the psycho-potent resins peculiar to cannabis. They also learned that the concentration dropped if the female plant became pollinated. It was crucial, therefore, to uproot the male plants as soon as they became identifiable.

From the work involved in just getting a one-acre site going, Becky became deeply impressed by the extent of Pablo's pot-growing operation. She knew he contracted with Indians to grow small fields along the Rio Conchos. He also operated at least one large field of his own that she knew of—and probably many more. She once visited a forty-acre hillside plantation south of San Carlos. The vast emerald field was irrigated with spring water that cascaded down a low cliff. The investment was enormous, she realized, but so were the profits.

Marco and Becky frequently visited their ranch to inspect the marijuana and to party. When harvest came in late October, they trucked fieldworkers out to the ranch. One afternoon during harvest time, they brought out a group of mariachis wearing broad sombreros with gold brocade. Pablo came that day with his own group of *pistoleros*. As the mariachis provided music, the traffickers barbecued a goat, drank case after case of beer, danced and made merry under the blue desert sky, and smoked an endless supply of crack-laced cigarettes.

Becky was the only woman among several dozen men. The way she shouted orders in a hybrid Spanish led the workers to start calling her *La Jefa*—The Boss. Everyone joked about her amusing errors in Spanish. Marco, whose alias DeHaro already showed his disdain for his humble origins, wanted everyone to call him *El Príncipe de León*—the Prince of Leon. But to Becky's ear, it sounded like they were calling him *Pinche Pelón*—Friggin' Baldy. As a sobriquet, *Pinche Pelón* prevailed.

One acre produced about a ton of valuable *colas*, the top part of the marijuana plant where most of the resin concentrates. The *colas*, loosely packed into bales, were wrapped in broad sheets of cellophane and secured with silver duct tape. Marco and Becky had all their bales flown across the border and unloaded at a ranch in New Mexico outside Jal. As far as she knew, none of that marijuana was ever seized by American authorities.

Even though Pablo did not have an investment in the field and did not lift a finger to help, he collected a percentage of the profits from the sale of the marijuana.

Theoretically, they were as untouchable as Pablo through his protection scheme, but there were occasional misunderstandings. One time during the midsummer of 1985, Marco, Becky and several others were detained by a squad of soldiers and taken to the downtown garrison for questioning. This arrest occurred while Marco, Becky, Armando, Armando's brother Joaquin, several *pistoleros* and a marijuana buyer from Hobbs were having a meeting in one of the rooms of the Hotel Rohana. The buyer wanted 500 pounds of marijuana. They were working out the details of the deal—the price, how and where it was to be delivered, how and when payment was to be made and other pressing business details. In the middle of the negotiations, there was a harsh pounding on the door. Four soldiers rushed in and an army officer barked, "Hands up!" The soldiers quickly disarmed everyone, bound their hands behind their backs with rope and marched them through the streets to the old adobe garrison a few blocks away.

With Pablo "fixed" with the military, they should not have been bothered by the army officer. Marco figured the officer was new in town and wanted to put the squeeze on them for money. Normally, Marco would simply whip out his police credentials and send the officer packing, but he never bothered to carry them with him in Ojinaga. He kept telling the officer that he worked with Pablo Acosta, that Pablo Acosta was fixed with the army. Finally, the officer allowed Marco to make a telephone call.

They fumed and muttered among themselves for about four hours. A furious Pablo finally strode into the room. He walked to one side with the officer. They went into another room as Pablo talked in a low voice. A short while later, Pablo came out with the confiscated weapons and handed them back to everyone.

"Let's go," he said.

They walked back to the Hotel Rohana. Pablo was still angry. Once in their room, he said: "Tell me what happened. I want to know everything that happened."

Marco gave him a rundown in rapid Spanish, Pablo nodding his head and interjecting questions. He said he was going to look into it. Becky never heard any more about it. But no one ever bothered them again.

Marco sometimes killed on the spur of the moment, in a fit of anger, according to Becky, or on orders from Pablo Acosta. She later claimed she saw him kill several people during a single summer.

On one occasion, Marco had fronted about ten pounds of marijuana to a man in his mid-twenties and told him he wanted the money on a certain day. That day had come when Marco and Becky pulled up in front of a shabby pastel green adobe house on an unpaved street at the foot of the steep slope that led to downtown Ojinaga. A new pickup truck was parked outside.

Marco honked the horn repeatedly. A woman in a faded dress came out with a baby in her arms and told Marco her husband was out of town. Marco brushed past her and found the man in a bedroom sitting on the edge of a dirty mattress. The two men came outside. Marco had the Latin habit of using his hands animatedly while he spoke. Becky heard him telling the young man not to make a fool of him, to give him the money he owed. The shirtless man kept insisting he did not have the money. Marco kept responding "Well, how much money do you have? Just give me that and we'll call the rest of it quits." And "Just give me *some* of the money."

Becky knew by then that Marco was obsessed with getting respect and could become infuriated if he felt slighted. Nevertheless, Becky was not expecting the lightening-quick motion of Marco's hand to his belt, where he kept his .45 semiautomatic. Marco put the barrel within inches of the young man's face and pulled the trigger. The bullet hit him between the eyes with the force of a sledgehammer and sent him flying backward into the dirt front yard.

Terrified, Becky quickly jumped back into the Bronco. She could not believe the swift, irreversible brutality. Marco coolly walked around the vehicle and slid in behind the wheel.

Later, at an apartment where Becky was staying, Marco explained that all the young man would have had to do was to give him something, anything, so he wouldn't feel like a fool. But the guy wouldn't do it. He was a scumbag who deserved to die. He didn't take care of his family. He had come to Marco with a sob story about being broke, that his family was starving, that his wife needed an operation. Marco had given him money, then fronted him the marijuana. He was being generous and helpful. Then it turned out the guy was driving a new truck, the one in front of the house. And he couldn't pay Marco back? He was making a fool out of him, and that was why he killed him, Marco explained.

Becky did not voice her opinion, but it was evident she did not think it was worth killing someone over ten pounds of marijuana. Marco, however, had often instructed Becky about his business philosophy. It did not matter if someone owed just one dollar or a million dollars, it should be handled the same way. If you let your guard down, someone is going to take advantage of you, or cheat you, and make a fool out of you. He had let his guard down, and—see—the guy tried to make a fool of him.

While lecturing Becky, Marco prepared some crack ciga-rettes. Apparently losing interest in the subject, he mentioned a small restaurant near the town center. It was midsummer and it *was* awfully hot in Ojinaga. They drove to the restau-rant and ordered a couple of cherry-lime sodas.

One day, Becky asked Marco if he ever felt remorse for the murders he had committed.

"No," he said. "They had to die."

"How do you live with yourself? I mean, how can you live with yourself knowing that you've taken husbands away from their families and you've taken young boys out of the life cycle. How do you feel? Don't you ever think about it?"

"No."

"Do you ever have bad dreams about it?"

"No, not really," Marco said. "They had to die."

Chapter Fifteen

FIRST WEEK OF JULY

The pace Pablo set was frenetic. His life was characterized by nonstop activity. He and those working with him sometimes went for two or three days without sleep as they took care of the business of drug trafficking: obtaining heroin, marijuana, cocaine; getting drugs to the border; cutting deals with clients; getting it across the border safely, collecting money, disposing of money. Then there were time-consuming ancillary activities to be attended to, such as arranging for vehicles and airplanes to be stolen and brought to Ojinaga, smoothing out production problems at some of the pot plantations, maintaining relationships with authority and a myriad of other tasks that placed heavy demands on Pablo's time.

The first week of July 1985 was typical in the lives of the Ojinaga traffickers.

Becky happened to be in Ojinaga preparing for another marijuana run. Pablo dropped by her motel room to talk over some business he needed her to take care of while she was up in New Mexico. A couple of pilots she had told him about earlier were supposed to be coming down from Albuquerque to talk to him about flying marijuana loads. Pablo wanted her to drive them down to Ojinaga, put them up at a motel and keep them there until he could arrange to meet with them.

While she was up there, Pablo had an equally urgent task for her: he wanted her help in getting an airplane and it needed to be delivered "within a week." He did not explain why this was needed so soon, but she knew better than to ask. Pablo wanted her personally to place the order for the aircraft with Sal, a professional airplane thief in Texas. Pablo did not use the word steal when he spoke to her about the aircraft, but that was always the implication. He almost never bought anything—at least, not from its rightful owner. He just sent someone to take it and then paid the thief, usually in marijuana or heroin. Pablo wanted Becky to help make the arrangements for the acquisition of the aircraft and he wanted her to be in Ojinaga when it was delivered.

Like Sammy Garcia, Sal was an Acosta pal from Pablo's construction and roofing days. He was now a heroin pusher who ran an auto body shop in Seagraves, a small Texas farming town about an hour's drive east of Hobbs. Sal could always be counted on to acquire the right kind of airplane.

"What kind of plane do you want?" Becky asked.

"A little twin engine," Pablo said.

"Any particular model?"

"It doesn't matter. As long as it has two engines."

Like automobiles, airplanes were regularly stolen from the United States and traded in Mexico for drugs. Some were stolen outright, as when Sal broke into a hanger at the Hobbs Industrial Airpark and stole a Cessna 182. For that particular theft, Sal brought a boltcutter and a set of large stick-on letters and numbers to cover up the tail number with a phony Mexican one. Then he and a pilot flew it down to Ojinaga and turned it over to Pablo's organization. The plane was later used to fly loads of marijuana. Or the thefts were part of an insurance scam. The plane disappeared with the knowledge of the owner, who filed a report of loss, collected the insurance and picked up a kickback once the "thief" had been paid for the airplane down in Mexico.

As soon as she delivered the propane tankload of marijuana to a customer and returned to Carlsbad, Becky contacted Sal and told him what Pablo wanted. She was not in a position to negotiate the price, she told him. Sal would have to go down to Mexico and work that out directly with Pablo.

When that task was accomplished, she called the pilots in Albuquerque to tell them Pablo had agreed to meet with them. These pilots were her discovery. An attorney she knew had introduced her to the aviators during one of her recent drug runs to Albuquerque. The two men—Charlie and Red were the names they used—had been members of the so-called Columbus Air Force, a notorious air-smuggling organization. When they learned Becky worked for Pablo Acosta, the big drug honcho of Ojinaga, the pilots understood she was connected to a big business opportunity.

When Becky told Pablo a few days later about meeting a couple of "Columbus Air Force guys," he paid attention.

Always looking for reliable pilots, Pablo had heard of the Yankee smuggling outfit—a bunch of American drug pilots who had taken their name from the small border town of Columbus, New Mexico, where they had once maintained hangars and headquarters. These air jockeys, some of whom had been military pilots in Vietnam, claimed they could take off and land just about anything blindfolded. They owned a private air force that included vintage World-War-II aircraft and had a reputation for doing what they were paid to do. The organization had been largely disbanded by 1985 through deaths, arrests and burnout, but some pilots, including Red and Charlie, still freelanced on their old Columbus Air Force connection.

Becky drove the two pilots down to the border town on July 3 of that year at breakneck speed. They checked in at the Motel Ojinaga. Once they had time to settle in, Marco dropped by the room and told them that Pablo Acosta would probably see them the following day. They asked Marco if he had any pot, and he came back an hour later with a one-ounce baggie.

Charlie and Red ended up waiting several days. There was just too much going on in Ojinaga during that first week of July, and nobody, particularly Pablo, had any time for them. Among other things, Pablo was throwing a farewell party for the outgoing *comandante* of the Directorate of Federal Security, the Interior Government Ministry police, scheduled to take place the following night; a load of cocaine was coming in from Colombia; Marco and Becky needed to go up into the mountains to escort a shipment of marijuana from Chihuahua City. To top it all off, the stolen airplane was due to be delivered as well.

Just before dawn the morning after Red and Charlie arrived in Ojinaga, the stolen twin-engine airplane landed at the municipal airport, piloted by an American accompanied by two other men. Marco and Becky and a flock of gunmen had been waiting in four Broncos at one end of the dirt airfield, smoking crack cigarettes to pass the time. As soon as the plane taxied up to the end of the runway, the four Broncos rushed up and formed a circle around it. Everyone got out of the vehicles with the usual show of weapons.

Three armed soldiers stood guard at the small cement-block guard shack near a tiedown area. The soldiers ignored the traffickers, the traffickers ignored the soldiers. Marco and Becky drove the pilot and his companions to a motel and dropped them off. Someone would drive them back to the United States later that day. From the motel Marco and Becky went to tell Pablo the plane had arrived.

By then the sun was coming up, yet Marco and Becky had no choice but to stay awake: a shipment of about 500 pounds of marijuana was coming from Chihuahua City through the mountains. First, they drove downstream to El Mulato to pick up Tito, one of Marco's pot buyers from Odessa. A thin, middle-aged man with gray hair, dark skin and sunken eyes, Tito had crossed the Rio Grande in a rowboat early that morning and was waiting on the riverbank for them. Tito planned to smuggle the marijuana across himself. He had hidden a load vehicle on the other side of the river.

It was the usual caravan of stolen Broncos. With Tito in the back of their vehicle, the smugglers drove south out of Ojinaga for about an hour, pulling into a secluded ranch house where they dropped Tito off. The caravan continued south to a rendezvous in the mountains with one of Marco's brothers who was driving the load up from Chihuahua City. Marco had called the brother the night before to find out what time he and an escort of armed men were leaving. Marco and Becky arranged their schedule accordingly.

Drug shipments frequently came directly on the two-lane highway connecting Chihuahua City and Ojinaga—if they did not come by air. At times, the Ojinaga traffickers found it prudent to bring the narcotics through desert and mountain back roads, more often than not to cheat the authorities involved in the protection scheme. The *plaza* payments Pablo made to the authorities were based on volume. The more narcotics Pablo and people under him moved, the more Pablo was supposed to pay. The drug traffickers, therefore, devised ingenious ways to get their shipments to the border without anyone being the wiser. The authorities, meanwhile, relied on informants to keep abreast of drug movements. It was a constant game of cat and mouse.

Once, for example, Pablo took about a dozen men along late one night to escort a big load of marijuana and heroin through the mountains. The caravan came to a dry creekbed somewhere in the mountains south of Ojinaga and was stopped by a small group of armed men who politely flashed Mexfed credentials. The Mexican federal police had somehow found out about Pablo's drug shipment and knew along which route it was being delivered to Ojinaga.

"They told us they were going to have to take the load. They knew it was coming and they weren't going to let us have it," Becky later recalled.

If it had come to a fight, the Mexican agents would have been blown to smithereens. The agents were outnumbered and way off the beaten track, but Becky quickly understood that nobody had planned on any gunplay. She watched Pablo, Marco and the Mexfeds jabber while standing in a small circle in the bright headlights of one of the vehicles. Pablo pointed in the direction of a yellow Chevrolet Silverado that one of his gunmen was driving. Becky saw a lot of heads nod up and down. Then she saw Pablo's *pistolero* slide out of the Silverado and two of the Mexfeds jump in and drive off. The rest of the Mexican federal police agents waved the drug caravan through.

Becky realized later that Pablo had brought the Silverado along on purpose, knowing there could be an attempt to intercept the load. The Silverado had been stolen in the United States and brought to Ojinaga just days before the mountain excursion and was brought along as tribute.

Such stolen vehicles, Becky knew, hardly cost Pablo anything. At most, he gave ten grams of uncut heroin to the thief, worth perhaps $500 to Pablo. Once the pusher cut the heroin—usually with chocolate-flavored powdered baby milk—he could sell it on the streets of Odessa or Hobbs or Albuquerque or Oklahoma City for $5,000 or $6,000.

This time, Marco and Becky did not find any troublesome Mexfed roadblocks. They waited in a narrow valley surrounded by pale-brown mountains and after an hour of waiting they saw a large pickup with rattly wooden sideboards rumbling down the dirt mountain road. A Jeep full of gunmen was not far behind.

With Marco and Becky's Bronco in the lead, the caravan drove out of the mountains and back to the ranch where Tito was waiting for them. The marijuana was in the back of the pickup truck in cellophane-wrapped bales, hidden under a tarpaulin. Tito inspected the pot carefully, smelling it, feeling it between his fingers, and finally rolling a joint and lighting up. He liked it. They drove back to the Rio Grande and left Tito and the bales at a stash site in El Mulato. Once in his hands, the marijuana was Tito's responsibility.

By the time they got back to Ojinaga, it was already the afternoon of July 4, and they had gone without sleep for two days in the non-stop whirl of activity. They crashed in their room at the Hotel Rohana.

Becky could have slept for sixteen hours straight, but along about ten o'clock that night, noise from a party in the carport next to their room kept waking her up. And so did Pedro Ramirez Acosta, Pablo's nephew. He kept coming into the room to get cocaine from a stash she and Marco had on the dresser. She got up once to get sandwiches for herself and Marco from the barbecue grill set up in the carport.

While preparing the sandwiches, Becky observed Pablo

chatting with the outgoing DFS *comandante*. One of Marco's brothers and more than a dozen other people who were linked in one way or another to Pablo's organization crowded around a few tables that had been set up for the event. There weren't any mariachis, but someone had tuned a radio to a local station and it was blaring *norteño* music—Mexican country and western. If any of the hotel patrons was upset by the racket, not a single one came forward to complain: all of the partygoers were armed with assault rifles or semi-automatic pistols.

One of the *pistoleros* was holding an AR-15 horizontally at chest level. On the flat of the grooved ammunition clip were white lines, and someone standing in front of the gunman was snorting the lines directly from the clip. It was a snort style considered *muy macho* by the gun-toting traffickers. Everyone else was smoking the crack Pedro Ramirez Acosta prepared from the cocaine in Becky's room.

Becky stayed with the partygoers just long enough to make sandwiches and went groggily back to the room.

She and Marco were awakened the following day at noon by Pedro, who needed more cocaine from their stash. Pablo was about to get up, Pedro explained, and would get upset if some cooked cocaine was not already prepared for him.

As Marco gave him some cocaine in a plastic bag, he asked Pedro what the "big deal" was the night before. Pedro told them the DFS *comandante* was leaving town and that Pablo had thrown a going-away party.

Marco had known in advance about it but had completely forgotten. If he had not been stretched to the limits of endurance by the hectic pace of recent days, he would have attended.

Becky had never spoken much to the *comandante*, but he always seemed to be with the traffickers. He was chubby, tall, charming and every time Becky had seen him, he had either Corona or a Tecate beer in his hand.

The DFS commander was always exceedingly polite with her, but due to her limited Spanish their conversations never went beyond elementary greetings:

"Como le va, señorita?"
"Muy bien, comandante. Y a usted?"

The Directorate of Federal Security or DFS was an internal political police force created in Mexico following World War II as a part of the powerful Interior Government Ministry. For several decades the agency kept track of anybody with political views at odds with Mexico's one-party political system. In the late 1960s and during the 1970s the agency helped quash several urban and rural guerrilla movements in both northern and southern Mexico, a war that resulted in the disappearance of some 1,500 people.

The United States began to suspect the DFS of engaging in criminal enterprises beginning in the early 1970s. Using their DFS credentials as shields, agents regularly escorted narcotics shipments through Mexico and provided other services, frequently even selling seized narcotics to favored organizations. Later intelligence showed that the DFS embarked on an ambitious project to organize protection on a national scale, bringing as much of the nation as possible under a unified system.

As with federal judicial police positions, gangsters frequently were able to buy their way into the agency, and then use their positions to engage in criminal activities. Former underworld players tell of a Juarez DFS commander, Rafael Aguilar, a trafficker prior to becoming a DFS agent, whose role was to fly around Mexico once a month in his Learjet to pick up protection money from favored groups. The payola was then taken to the attorney general's office in Mexico City or to a mansion in Cuernavaca that Aguilar was building for the official.

Some high-ranking DFS officials were later accused of managing auto-theft rings that preyed on the southwestern United States. In May 1981, a federal grand jury in San Diego indicted Miguel Nazar Haro, then director of the DFS, on charges of auto theft. He was arrested in San Diego, but disappeared after posting a $200,000 bond. As DFS director during the administration of Miguel de La Madrid, president of Mexico from 1982 to 1988, Nazar allegedly sold

DFS credentials to powerful Guadalajara traffickers later involved in the murder of Enrique Camarena Salazar, the DEA agent who was kidnapped and tortured to death in Guadalajara in February 1985.

The head of the agency was fired in the months following that murder, as were several hundred agents, including Rafael Aguilar Guajardo, the Juarez-based drug trafficker who had been DFS coordinator for Chihuahua and Coahuila. The DFS was then reorganized and renamed the General Directorate of Investigation and National Security. But before the year was out, drug traffickers, including Pablo Acosta and Ismael Espudo, the former Culberson County commissioner, possessed credentials bearing the name of the new organization. Additionally, one of Rafael Aguilar's lieutenants took over as the secret police agency's *comandante* in Ciudad Juarez.

U.S. Customs later learned about Pablo's going-away party for the Ojinaga DFS *comandante* from an informant. In an interview later with American contacts, the source said Pablo and the *comandante* first tried to outdo one another drinking tequila, then smoking cocaine. Pablo had reserved a room for the federal official at the Hotel Rohana and had stocked it full of surprises: he had sent someone to the *zona* to fetch three of the best looking hookers and had them hide in the hotel room. With a broad smile, Pablo escorted the guest of honor to the room and opened the door. If the federal dignitary could barely stand up on the way into the room, he was considerably less steady on his feet when he eventually came out.

The source, who later passed government polygraph tests, told U.S. Customs and the DEA that the farewells between the *comandante* and Pablo Acosta did not end at the hotel-room door. Much later in the evening the two men staggered out to the airfield. A twin-engine airplane was waiting with propellers spinning to take the *comandante* to Mexico City. Pablo bundled him into to plane, possibly the same one Becky had arranged to be stolen from the United States, after giving him a gold watch and exchanging warmhearted *abrazos*.

The *comandante* boarded the airplane with a "big old silly grin on his face," the informant said.

Toward the end of the first week of July, two days after the going-away party, Pablo finally disposed of enough free time to see Charlie and Red, the two Colombus Air Force pilots. Red was a tall burly man who got his nickname from his flaming hair—red hair, red mustache, red beard. Charlie was slender, with handsome Italian features.

About noon, Marco and Becky stopped by the motel for them. The two airmen climbed into the back of their Bronco. They drove the fliers up the road to Casa Chavez, Pablo's drug warehouse.

The adobe building was full of Pablo's gunmen. At the snap of Pablo's finger, all the gunmen were on their feet. They were armed with AR-15s, AK-47s, Uzis, .45-caliber pistols and knives. His bunch of gunmen knew what they were supposed to do the moment they picked up a gun: shoot to kill if they had to. The rest of the time they were supposed to keep their eyes open and their mouths shut and stare with cold hostility when strangers were around—something they did well without any prompting.

Becky had pumped the pilots during the trip to Ojinaga from the United States to find out the prices they had in mind. She passed the information on to Pablo. They had been getting $10,000 a load from other traffickers, they told her, but they were convinced they could get $40,000 per load out of Pablo Acosta. The pilots had a package deal in mind for the amount. They proposed to fly loads of up to 1,100 pounds of marijuana in a twin-engine airplane to New Mexico. They could promise a ground crew in Mexico to load the drug, another crew in New Mexico to offload it, and a storage place somewhere in the mountains of southwestern New Mexico to keep it until Pablo sent someone to pick it up. They would even deliver the marijuana to its final destination for an additional fee.

They also wanted their payment in drugs, not cash.

Before they were brought in, Pablo prepared the props

that in his mind befitted a drug lord of his stature. He was sitting on the edge of a narrow bed in the living room and had an assault rifle next to him, barrel pointing forward. His pants were tucked into his boots to reveal a knife handle sticking out of one boot, the grip of a pistol jutting from the other. He looked just like the man he was—a real badass Mexican bandit who controlled crime along a big stretch of the border.

It took a lot to unnerve a couple of experienced drug-smuggling pilots like Red and Charlie. Constant danger made them about as cocky as World-War fighter aces. At one time, some twenty drug-laden planes were crashing somewhere in northern Mexico every month, and both men had had their share of mishaps. Usually the accidents happened because of greedy pilots or drug buyers overloading their planes, or pilots trying to fly for extended periods with the aid of amphetamines or cocaine. Even the concentrated odor emanating from a planeload of marijuana could be fatally intoxicating. Such pilots not only flew drugs out of Mexico, but also augmented their income by flying contraband electronics goods *into* Mexico from the United States. That entailed bigger risks than the northward flights. During those years, a small airforce of pursuit planes led by a Mexican Customs *comandante* nicknamed The Red Baron was routinely shooting down such smuggler airplanes over northern Mexico.

The Ojinaga area had had its share of aircraft crack-ups. An airplane had recently crashed and burned on a ranch east of El Mulato. The aircraft had enough fuel to fly non-stop to Michigan, its destination. But the field was dangerous due to the shortness of the runway and the hills that hemmed it in on all sides. Additionally, the plane was overloaded with marijuana. When the pilot climbed steeply to make it over a hill, the bales shifted. The plane stalled and pilot and cargo nosedived into the desert. There was not much left to bury, but what was left of the pilot joined some others who had not made it either.

That particular ranch belonged to one of Manuel Carrasco's cousins and was said to hold the graves of five or six American pilots. Mexican traffickers would usually try to contact the relatives of a dead pilot if there was any kind of documentation available. But there usually was not any, and the Mexicans buried the remains with a cross bearing the name the pilot had used—often just a first name—in case anyone ever came asking about a missing relative.

Making their pitch to Pablo, the pilots talked about their years of flying with the Colombus Air Force and entertained him with accounts of their exploits. Red did most of the talking. He described their airplane and went over the technical details about payload capacity, range, the kind of a runway they needed, their unloading, storage and courier services once the marijuana was in the United States, and so forth. They had a secret landing strip in the mountains somewhere in southwestern New Mexico.

Except for the hippy scruffiness and the references to *mota*, the pilots could have been taken for a couple of high-pressure sales reps making a pitch for an airfreight company. Pablo asked a lot of questions, laughed over some of the anecdotes, and told some of his own. But once it came down to bargaining, the smiles vanished. When Red mentioned the $40,000 fee for the entire package, Pablo pretended he had heard the figure for the first time. He shook his head. He wanted to give them $10,000 a load.

From experience, Becky knew how Pablo operated. When drug buyers came to him for the first time, he usually hiked the price to about twice what he sold to other people. When he was satisfied the newcomers knew what they were doing and had good connections on the American side for moving the drug, he would bring the price down. Becky figured Pablo was going to use the same approach with these pilots. He would test them out on a couple of loads and if they really did everything they said they could do, then he would give them $40,000 a load. But not before.

The pilots, however, kept insisting, and kept raising their Colombus Air Force connection.

"I don't care," Pablo said. "I have people that aren't anybody's air force, and they do a good job for me. And they don't cost me what you guys want."

They dickered for a long time. Pablo hinted that he would pay them more once he had tried them out. Finally, he folded his arms and looked at them coolly.

Becky could see the two pilots were getting frustrated. She leaned forward and said, "If you'll just listen to him and quit interrupting, you'll understand what he's saying."

The redhead replied, without even looking at her. "We don't need no women discussing our business."

It was the wrong thing to say. Marco's eyes narrowed. Pablo stood up and said, "I'd listen to her any day before I'd listen to you." He went into the kitchen. He came back into the living room with a crack-laced cigarette between his lips and said, "We'll discuss it some other time. I'll call you."

There was a rattling of weapons in the background. The pilots got up and marched through the screen door to the Bronco. They got into the back seat. Marco and Becky got into the front to take them back to the hotel.

Becky turned around in the passenger seat as Marco sped down the dirt streets. "Understand his side," she said. "This is a very powerful man in his own territory here. He's never seen you before. And I'm not sure you made much of an impression, the way you talked to me in front of him. He sees that you have no respect for me and I'm the one that introduced you to him. You can't do that."

Red said, "Ah, you made him sound like he owned northern Mexico. He's just a penny-ass border punk. We didn't come here to play kid games."

Marco had not said anything the whole time. Now he leaned forward against the steering wheel, reached behind his back, and pulled the .45 out of his belt. He put it on the seat in plain view of the pilots and put his hand over it. They could see his fingers tapping on the shiny barrel, near the trigger.

Becky turned around, batted her eyes, and said with an exaggerated sweetness, "We don't play games either."

Nobody said anything for the rest of the trip to the motel. Once there, Marco and Becky followed the pilots up the stairs. Marco was still holding the pistol and Becky was hoping he would not do something stupid.

With the pistol in Marco's hand, it looked like they had taken a couple of hostages; but they were climbing the stairs to the motel room adjacent to the pilots' room, which Becky had rented that morning.

They separated at the top of the landing. The pilots had their eyes on Marco's pistol. Becky said cheerfully, "Talk to you later."

Once in their room, Marco exploded. He grabbed a chair and flung it against the wall. He aimed the pistol at the wall, as if he were really going to shoot.

"Nobody gets away with talking that way," he yelled.

Becky tried to calm him down. "What are you getting so upset about? They're just cocky sons a bitches who think they can get their own way by flaunting their Columbus Air Force connections. Pablo wouldn't give a damn if they were the United States Air Force. They're going to have to do it his way if they want his business."

Marco finally called Pablo at Casa Chavez. He told him about the conversation.

Pablo said, "We're not going to play kid games. I'm going to let them take a load for ten thousand, but only pay them five thousand. Then they're going to have to work another load for ten thousand, and I'll give them five thousand for that. The third load they take, if they're still willing to run for me, I'll give them the forty thousand plus the ten thousand I owe them."

"When do you want to see them again?" Marco asked.

"Tell them in four of five days. Make them wait."

Later in the day, Becky went alone to talk to Red and Charlie. They finally agreed to Pablo's terms.

Chapter Sixteen

SEARCH AND RESCUE

Marco and Becky knew the Lomas de Arena—the Sand Hills—river crossing like the back of their hands. A relatively safe route some fifty miles upstream from Ojinaga, it was one of many crossings Pablo had used over the years. It took three to four hours of rough driving to get there along a narrow dirt road that wound around low, barren mountains. On the U.S. side, a rancher had erected a fence with a gate. Pablo's people had a key, as well as keys to other gates through the mountainous ranches between the river and Interstate 10, some twenty miles north of the border. Once on the busy interstate, Pablo's smugglers merged with the ceaseless flow of trucks, cars, vans, recreational vehicles, campers, trailers and motorcycles and drove on easily to their destination.

The river crossing took its name from the nearby village of Lomas de Arena, a sun-baked agricultural hamlet consisting of a scattering of adobe shacks without running water or electricity. Perched on a low sandy hill less than a mile from the river, the village had taken on a strategic importance to the traffickers because of its remoteness and the fact that it was at the extreme end of both Mexican and American police jurisdictions. One of the villagers made good money storing 55-gallon drums of gasoline for Pablo in a shed next to his adobe. When the fuel cache ran low, Pablo had fresh drums trucked in and the empty barrels brought back to Ojinaga for refilling.

The crossing had always been important to Pablo's organization for smuggling narcotics north into the United States, but in 1985 Pablo also began using it to smuggle weapons south into Mexico.

For several years, gunrunners had simply driven weapons and ammunition into Mexico across the international bridge between Presidio and Ojinaga. The Americans never searched vehicles leaving the United States, and Mexican customs authorities on Pablo's payroll simply looked the other way when weapons and ammunition destined for the drug lord came across.

But then two events brought the brazen gunrunning at the international bridge to an end. One was a shootout on the international bridge between one of Becky's runners and a Mexican customs inspector. "Jimmy" was supposed to bring a load of weapons across, and the right amount of money had already flowed into the right number of hands. What nobody had foreseen was Jimmy getting soused on tequila before driving to Mexico. He got surly with a young Mexican Customs inspector who insisted on taking a *pro forma* peek under the tarpaulin covering the weapons cache. The officer put up with the sass until the inebriated runner told him to go screw his mother. The men drew and began blasting away at one another, even though the bridge was crowded with afternoon traffic. Miraculously, no one got even a scratch, although there was a lot of shrieking and diving for cover.

The Mexicans let Jimmy go after Marco arrived on the scene to calm things down, but kept the weapons. Getting the weapons released by the Mexican authorities cost Pablo a lot of money and he was upset.

"Good help is hard to find," Becky told Pablo, shamefaced over her runner's comportment.

Possibly as a result of the international bridge shootout, Americans began without warning or explanation to search vehicles going south. In one of those searches, Amado Carrillo Fuentes, one of Pablo's partners, was detained for taking an AR-15 *into* Mexico. Customs inspectors found the rifle in the trunk of Amado's vehicle. After photographing and questioning Carrillo Fuentes, the Americans let him go but kept the assault rifle.

Though a longer route, the Lomas de Arena crossing presented fewer hassles for bringing weapons into Mexico, and making the trip out there was usually a welcome opportunity for everyone to get out of blistering Ojinaga and take a splash in the river. Any time Becky had weapons or ammunition or anything else to bring down to Mexico, she called ahead from Carlsbad to notify Pablo or Marco. It took her exactly four hours to make the trip, and by the time she got to the edge of the river someone would always be there waiting for her. Often both Marco and Pablo would make the trip. If they could not go themselves, they always sent a trusted gunman to escort Becky back to Ojinaga.

As a smuggling route for narcotics, the Lomas de Arena river crossing was ideal. Though the roads were murderously rough, a flat tire was the greatest mishap that had ever befallen anyone. But then one day in August 1985, a truck that had crossed at Lomas de Arena with a 700-pound load of marijuana disappeared, leading to a search-and-rescue mission by a troop of traffickers. The marijuana was destined for a pot buyer from New Mexico who wanted the marijuana delivered to him at a ranch house outside Hobbs. The load was to go in a fruit truck, hidden in a compartment under a ton of Chihuahua cantaloupes.

The day the load was supposed to leave all of Pablo's experienced runners were already on the road or were not available for one reason or another.

"Find me somebody to run this load," Pablo told his sullen nephew, Pedro Ramirez Acosta.

Pedro came back with two farm workers from the San Carlos area. One of them had light brown hair and freckles, the other dark skin and coal-black hair and eyes. Both were cornstalk thin from fieldwork and the spare *campesino* diet of maize, beans and chili. Like most adult males in the region, they had worked illegally at one time or another in the United States and were reasonably familiar with West Texas and New Mexico and the route they would have to take once they made it to Van Horn. The freckle-faced one had already driven a load of marijuana for somebody else to Odessa, proving to

Pablo that at least he had the nerves. It was clear they were eager to work for the famed *mafioso*, and even more eager for the money two days of driving would bring them—more than they could ever make in a year of back-breaking labor in the fields.

The truck was loaded up at Casa Chavez on a thermometer-busting August afternoon. Pablo leaned against a shady wall of Casa Chavez and shouted orders to the two *campesinos* and several warehouse workers assigned to help load the truck. As usual, Marco, Becky, Pedro and some of Marco's brothers accompanied Pablo.

The two farm workers stashed marijuana bales quickly into a phony compartment in the flatbed, then loaded nearly a ton of sweet-smelling cantaloupe between the wooden sideboards. Every once in a while they glanced over at the traffickers, noting with envy the machine guns leaning against the wall and the .45 semiautomatics stuffed in their belts. Even the *gringa*, blond Becky, had an arsenal.

The loading was finished by late afternoon. Marco gave them some expense money, detailed instructions and some marijuana in a baggie—which later proved a mistake. Soon they were off to the canals and the dirt road that led to Lomas de Arena. Two gunmen followed them in another vehicle to make sure they got to the crossing without any trouble. By the time they arrived it would already be dark and safe to cross into the United States.

Once they got to Lomas de Arenas, the runners and their escort stopped at the makeshift gas station to top off the melon truck. The gunmen accompanied them to the banks of the river and waved them through after unlocking a gate on the American side.

From then on until the delivery, the rookie marijuana runners were on their own.

Back in Ojinaga, Pablo was busy arranging other dope deals, getting other loads ready for crossing, and he quickly forgot about the 700-pound load in the melon truck. He had his money, the pot was on its way, the deal was already ancient history.

But late the next day Pablo got a telephone call. The marijuana buyer from Hobbs was *muy* upset. "Where are my fucking birds?" he demanded, referring to the marijuana. "Did they fly away, or what?"

"Goddamn, don't get so excited," said Pablo. "I'll call you back."

He told Becky and several others to find out what happened to "those two fucking guys" with the cantaloupe truck. Becky made calls to the United States while others paid visits to anybody even remotely related to the two men to find out if they had been busted in the United States. If anybody would know, it would be one of the relatives. But no, nobody had heard anything about the runners one way or the other.

Pablo was beside himself with anger. If they had not been busted, the only other possible explanation was that they had stolen the load. That's what he got for using someone he didn't know well. If they had ripped him off, he would have to make good on the load by replacing it. That meant breaking even on the deal at best, and looking stupid and not in control if word got around he had been ripped off by a couple of peons.

He knew that the runners would sooner or later flutter back to their *pueblito* like homing pigeons. Then they would have some explaining to do. It did not matter if it was thirty pounds, 300 pounds or 3,000 pounds. If they had stolen from him, he would make them pay for it.

"I'm gonna kill those sons of bitches!" Pablo said.

Two days after the runners first left Ojinaga for Lomas de Arena and the trek north, Pablo got a call that they were in a room at Motel Ojinaga. He quickly got a hold of his top people by radio.

The two failed runners sat with glazed eyes and dry throats in their motel room. They themselves had called everywhere they could in town trying to locate Pablo. They were expecting the worst to happen when they explained about the truck. They had been smoking the pot Marco had given them. The driver was not paying sufficient attention to the road. Then suddenly, *bang!* They were in a ditch, nearly tipped over. They were not experienced as runners, but they knew they had put their lives up as security for the load the moment they agreed to run it. It was a code they had absorbed practically with their mother's milk. They knew they could run, but they could not hide. The only solution was to come back and tell Pablo the truth and hope for the best.

The two peasants were discussing how to explain it to Pablo when suddenly the door of their motel room burst open to reveal Pablo, Marco, Pedro, Becky, four gunmen and a few other people.

Pablo and Marco grabbed the young men by the shirt collars and began shaking and slapping them.

"What did you do with the dope? What did you do with the dope?"

Pablo and Marco kept shouting variations of the same question without giving the young men a chance even to speak. Everyone was shouting like the crowd at a wrestling match The two trembling *campesinos* begged for a chance to speak.

Pablo's grip on the collar of the freckle-faced youth finally relaxed. He turned to Marco. "That's enough. Let them talk and let's see what they have to say. And *then* we kill them."

Almost in unison, the two gasped: "We didn't steal the stuff. We had an accident!"

They explained to Pablo they had run into a ditch ten miles after crossing the river. It was pitch black out there, the trail was difficult to follow, and they drove off the road when it curved suddenly. The truck didn't tip over, but part of the load of cantaloupe had spilled out. They had tried without success to back the truck out.

"You lying bastards. What took you so long to call me?" Pablo demanded.

"It took us that long to get back to Ojinaga. We had to walk through the desert," said Freckle-face.

Pablo's eyes narrowed. "You better be able to take us to that truck and that stuff better be there, because if it's not, you're going to die."

The two men were dragged out of the motel and shoved into one of several Jeeps parked in front of the hotel restaurant.

Including the *campesinos*, there were twelve people in the group. The three Jeeps and one pickup truck in the caravan bristled with weaponry. Everyone had a .45-caliber semiautomatic pistol and was armed with either an AR-15 or a banana-clip Kalashnikov. They drove by Pablo's warehouse to pick up ammunition, then headed west to the dirt road leading to Lomas de Arena.

The dirt road was deeply rutted, and tips of boulders projected here and there. The trip was bumpy and dusty. Pablo always rode in the lead car. From a distance, his convoys looked like furious dust devils streaking across the desert. An ongoing joke among Pablo's men was that they would die from only one of two things: lead poisoning or Pablo's dust.

Amado Carrillo Fuentes rode with Pablo. Like Marco De-Haro, Amado had either worked for a time as a Mexican federal agent of some kind, or had been given police credentials. American investigators later learned that Amado himself claimed to have worked as a DFS agent for five years. He was the nephew of a powerful Guadalajara drug trafficker and had important contacts there and in Mexico City. Amado had no financial stake in this particular marijuana load, but had decided to go along for the ride.

Arriving at the river just before midnight, the traffickers parked all four vehicles at the edge of the river with headlights shining on the brown, swirling water. Weapons clattered as everyone except the two peasants got out of the Jeeps. The captive runners sat in glum silence.

A tall man with a plump, boyish face, Amado had been having second thoughts about crossing. He strode to the edge of the river and looked across the muddy water. "This idea sucks," he said. "We don't know what's up the road. Those two jerks could have been caught and then worked out a deal to get us across. Or the truck could really be in a ditch, but it's been found and they're waiting for someone to come for it."

They decided to turn off the headlights. The moon was not out but the sky was bright with stars. They could barely make out the crests of the Van Horn Mountains that lay between them and the town of Van Horn and Interstate 10, some twenty miles directly north through a mountain pass.

With them was a stock of crack cigarettes Pedro had prepared earlier that day. They took out a pack and everyone lit up. The orange tips of the cigarettes moved around in the darkness like crazy fireflies. For about ten minutes they debated who if anybody should go to see about the truck.

Pablo fell into a reflective silence. He knew one day he was going to die a violent death. That was the way it had to be. But was it going to be tonight? Over a chickenshit cantaloupe truck? He formed a mental image of a tiny army of smugglers in a machine-gun battle with a platoon of American narcs. The great melon war. It appealed to him.

Finally he spoke. "Screw it. We all go. If they're out there waiting for us, we're going to take a bunch of them with us."

Having crossed there several times a week shuttling weapons or drugs between Ojinaga and Carlsbad, Becky knew the trail on the American side better than anybody else. But she suddenly got cold feet at the thought of a suicidal showdown in the desert with American narcotics agents. If there were any agents waiting to bust them, she knew there would be a shootout. Pablo had always made it clear: nobody with a badge was ever going to take him alive.

"I don't really want to do this," she said. "I'll wait over here."

But Marco said firmly, "You're coming with us. We all go together."

They decided to split into two groups and take two separate roads that further on merged into the one the *campesinos* said they had taken. Two of the Jeeps with Pablo, Amado, several gunmen and the two trembling peasants drove up the river a few miles and splashed across the shallow Rio Grande into the United States. Each of the Jeeps was equipped with a spotlight mounted on the driver's side. Pablo's gunmen stood up once they had bounced over the embankment and aimed their machine guns in the same direction as the spotlights.

Their purpose for splitting up was to make sure the roads were clear in case they later had to beat a hasty retreat back to the river and the safety of Mexico. If it was a setup, it would have to happen in the area of the cantaloupe truck somewhere up the road. They knew how the *gringos* operated. The Americans would have to wait for them to get to the cantaloupe truck, unload the melons and uncover the marijuana before making a bust that had a chance of standing up in court.

The spotlights swept across mesquite bushes, dry creekbeds and boulders as they slowly drove to a fork where two dirt roads met. Marco, Becky and their gunmen were already at the junction when Pablo's vehicles pulled up. They drove in single file three miles further into U.S. territory before spotting the cantaloupe truck. It was leaning at a dangerous angle into an arroyo next to the road, just as the runners had described it. Cantaloupes were scattered everywhere.

Pablo sent two of the Jeeps to scout around. They came back fifteen minutes later. The coast was clear.

Everyone pitched in to unload the melons. When the truck was finally unloaded, Marco loosened one of the floorboards covering the hidden compartment and the pot.

"It's all here!"

Clearly, the only way to recover the truck was to build up a path leading back to the road. The farm workers and the gunmen were put to work building a base of rocks so the truck could be jacked up higher and higher.

Pablo sat on the hood of one of the Jeeps, patiently smoking crack-laced cigarettes with Amado and Marco and watched the work, illuminated by the headlamps of one of the Jeeps. Hours later, when the work was finally done, Marco jumped behind the wheel and expertly backed the truck onto the road. They quickly reloaded the melons.

The two *campesinos* had done most of the hard labor and were as filthy as coal miners. They stood near the truck after it was back on the road. They watched Pablo slide from the hood of the Jeep, then walk toward them, holding his AR-15. A crack-laced Marlboro dangled from his lips.

"That was stupid of you to drive into a ditch," he said, his eyes narrow and unsmiling.

The two runners stood before him. Their faces showed they expected the worst.

"But you did the right thing going back to Ojinaga to find me," Pablo continued.

The drug lord apologized: he was sorry for mistrusting them. He broke into a long, convoluted explanation about how he had become mistrustful of people. He had trusted people again and again, and how many times had he been ripped off? How much money had he lost by trusting people he shouldn't have trusted? The two runners had been victims of other people's untrustworthiness.

Becky and Marco had heard the same complaint again and again, as had anyone who had spent an evening with the *padrino*, smoking cocaine and drinking whiskey until morning. But more than others, Marco and Becky knew what *really* happened to people who had tried to double-cross Pablo.

"Do you have any money?" Pablo asked.

"*No, señor.*"

He pulled a wad of American money from his pocket and gave the grimy men $500 each.

"Then take this. And be careful not to screw up by driving into any more ditches. God be with you."

"*Vayan con Dios!*" —like the benediction of a rural priest. Becky thought for an instant that the peasants would go to their knees and kiss Pablo's hands.

They were hicks but not fools. They hopped into the cantaloupe truck, shouted "*Adiós, señores,*" slammed the truck into gear, and rumbled north as fast as they could without skidding into another ditch.

Pablo and his entourage stood in the road and watched the truck's taillights until they disappeared over a hill. Then everyone piled back into the Jeeps and returned leisurely to Ojinaga.

Later that day, a twin-engine turboprop flew low over the desert of northern Chihuahua. Just before midnight, the pilot, expert at landing on dirt runways at night, spotted the

string of lanterns. He set the plane down smoothly and taxied to the far end near a cement-block guard shack.

A small fleet of Broncos and pickup trucks quickly surrounded the airplane. Men with assault rifles jumped out
and stood aside as Pablo walked up to the plane. The pilot
cut the engines and Pablo signaled to his men to clamber
aboard. Working quickly, his men unloaded the cargo: sturdy cardboard boxes, each four feet long, three feet wide,
and a foot deep. As each box was slid onto the bed of one of
the pickup trucks, Pablo opened them to ensure the contents.
Each of the boxes contained kilogram packages about the
size and shape of a thick hardbound book. The packages
were sturdily wrapped with green, silver or gray plastic tape.
Each had markings in indelible ink. When all the boxes were
loaded onto the pickups, Pablo signaled to the pilot to leave.

Three soldiers had come out of the guard shack when the
plane arrived, Indian conscripts with black, expressionless
eyes who stood silently with their rifles slung over their shoulders. They stiffened at the approach of the *narcotraficante*
with the big nose and scarred face. The drug lord gave them
$20 each, his custom even though he was "fixed" with the
military. Their helmeted heads nodded as they took the bills
and shoved them into the pockets of their fatigues.

The empty plane was already bouncing down the runway for takeoff when the pickup trucks and Broncos left the
airfield and rumbled through the dirt streets to Casa Chavez.
Pablo had the boxes carried inside the adobe house. He pulled
one of the book-sized bricks out and sliced it with a knife. As
everyone gathered around, he scooped a couple of ounces of
white powder into a plastic bag.

It was time to sample a load of about 1,800 pounds of
pure cocaine that had just arrived from Colombia.

"You cook," Pablo said to his nephew Pedro.

Chapter Seventeen

NORTH-SOUTH DIALOGUE

In the early 1980s, forces were at work in South Florida that propelled Pablo Acosta into the cocaine smuggling business and converted Ojinaga into possibly the biggest cocaine depot ever in North America.

For years most of the cocaine smuggled into the United States had been coming through the hundreds of isolated coves and inlets of south Florida. Miami was the control center of the trafficking operations in the United States for all of the big-name Colombian traffickers. The presence of their organizations transformed the balmy resort town into one of the murder capitals of the United States.

In 1982, the United States created the South Florida Task Force to concentrate federal anti-narcotics personnel in Miami. Their job was to disrupt the cocaine supply lines that had their beginnings in the steamy, snake-infested jungles of South America. The Task Force counted on help from the DEA, FBI, U.S. Customs, the Coast Guard, the Bureau of Alcohol, Tobacco and Firearms and other federal agencies, not to mention state and local narcotics agents. The concentration of resources and manpower lead to one record-breaking cocaine seizure after another. But the effort was as frustrating as fighting an infestation of cockroaches with a rolled-up newspaper. A few big ones got taken down; the rest just scurried away.

Since the early 1970s, Colombian and Mexican traffickers were known to collaborate to supply cocaine to the West Coast

By 1985, Amado Carrillo Fuentes was only beginning to be known by American intelligence as a key player in Ojinaga. He was positioning himself to take over and eventually became the most powerful trafficker in Mexico. He accompanied Pablo Acosta, Marco DeHaro and Becky Garcia on many of their smuggling activities, including the rescue of the broken-down marijuana truck near Lomas de Arena. The left photograph of Carrillo Fuentes was taken by a U.S. Customs agent after the trafficker was detained for possessing an assault rifle while crossing the international bridge into Mexico. It was found in the trunk of his car. The right photo was taken after Carrillo Fuentes was jailed in Mexico for several weeks in 1989. By then, he had undergone plastic surgery at least once to alter his appearance.

of the United States. The Colombians "piggybacked" Mexican organizations with complex smuggling networks that had been set up for marijuana and heroin, but these transactions had been relatively small scale. As it became more costly to do business through Florida, however, the Colombian traffickers began to seek out promising smuggling organizations along the U.S.-Mexican border and shifted much, though not all, of their operations.

Exactly how the Colombians and Pablo Acosta came together did not become clear until much later. But the presence of Amado Carrillo Fuentes provided a clue. Amado was the nephew of Ernesto Fonseca, a powerful Guadalajara trafficker of the same bandit-gangster-peasant mold as Pablo Acosta.

Pablo was believed to have had long-standing business dealings with Fonseca and other traffickers in Guadalajara, a city that is to Mexican organized crime what New York City is to the American Cosa Nostra. Colombian traffickers had unsuccessfully attempted to gain an independent foothold in Mexico, but only began to flourish through their Guadalajara contacts.

American narcotics agents familiar with the border speculate that in their search for business relationships, the Colombians were told, "Go see Pablo Acosta in Ojinaga." They would have approached him, therefore, with a deal he could not turn down. It is now believed that as the relationship progressed, Amado, was sent to work with Acosta and oversee cocaine deals that had originated in Guadalajara. Agents have speculated that a Colombian presence was inevitable and that Acosta, realizing that he could be bypassed or removed, made a virtue out of a necessity.

However it came about, in late 1984 or early 1985 planeloads of cocaine began arriving in Ojinaga, or at surrounding ranches, like clockwork. The traffickers used long-range, twin-engine executive turboprops that flew directly from Colombia to northern Mexico. At times, the aircraft landed brazenly at the Ojinaga municipal airport. At other times, they landed on dirt runways at remote ranches. Pablo received and stored the cocaine in the Ojinaga region for the Colombians.

Informants later told American police it was Pablo's responsibility to ensure protection for the drug shipments with Mexican authorities, particularly through his connections with the military. His own organization smuggled some of the cocaine to the United States; the remainder he held for other important traffickers—for organizations downstream as far as Matamoros, upstream and across the great Sonoran desert as far as Tijuana, and down south as far as Guadalajara. These groups came to Pablo to pick up their merchandise. For doing nothing more than warehousing it and ensuring the safety of the cocaine while it was in his jurisdiction, Pablo was paid anywhere from $1,000 to $1,500 per kilogram.

U.S. government informants later said Pablo met directly

with Carlos Lehder Rivas in Colombia. Until he was extradited to the United States in February 1987, Lehder was one of the most notorious members of the so-called Medellin Cartel, a powerful group of Colombian traffickers believed at the time to be responsible for producing eighty percent of the cocaine consumed in the United States.

While a cocaine producer himself, Lehder's importance was thought to consist in arranging smuggling networks for other cartel members. Pablo reportedly made several trips to Colombia, evidently to work out details of the Ojinaga warehousing operation. Informants said that Lehder himself may have visited Pablo Acosta several times in Ojinaga, but used the name Carlos "Rivas," the Colombian trafficker's maternal last name that he sometimes used as an alias.

When the cocaine arrived in Ojinaga, Pablo had sophisticated ways of storing it. A confidential informant working for the U.S. Drug Enforcement Administration described how a twin-engine plane landed about May 1985 at a ranch thirty miles southeast of Ojinaga with 1,800 pounds of cocaine aboard. The cocaine was wrapped in circular or rectangular one-kilogram bricks that looked like wax-enclosed wafers of imported cheese. To unload the cargo, Pablo's men formed a "bucket brigade" between the airplane and a three-foot deep hole next to a livestock watering tank near the runway. At the bottom of the hole was a rusty metal hatch—the entrance to a cylindrical metal tank buried beneath the desert floor. One of the traffickers squeezed down into the storage tank through the circular hatch and stacked the packages inside the tank. When the last of the bricks was stashed, the hatch was slammed shut and locked. Then the traffickers filled the hole back up and dusted it down with caliche and threw a few rocks on top. No one besides the traffickers could ever know that a Montezuma's fortune was buried down there.

Present at that particular delivery, the informant reported, was Marco DeHaro and Ismael Espudo, the former Culberson County commissioner. During the operation,

Marco sent men to patrol the ranch, and helped Espudo supervise the unloading and storage of the cocaine.

Parked next to the desert landing strip was a tanker-truck holding 1,500 gallons of jet fuel. Once the unloading was accomplished, some of the men under Marco's command shoveled dirt into the access hole to the underground tank, while others pumped fuel into the turboprop. When the refueling was completed, the aircraft swirled around in a blast of dust and took off in a high-rpm roar up the long runway.

The same informant who had observed the unloading said he was present a few weeks later when the cocaine was unearthed and transferred to Ojinaga. A platoon of Pablo's men dug back down to the tank hatch. Someone climbed into the tank and handed up the cocaine. The cheese-like bricks were put into cardboard boxes in the back of two pickup trucks. This time, a squad of Mexican soldiers was present to provide security. The soldiers escorted the traffickers from the desert ranch to the outskirts of Ojinaga. Pablo and a group of his *pistoleros* were waiting for the convoy alongside the dirt road. Following his custom, Pablo pulled out a wad of bills from his shirt pocket and gave each of the soldiers a crisp $20 bill. He dismissed them, and the soldiers made their way back to their garrison in Ojinaga by a different route.

Pablo's men drove the cocaine to a warehouse in Ojinaga a few blocks away from Casa Chavez where Pablo still stored much of his pot. This warehouse was inside a large lot enclosed by high cement-block walls. The compound was strewn with propane tanks that were in the process of being modified and fitted with a smaller tank—just as Sammy Garcia had done it. It was like a small factory, bustling with employees working overtime to meet a production deadline.

The same informant observed how, over the next few days, the cocaine from the underground storage tank was broken down into seven separate loads. Each load was packed inside one of the modified propane tanks. Once the tank was sealed with Bondo, it was bolted to the floor of a pickup truck and hooked up to look like a functioning propane tank. When the shipment was ready, a trusted runner would drive the truck to Lomas de Arena or some other low spot, cross the river, and drive north to the interstate and on to the destination.

During 1985 and 1986, as much as five tons of cocaine a month—possibly one-third of the amount consumed in the United States—was passing through Ojinaga.

Marco and Becky essentially worked for themselves, paying Pablo a percentage of their profits for the right to operate in his territory. They gave Pablo a hand whenever they were in Ojinaga. In the summer of 1985, they decided to move their base of operations to Carlsbad, after obtaining Pablo's blessings. Without his approval, they would have had a tough time bringing their shipments through Ojinaga.

When Marco told him about their decision, Pablo tried to talk him out of it. Marco did not know the United States well enough, Pablo pointed out. It would not take long for the cops to know who he was, and they would end up tailing him everywhere to look for a way to bust him. He could end up in the slammer for twenty years. He could not get protection like in Mexico. It was best just to stay in Ojinaga and let the runners take all the risks, Pablo insisted.

But Marco was adamant. Pablo relented. He sent for Becky and lectured her sternly, like a father. "Just make sure that he's all right," he said about Marco. "If you need anything, give me a call."

In Carlsbad, they lived in the same apartment Becky had moved into after separating from Sammy. It was in an apartment complex on the upscale north end of Carlsbad. Marco and Becky had the appearance of respectability. They dressed well, drove new vehicles, and gave off an aura of successful entrepreneurs. The only thing that did not add up for neighbors were the stressed-out lowlifes who were seen going in and out of the apartment at all hours of the day and night.

Marco and Becky did indeed have a major enterprise in mind. Between the two of them, they expected to clear $2.5 million in less than six months from the frenetic pace of their drug deals. Much of the money would come from the single acre of marijuana they had under cultivation south of Ojinaga. Once the pot was sold, they were going to invest the entire $2.5 million wad in the purchase of a ton of cocaine from Carlos Lehder, a connection Marco had made through Pablo.

Between the summer of 1985 and November when they were arrested in Odessa, they made four trips to Colombia to work out the cocaine deal. Becky later described the journeys to American police and others. On the first trip, Pablo joined them in Bogota and drove with them to visit Lehder in Medellin. Lehder invited them to a palatial estate, and the next day took them to visit a cocaine "factory" the Colombian trafficker was overseeing deep in the jungle. It was Marco's deal, but Pablo went along for the ride. An *aficionado*, Pablo knew that cocaine was extracted through a long, tedious chemical process involving highly flammable industrial solvents, but he had never seen it done.

The "factory" consisted of sheds with corrugated iron roofs and large tents spread over several acres of jungle clearing. It was midsummer and the jungle was as humid as a steam bath and the air abuzz with mosquitoes. People at work near vats and barrels of chemicals paid little attention to the visitors, whom Lehder guided through the production labyrinth step by step. Everywhere was the telltale odor of acetone.

Pablo and Marco, both dressed expensively in western clothes and absorbed by the complexity of the operation, asked questions.

Becky was impressed by the cleanliness, the organization, the attention to the smallest detail. Though it was a shanty-village in the heart of the jungle and could be torn down and moved overnight if necessary, the dirt streets were litter-free. A water truck made the rounds sprinkling the bare earth to keep the dust under control.

Lehder showed them a ton of cocaine, the facility's most recent production. It was stored inside a tent near what appeared to be the main building. Workers had already wrapped the cocaine in kilogram bricks and piled them inside wooden crates. The bricks had letters or symbols written on them with permanent markers. The crates were stacked on pallets.

Nearby was a forklift. The Colombian picked up a clear plastic bag full of cocaine from a bench and scooped out a couple of ounces into another bag. He handed it to his visitors as a sample. They snorted some on the spot. Inside the main building, they prepared some crack and smoked it *a la mexicana*—in cigarettes. There were grunts and groans of approval.

Instead of shipping the cocaine through northern Mexico, a logical route given their connections to Pablo, Marco and Becky made arrangements with a Colombian named Jaime Herrera, thin-faced scion of a trafficking family in Bogota, to ship the load through Florida. The Herrera family was connected to Lehder's organization; Jaime Herrera's sister, who lived in Miami, was to receive the load and Jaime was to escort it to San Antonio after taking charge of it in Miami.

The plan was for Jaime to fly to Ojinaga and to be picked up by Marco and Becky at the Lomas de Arena crossing. As soon as Jaime's sister got the load in Miami, they would put Jaime on a flight to Florida. Once the cocaine shipment arrived at a stash house in San Antonio, they would take possession of it, break it down into smaller loads and run it to customers they had already lined up.

Marco and Becky made two more trips to Colombia to work out further details of the deal and a final trip in early November when the deal was sealed. They visited the jungle factory one more time, and saw the cocaine they would receive being packaged and marked MB—for Marco and Becky. On the way back, they flew to Jamaica to work out details of a money laundering scheme with a tall, distinguished looking Jamaican banker who spoke English with a British accent.

When they returned to Carlsbad, they were ecstatic. If everything went smoothly, they were going to quadruple their investment, they calculated.

But things were not destined to go as planned. Pablo turned out to be right about the dangers of operating a narcotics organization in the United States. Only a few months after they began operating out of the Carlsbad apartment, Carlsbad police were on to them. Police informants not only identified Marco and Becky as important drug traffickers but also as high-ranking members of Pablo Acosta's organization. This brought even greater police scrutiny.

Even more, the informants stated that Marco had boasted of killing people for Pablo Acosta, among them two young Mexican men shot to death in a house in nearby Hobbs in September 1983. Just as Pablo had predicted, police soon were tailing Marco and Becky, gathering intelligence about their movements and looking for a chink in their armor. The city police subpoenaed telephone company records for Becky's telephone number and found 180 long-distance calls placed from the middle of May to the end of August to Mexico, Texas, Oklahoma, Wyoming and New Mexico. Many of the telephone numbers turned out to be "hits," numbers belonging to suspected drug traffickers. In October, a state judge authorized a wiretap of Becky's Carlsbad telephone and the bugging of her apartment.

Through the eavesdropping, the authorities soon became aware that a major cocaine deal was in the works. The language Marco and Becky used was vague and coded. The police could only guess at the details. But the wiretap did pick up Becky's optimism and a hint of the size of the transaction: "We will be set up. No more worries forever. None," Becky said in one conversation.

While their business venture seemingly was on firm ground, Marco and Becky's personal relationship had begun to deteriorate. Their arguments, frequently disagreements over business, were becoming daily occurrences.

They both were smoking a lot of crack, making the arguments potentially dangerous. During one argument, with police listening through a bug hidden in the living room, Becky threw a paper bag full of money at Marco. He threw it back, hitting her above the eye. They started shoving one another. Becky grabbed her pistol, aimed at Marco's head and pulled the trigger. But she had not chambered a round and had accidentally released the ammunition clip.

Marco did not give her a second chance. He put his .45 to her head.

"Do you want to see how it feels to die?" he snarled.

Carlsbad police and DEA agents in a van outside started sweating. What were they to do? If they rushed into the apartment, then the surveillance was blown. When it really did sound like Marco and Becky were about to kill each other, they decided to grab Becky's nine-year-old son, Chase, who was playing on the landing of the apartment, to get him out of harm's way. Just as the agents jumped out of the van, Marco got a hold of himself and threw down the pistol he had been holding to Becky's head.

After that nearly fatal argument, Marco and Becky cut down on their crack consumption, but their relationship was never again the same.

During one of her later trips to Ojinaga, Becky told Pablo about the argument.

"You're probably the only person who's ever gotten that close to killing him and lived to tell about it," Pablo said.

Not long after, a surveillance team followed Marco and Becky from Carlsbad to a dirt road south of Van Horn, but the officers dared not follow any further for fear of giving themselves away. The dirt road cut straight south through the Van Horn mountains and led to the Lomas de Arena river crossing. They waited instead along the highway to see if Marco and Becky would return. Sure enough, several hours later, the dusty black Bronco that Marco and Becky were driving reappeared on the highway. But this time, there was a third person in the vehicle, a pale, thin-faced man who later checked into the Driftwood Motel in Carlsbad under the name of Jaime Herrera.

A week later, the wiretap picked up Jaime Herrera using Becky's telephone. Jaime called Bogota, Colombia. A woman answered. Jaime asked politely if the "lady" had been sent.

"Yes, the 'lady' has already left," the female voice said.

The next day, Marco, Becky, Jaime, and Becky's nine-year-old son drove to Odessa and checked into a motel. They needed to collect $140,000 from an Odessa heroin dealer, and make another heroin delivery. Afterwards, it was their plan to take Jaime to the Odessa airport to catch a plane to Florida. The following day, Marco and Becky intended to drive to Ojinaga to wrap up some business with Pablo, then drive to San Antonio to meet Jaime and take charge of the cocaine.

Marco and Becky agreed on every aspect of the deal except for one—whether or not to cut in Pablo Acosta. Marco wanted to give him the usual percentage even though they were not going through Pablo's *plaza*. With Marco, it was a matter of loyalty. With Becky, it was strictly business. Why pay for protection they were not even going to use?

Just after checking into the motel, they began shouting at one another again. Marco stepped out of the motel to cool off. He walked up to the Bronco. Just as he did, a swarm of DEA agents and city policemen moved in to arrest him.

Marco usually carried a gun with him wherever he went. For some reason, he had left his .45 in the Bronco. DEA agents shoved him to his knees. One of the agents ordered him to lie facedown on the ground. It was cold outside, and Marco was already kneeling in a puddle of water.

"Hit the position—face down!" the agent repeated.

Marco looked at him with contempt and said, "You know who you're talking to?"

The agent shoved the muzzle of an M-14 to the back of Marco's head, and pushed until Marco's face was pressed into the puddle.

"Yeah, I know who you are," the DEA agent said.

Only later, the authorities realized they had acted too quickly. If they had continued the surveillance for several more days, they could have caught Marco, Becky and Jaime with a major load of cocaine.

As it was, the couple was charged in New Mexico state district court with twelve felony counts ranging from racketeering to conspiracy to traffic in cocaine and heroin. Marco was additionally charged in federal court for weapons possession and illegal entry into the United States.

Becky was released on bond and realized she was out of money after paying attorney fees in Texas and New Mexico. She was wiped out. All of the money she and Marco had raised over the previous six months—$2.5 million—was in Colombia and she figured she was never going to see any of it again. In February 1986, she drove down to Ojinaga to see Pablo about getting fronted some loads of marijuana. She needed to make money, and she needed to make money fast, she told him. Pablo cleared out the downtown Bikini Bar so they could talk, just as he did the first time she went to Ojinaga. Pablo had his nephew fetch some musicians from the *zona*, and his nephew came back half an hour later with a group. The musicians crowded onto a low dais in one of the corners and played softly while Pablo's gunmen kept watch at the front and back doors.

Pablo wanted to know what had happened. How had the authorities caught on? And how did Becky manage to get out of jail and not Marco?

Becky explained: The Carlsbad police had four informants who evidently knew a lot about them and a lot about Pablo. If Marco was not allowed out on bond, it was because he was a foreign national and was considered a flight risk. She was not.

Becky had brought along two copies of a twenty-nine-page wiretap affidavit, the document Carlsbad authorities had presented in court requesting an extension of the original one-month wiretap authorization. The document went into detail describing Marco and Becky's suspected criminal background, and their role in Pablo Acosta's drug trafficking organization. The affidavit summarized information obtained from four confidential informants who were identified in the wiretap affidavit only by numbers.

Between drinks from a bottle of El Presidente brandy and long drags on his crack-laced cigarettes, Pablo read the entire document, asking Becky to explain words he did not understand. They tried to deduce who the informants were and came up with several possibilities. Pablo never said what he was going to do about them. All he said to Becky was, "Don't worry about it," and kept the document.

They got down to business: Becky wanted a load of marijuana; she had some customers who would buy as much pot as she could supply them, but she hardly had a dime to her name. All of her vehicles had been confiscated. The only vehicle remaining to her was the truck with a propane tank that she had left with Pablo not long before her arrest. Pablo had recently sent the truck off with a load, and it was not back yet. So Pablo would have to give her the load on credit and provide the truck and propane tank. "When are you going to need it?" he asked.

"Right now. I need it now."

"Do you have somebody to drive?"

"No, I'll drive it myself."

"I don't want you to get caught. I'll give you a driver," Pablo said.

"I don't have money to pay a driver," Becky said. "Every dime that I have went for those attorneys. So I'd rather do it myself."

"I'll pay the driver," Pablo said. "When do you want to go?"

She loaded up a propane tank with a hundred pounds of marijuana the next day at Pablo's Casa Chavez *bodega*. The driver assigned by Pablo drove the truck across the river and took it to the destination Becky indicated. She collected the money and returned to Ojinaga with Pablo's share.

She made about four loads, making a quick $20,000 to $25,000 each time. But the money vanished almost as quickly in attorney fees. To her despair, her expensive legal help was not getting her anywhere. Her case took a turn for the worse when one of her former runners agreed to testify against her and Marco. She could see she was going to spend at least the next ten years in jail; either that, or she would have to flee to Mexico, an alternative that was not very appealing: her welfare and security in Mexico would depend almost entirely on Pablo, and she was not sure that Pablo was going to last much longer as the drug lord of Ojinaga.

Each time she saw him, she noted the effects of Pablo's growing cocaine addiction. The last time she saw him was in June. It was late in the evening. He mumbled a lot, and it was hard to understand him; he kept repeating himself. It just was not the same alert, commanding, sharp-as-a-whip Pablo that she had met after Sammy's arrest. Someone in his condition could not remain in power indefinitely.

Even before that last meeting with Pablo in June, she had already considered plea bargaining with the district attorney in Carlsbad where the charges were filed—a guilty plea in exchange for a lighter sentence.

She felt so tired of the life she had been living. It seemed like her life was slipping away, and that it could easily end with a bullet. What if she had not been arrested in November? Very likely, she and Marco would have been with Pablo two months later when he was ambushed in front of a corner market by several carloads of gunmen. And if they had been with Pablo that fateful night, would she have been killed? Now, she was hustling to make money by trafficking to pay attorneys to get her off the hook for trafficking. It was a vicious circle that led nowhere except to the grave or to jail.

The day after that last visit with Pablo, she drove to Carlsbad to see about entering a guilty plea.

As it turned out, the New Mexico authorities and the DEA considered her an important drug operative and potential source of information. Over the next few months, an agreement was reached. Becky was granted immunity from prosecution for each and every crime she had ever committed provided she admit to the crime and go into detail about it. In exchange for a probated sentence after pleading guilty to the trafficking charges, she agreed to cooperate in investigations stemming from the information she provided. The only thing she refused to do for the authorities was set up Pablo Acosta.

DEA agents asked her to figure out a plan to lure him to the American side of the river. It would not have been too difficult, she thought. All she would have to do would be to arrange for a big load of marijuana to come across at Lomas de Arena, then fake a breakdown on the American side of the river—just like the summer before when the melon truck broke down and the two *campesinos* had to trek back to Ojinaga across the desert to fetch help. Pablo would surely form an expedition to recover the truck.

But she knew that Pablo would never surrender, would never allow American police to take him alive. A small army of his men—Pedro, Hector, Armando, Joaquin, Miguel and some of the nameless gunmen who had been with him lately—would be there. The traffickers would have an arsenal of machine guns and boxes of ammunition. It would end up in a big shootout, the biggest the border had ever seen, with blood and bodies and more blood. That would be Pablo's parting style.

She believed that Pablo was going to die a violent death sooner or later anyway—probably sooner than later. But she did not want to be the one to bring it about.

"I didn't think that was the way he should be killed, not Pablo Acosta. Not by a woman," Becky would later say.

Chapter Eighteen

REIGN OF TERROR

Many Ojinaga citizens sighed with relief when Fermin Arevalo was killed, thinking the shootings would stop now that Pablo's archrival was out of the way.

But the murders continued as new adversaries came into the picture or old scores were settled. A body a month was turning up in the river, sometimes with the face nibbled away by fish. In 1985, someone spotted a dog trotting along the Chihuahua highway with an arm dangling from its mouth. It took a day of searching to connect the arm with what was left of the body, found out in the desert in a shallow grave that had been dug up by coyotes or wild dogs. Another man was kidnapped in broad daylight from Samborn's Restaurant, never to be seen again.

About the same month as the kidnapping, a lone gunman tried to kill Pablo at the intersection in front of the Motel Ojinaga. Though firing six rounds at a distance of only a few yards, the gunman missed. He paid with his life when Pablo and his nephew chased him through town and machine-gunned him to death down by the railroad station.

For the people of Ojinaga, the only satisfaction from all the murders came from the fact that the hoodlums were bumping one another off. Innocent citizens, at least, were not in danger.

However, on January 20, 1986, the people of Ojinaga found out that innocence was no longer a shield. About midnight, Pablo, his nephew Pedro Ramirez Acosta and a Cuban called

El Charley stopped for the traffic light at the intersection of the Camargo and Chihuahua highways. A four-way stoplight dangled above the busy intersection. On one corner was a market. Cars and trucks were driving in and out of a the parking lot.

The moment they pulled up to the intersection, Pablo and his companions were suddenly caught in an ambush. At least a dozen assailants in several vehicles on the opposite side of the intersection sprayed volleys of deadly automatic fire at them.

All that saved Pablo from instant death was the fact that two ranchers in a pickup truck drove into the middle of the intersection the instant the shooting began. The men were turning into the market and were hit in the initial fusillade. That gave Pablo and his men enough time to jump out and take cover between their truck and that of the two ranchers, who were slumped over and covered with blood.

Inside the market, the cashiers, customers and a guard dropped to the floor or ducked behind counters and shelves as bullets tore into the store's ceramic-tile facade and sprayed through the windows into the store. Vehicles that had been approaching the intersection spun around and vanished in a roar down side streets. One witness heard Pablo shouting for reinforcements into the microphone of his radio. In less than a minute Pablo's younger brother, Hector Manuel, skidded to a halt nearby and he and several gunmen jumped out of their Bronco and joined the fight.

At one point, Pablo turned his machine gun on a pickup truck that backed out of a parking stall directly in front of the market, thinking it was another truckload of gunmen. In the truck were four young men who had come out of the market just as the firing began and had ducked into the truck for cover. When bullets tore through the sheet metal and hit one of them in the foot, the driver frantically backed out to try to get away. That is when Pablo opened fire, hitting the pickup seventeen times. Hector Manuel chased them and shot out one of the tires, but the terrified youths fled on foot and escaped down a residential street.

The clatter of machine-gun fire continued until Pablo, his

Pablo Acosta posed in front of the Ford Bronco he and his men had been in when they were ambushed by Fermin Arevalo at the entrance to the El Salto ranch. The photograph was taken on October 28, 1986, six months before Acosta was killed in the Rio Grande village of Santa Elena. (Photo by Terrence Poppa)

nephew and the Cuban jumped back into their truck and launched a frontal attack on one of the remaining vehicles, a black Firebird. The attackers appeared to be young, inexperienced gunmen. They were aiming high. Several were shooting from behind the Firebird while two others fired from within the car. Pablo raced through the intersection, bounced over the center island and sped straight for the Firebird, an audacious counterattack that allowed Pablo, Pedro and the Cuban to shoot the assailants to pieces. "I don't know how many of them we killed, but I know we hit a lot of them," Pablo later told a visitor.

The shooting continued elsewhere in town. According to witnesses, the furious gunbattles lasted on and off for two hours and the staccato of automatic gunfire was heard even across the Rio Grande in Presidio.

Rumors circulated that the shootout had actually begun earlier that night outside the home of Amado Carrillo Fuentes on a hill north of downtown Ojinaga overlooking the United States. Pablo, Ismael Espudo, Amado and several others had been holding a meeting about upcoming cocaine shipments. Afterward, Pablo and some of his men got into a Bronco on the street in front of Amado's home when suddenly a truck careened out of the darkness and the shooting started. What happened later in front of the market was merely a continuation.

No one was able to say exactly how many people had died, but it was a massacre. When it was over, people inside the market looked up from their hiding places and observed men with rifles throwing bodies into the back of pickup trucks. Either the surviving ambushers were carting off their dead or Pablo's men were cleaning up the mess. The citizens did not dare step outside to ask.

One underworld account says the death toll mounted further after Pablo and his men set up a roadblock on a curve of the Chihuahua highway near Samborn's Restaurant. Pablo flashed his federal police credentials and searched all vehicles. Men found in possession of assault rifles but with no satisfactory explanation for possessing them were taken out into the desert to be questioned and shot. That story was never corroborated, but the U.S. Customs Office of Enforcement in Presidio picked up reports that as many as thirteen people died that night.

Federal and state authorities from Chihuahua City and Mexico City arrived the next day to investigate. As usual, the public was never informed of the results, nor was anyone ever arrested. The morning after the attack, soldiers surrounded Pablo's home on Calle Sexta. At first, people thought they had been sent to arrest Pablo. But in fact the troops had been dispatched to protect the drug kingpin from another murder attempt.

Officially, the only dead were the two ranchers, Adolfo

Lujan and his brother Pablo. They had been hit repeatedly in the head, chest, legs and hands. According to Mexican court documents, earlier that night they had visited their father at an Ojinaga hospital. They were pulling into the market to buy a box of disposable diapers before returning home.

Pablo tried furiously to find out who was behind the *supermercado* ambush, as it came to be known. To him, the ambush had Arevalo markings—young, inexperienced gunmen. Pablo was sure Lupe Arevalo, Lili's brother and Fermin's only remaining son, was behind it.

No one with any shred of knowledge about the incident was spared Pablo's inquisition. Ojinaga residents recall outbreaks of machine-gun fire in different parts of town almost every night for the week following the street-corner ambush. Innocent people who had been seen near the market when the shooting started were kidnapped and interrogated.

One week after the ambush, Pablo's paranoid fury reached Jesus Salinas, a rancher who lived in Ojinaga, and his wife, Noemi. They were awakened well past midnight by a banging on their back door. A matronly woman with kind eyes and streaks of gray in her hair, Naomi hastily threw on a robe and leaned her head against the door.

"Who is it?"

"Police! Open up!" came a harsh voice from the other side.

There was absolutely no reason for the police to be banging on the door at three in the morning at the home of the Salinas family. They were known in the neighborhood as God-loving people and mindful of the law. And even if there were cause for the police to be there, wouldn't the police have knocked on the front door?

"You can't be the police," Noemi said through the door.

The banging started over again. "Open up, goddamn it, or we'll shoot the fucking door down!"

By then, her husband Jesus had gotten up and slipped on trousers and a shirt. He walked to the back door in his bare feet and saw the worried expression on his wife's face. He opened the door.

It was freezing outside. It was January, and Ojinaga winters were the flip side of the summers: unbearably cold. Jesus recognized Pablo Acosta immediately. Behind him were a lot of men with machine guns. Pablo had a machine gun slung over his shoulder with the barrel pointing down. The husband stepped out into the concrete patio of the backyard and felt the cold through his thin shirt and his bare feet.

Pablo's voice was menacing. In a few words, Pablo said that he knew that Jesus' son Alberto had been in a truck in front of the market when the ambush took place.

"Why didn't you notify the authorities about the shooting?" Pablo demanded.

"We were afraid to. We're afraid to tell the authorities anything," Jesus said.

"Where's your son?"

"He's sleeping."

"Then wake him up!"

Jesus Salinas hesitated.

"Move, goddamn it, or I'll wake him myself!"

Filled with panic, the mother went to rouse her son. But her son had been awakened by the noise and was already getting his trousers on. She heard a voice that was not Pablo's shouting from the back door "Make it fast!"

Noemi Salinas was a pious woman, member of an evangelical Catholic movement, as were her husband and son. She believed fervently that there was good in everyone. She told her son, "Don't worry, they won't hurt you. They just want to talk to you."

Once back at the door, she spoke in a quivering voice. "We're not bad people. We don't have any weapons, we don't have anything to do with bad people."

"You're coming with us," Pablo told the man and his son.

The house was completely surrounded; men were standing everywhere with machine guns and there were four or five dark-colored Ford Broncos in the street. As they walked around front, the older Salinas recognized one of his neighbors standing to one side, his eyes cast down. Later, the neighbor

would tell about being abducted from his own home, saying
that he recognized some of the abductors to be federal agents
and that they and the traffickers had forced him through
death threats to point out the Salinas house.

After pushing the two terrified men into one of the Broncos, the traffickers blindfolded them and sped out of the
neighborhood, but the younger man could still see from under his blindfold. They were being taken to the Progreso
neighborhood of Ojinaga, one of the residential areas closest to
the United States, about a thousand yards from the international bridge. The car stopped in front of the federal police
headquarters. The young man and his father were pulled
from the Bronco and pushed inside the federal building.

Once inside, they heard the voice of Pablo order, "Get
them ready!"

Father and son were put into separate rooms. The traffickers wrapped towels around their heads and secured the towels
with bailing wire. Their hands were tied behind with bailing
wire too. They were shoved to the ground and made to lie on
their backs. Their interrogators kicked them in the sides and
hit them with rifle butts. Though blindfolded, Jesus realized
from the voice that Pablo was doing the interrogating.

After questioning the father, Pablo went to the son to see
if there were any discrepancies.

The worst of the beating was reserved for the son. Pablo
kept grilling him, "Why did you shoot at us? Who paid you
to try to kill me?"

All the young man could do was to relate what had truly
happened. Each time he declared his innocence, he was showered with punches, kicks and jabs with an electric cattle prod.
Over and over the young man repeated what had happened:
he had driven up to the market with some friends to buy soft
drinks; they had been cruising up and down Trasviña y Retes, like all the other young people did on a Sunday night;
they came out of the store and got into the pickup just as the
shooting started. Sure they ran off. Who wouldn't? Someone was shooting at them and bullets were coming right
through the sheet metal, the young man told the interrogators.

Then Pablo was back with the father, asking about his background, about his family, about his ranch, about how he got the money to buy his pumps, his tractor and other farm equipment. Pablo threw out dozens of names and asked the older man questions about each one of them. Most were unfamiliar, but some of them were names of friends or acquaintances. He wondered if they had gone through the same treatment. Jesus had the impression someone was taking notes, because there were pauses and he could hear the sound of a pen scribbling on paper.

Pablo asked him about people in Guadalajara. A trafficking family with the same family name operated out of Guadalajara. "They sent you, didn't they?" was the snarled question.

Then more questions, more beatings, more savagery.

The brutality lasted for three hours. Each time the inquisitors came back into the room, the father begged Pablo to spare his son, the son begged Pablo to spare his father.

Finally, Pablo ordered, "Get them out of here."

The two men were lifted to their feet, taken outside and pushed into a vehicle. The towels were still wrapped tightly around their heads and now neither could see anything. Their hands were still bound behind their backs. The vehicle bounced up and down the dirt roads, and it was difficult for them to keep upright. The older man wondered if they were being taken to the edge of the river to be shot in the back of the head.

Ten minutes after they had been shoved into the vehicle, it stopped. A voice snapped, "Get out. And make it fast."

They did as they were told, trembling. Except for the idling of the motor, all was silent outside. And bitterly cold. The older man was still barefoot. The muscles of his neck and upper back stiffened involuntarily. Any second now, he thought, a bullet would crash into the back of his head. He wanted to touch his son one last time, but his hands were bound too tightly.

Then he heard a clutch engage, a motor rev. The vehicle drove away. It drove farther and farther away until they could not hear it any more. The younger man managed to work his own hands free and he ripped the towels off his head. He freed his father.

Rubbing their eyes and looking around in the darkness, the father and son realized they were only a few blocks away from home.

About a month after the January 1986 shootout Pablo visited the widow of one of the unlucky ranchers who had been caught in the crossfire. Pablo's wife had known the dead men, who were the sons of one of her father's best friends back in the village of Mesquite. Olivia urged Pablo to go a step further than just paying for the funerals.

The day of the visit, Aida Lujan was doing chores in the modest Ojinaga home she shared with her parents, some younger brothers and sisters, and several nephews and nieces. Her young face still sagged from grief. Sometimes just the sight of her year-old, now-fatherless daughter was sufficient to make her crumble onto the sofa in tears.

At first, Aida did not understand that the man standing in the doorframe was the person who had caused the death of her husband. Pablo had knocked politely and stated he wanted to speak "to the wife of the deceased."

When she let him into the front room, he identified himself. He was apologetic. He said the two men were innocent, that they did not have anything to do with the ambush, that they happened to drive into the fusillade the moment it started and by so doing saved his life. He was sorry, so very sorry, and he wanted to help the family by setting up a trust fund at one of the local banks. He had empowered someone in the district attorney's office to start a fund of 800,000 pesos, then worth about $1,000, in the name of the widow's daughter. The widow would be able to draw the interest from the account each month. Pablo also offered to replace the truck, which had been shot up so badly that it was now useless.

Aida Lujan had been raised in a rural family where women were taught submissiveness, and practiced a religion that preached forgiveness and humility. The sight of Pablo Acosta in her home, nevertheless, caused a confusion of violent emotions in her. She struggled against a desire to shriek aloud the thoughts that had raged in her mind since her husband died. She wanted to scream how much she longed for his death, for his family to suffer as she was suffering. Instead, her dark eyes filled with tears as they searched the concrete floor, as if for guidance.

"As you wish," she said at last.

Pablo never found out for sure who was behind the ambush. At one point he thought the attempt on his life may have been the work of a drug faction from Guadalajara that wanted to put its own man in charge of the Ojinaga *plaza*, but Pablo's investigation had ruled out that theory.

The drug lord became convinced Lupe Arevalo had hired a dozen men to kill him in revenge for the deaths of his father and brother. Lupe had employed young, inexperienced shooters and so the attempt had failed, just as Fermin had failed when he hired three men to ambush Pablo in front of Samborn's Restaurant.

Several weeks after the January 1986 ambush, he told acquaintances he was certain Fermin's son Lupe was behind it. "Who else could it be?" he kept saying.

Pablo vowed he was going to make Lupe pay.

Chapter Nineteen

THE NEW MIAMI

With so much cocaine being smuggled through the region, sooner or a load was going to get busted and the Ojinaga conduit exposed.

It happened about five in the afternoon of July 13, 1985, six months before the bloody *supermercado* ambush, at a U.S. Border Patrol checkpoint between Las Cruces and Alamogordo, right across the highway from the entrance to White Sands National Monument and the blinding whiteness of the gypsum sand dunes that stretch north for miles.

New Mexico state patrol officers made a point of setting up at the checkpoint during each shift. At this roadside station an officer was always sure to write up reams of citations for expired driver's licenses, broken taillights, missing vehicle registration documents, failure to wear a seat belt and other minor violations. Officers several times had nabbed drunk drivers and had also recovered stolen vehicles.

On this day, Sgt. James Woods, a twelve-year state police veteran, was mopping his brow under the intense sun when he saw a blue-and-white Ford pickup truck pull into the highway checkpoint. The vehicle had a large propane tank in the back. Just as it drove up to the officer, the truck stalled.

The driver, a Hispanic teenager, started the truck up again, but as soon as he put it into gear it stalled once more.

"May I see your driver's license, please?" Woods said.

While the young man searched through his wallet, Woods reached to the top of the propane tank. He knew a lot about propane systems, having installed one recently on his own pickup.

"Your truck will run better if you open the valve completely, young man," he said as he tried to turn the valve handle. It was shut tight.

"What are you running on?"

"Propane," said the young man politely.

Woods glanced inside the cab at a dashboard fuel-selector switch. It was on the gasoline mode. The state police sergeant looked at the man closely. The driver was clean-cut, friendly, relaxed. Nothing in his manner suggested he was hiding anything. Perhaps he just did not know anything about propane tanks.

The driver fished for his license for a moment, then rummaged through the glove compartment for the vehicle registration, but could not find either one.

"I think I forgot them in El Paso," he said.

The young man told the New Mexico patrolman he was on his way to visit his mother up in Las Vegas, a small town in northeastern New Mexico, where she had been in a bad car accident and was in the hospital. "I found out about it when I got off work and I borrowed this truck because my car wasn't running right."

He gave his name as Henry Harrison Flores, nineteen years old. The truck belonged to his wife's brother, he said. It had a Texas dealer's tag on the rear window with the address of an El Paso dealership, indicating it had been recently purchased.

Woods checked the identification number on the tag against the vehicle identification number on the dashboard just behind the windshield. The numbers did not match.

After jotting down the tag numbers, he ran his hand down the tank. There wasn't a temperature variation, the trooper noted, even thought the gauge read about half full. He tapped the tank with his wedding ring and noticed a dull, hollow sound. He leaned against the side of the truck, bending forward to examine the tank closely.

The tank had been freshly painted and the trooper saw

that droplets of paint had speckled the threading of the filler nozzle.

Just then, Woods' partner, Sgt. Dave Skinner, walked up after ticketing another motorist.

"What have you got?" he asked Woods.

"He doesn't have a driver's license. The tag doesn't belong to this truck. And there's something screwy about this propane tank."

"What do you mean?" said Skinner, a man with the build of an NFL linebacker.

"Tap it."

Woods had recently talked with a state patrolman in Hobbs who had busted a propane load of marijuana and was wondering if they had stumbled across another. Skinner hopped into the bed of the pickup and tapped the tank a few times, then opened the bleeder valve. A jet of gas spewed out. He put his ear against the tank and told Woods to rock the truck.

"I don't hear any sloshing."

None of Harrison Flores' stories checked out by radio. The El Paso dealership was nonexistent; nobody matching his description of his mother had been involved in an accident in Las Vegas or was in the hospital there. There had not even been a traffic accident anywhere near the small New Mexico town in more than a week.

"You're coming with us," Woods said to the driver.

Henry Harrison Flores followed them twenty-five miles up the road to Alamogordo, the site of America's postwar rocket-development program. They drove into the service shop of a Chevrolet dealership. A mechanic slid under the truck and unbolted the tank. Skinner strained all his muscles attempting to lift the tank but he could not budge it. "Hey, there's got to be another bolt under there. I can't move this."

The mechanic slid back under. "No, there's no other bolt under here."

The sturdy patrolman kept lifting and tugging. Finally, he was able to move the tank away from the cab wall. By then, a magistrate judge and his secretary had arrived.

Before reaching Alamogordo, the officers had radioed to say they were going to need a search warrant to open the tank. When the warrant was written up and signed by the judge, the officers began scraping paint off the back of the tank. They soon found what they thought they were going to find—a thin line of sanded Bondo. With hammer and chisel they punched out a rectangular plate.

Woods and Skinner had expected to find a load of pot, just as one of their fellow patrolmen had recently in Hobbs. But when Skinner reached in and pulled out a plastic package tightly wrapped in tape with the letters NINFA written on it, they knew it was not marijuana. They sliced opened the container and saw white crystalline powder.

"Cocaine!" they exclaimed.

When the tank was finally empty they had counted 111 plastic containers. Each held about a kilogram of cocaine—246 pounds in all, with an estimated street value of $50 million. The two New Mexico patrolmen had made the biggest cocaine seizure ever in New Mexico and one of the largest cocaine busts ever on one of the nation's highways.

Inside the large tank they found a two-gallon propane tank partially wrapped in an army duffel bag. The smaller tank was hooked up to the gauges and valves of the bigger tank.

One of the officers walked up to the driver to read him his rights and slap handcuffs on him. Up to that moment, Harrison Flores had behaved like someone with nothing to hide. He had even curled up in a corner of the garage to take a snooze while the police went through the truck.

But as an officer read from a wallet-sized card informing him of his right to remain silent, the nineteen-year-old cocaine courier suddenly burst into tears. "Why don't you just take your gun out and kill me now," he blubbered. "They're going to kill me anyway."

The size of the load was already a clear indication that Harrison Flores worked for a big smuggling ring. Investigators quickly saw how well organized it was. The morning after the bust two criminal defense lawyers from El Paso

showed up in Alamogordo to represent the low-ranking courier, the cannon fodder of drug distribution networks.

The investigation spread to El Paso where four days later police found another drug cache in a red and white truck
in front of Harrison Flores' apartment. That truck also had
a propane tank bolted to the back. Inside, police found 263
pounds of cocaine in kilogram bricks with the same markings as the packaging found in the Alamogordo bust. At least
three other pickup trucks with the characteristics of the two
seized vehicles had been seen parked outside the Harrison
Flores residence, neighbors told the police.

Soon after the record-setting twin seizures, narcotics investigators from Los Angeles began making inquiries. In
May, just two months before Harrison Flores was arrested,
Los Angeles police had seized 556 pounds of cocaine in a
stash house in a suburb of Los Angeles—up to that time the
largest cocaine seizure in Southern California.

There were intriguing similarities between the Los Angeles bust in May and the Alamogordo and El Paso seizures in
July. In the Los Angeles case, the cocaine had been delivered in propane tanks in the back of pickup trucks bearing
Texas license plates. Were they from the same source as the
trucks seized in Alamogordo and El Paso? Most of the twenty-one people arrested in the Los Angeles bust were Mexican
nationals; the rest were from Colombia. Were these people
part of one of the already established Mexican-Colombian
smuggling combines that operated through Sinaloa and Baja
California? Or was there a new organization at work here?
How were the Texas license plates to be explained?

William T. Frensley and William Segarra, two El Paso DEA
agents, followed up leads from telephone bills, business cards
and scraps of paper confiscated from Harrison Flores' apartment. The investigation took them to a cabinet shop in a
rundown redbrick neighborhood near downtown El Paso.

Frensley's heart began beating faster when he peered in
through the shop window and spotted a couple of 110-gal-
lon propane tanks, one of them with a hole cut out of one
side. Searching one of the desks, the narcotics agent picked up

a telephone bill with some scribbling on the other side and a map.

"Why, lookee here!" said Frensley, an east Texas native who bore a resemblance to *Gunsmoke's* Dennis Weaver. "I think I can tell you right now who's behind all this cocaine shit."

The map showed directions to a garage owned by Ismael Espudo in Van Horn, about a hundred twenty miles east of El Paso on Interstate 10 in sparsely populated Culberson County. Espudo's telephone number was scribbled above the map. Originally from the Ojinaga area, Espudo had become an American citizen and raised his family in Van Horn. He ran a garage, a wrecking yard and a towing service. He was actively involved in community affairs and in 1982 was elected to a four-year term to the five-member commissioner's court of Culberson Country.

Then, in early 1985, Espudo suddenly vanished. When he missed four consecutive county commission meetings, his seat was declared vacant.

Several months before the propane tank busts, a Culberson County attorney had told Frensley his opinion that Ismael Espudo was "as crooked as a dog's hind leg." Among other things, Espudo was a suspect in a homicide and of a scheme to defraud a bank. He was also suspected of having major drug dealings with important Ojinaga narcotics traffickers. Additionally, Espudo was supposedly related by marriage to Pablo Acosta, the narco-honcho of Ojinaga.

Frensley had filed the information away in the back of his mind. When he found the map to Espudo's garage in the cabinet shop in El Paso, he recalled the conversation with the county attorney. It all clicked. He was certain that the cocaine seized in Alamogordo and El Paso had originated in Ojinaga. If so, Pablo Acosta, a DEA fugitive everyone had been after for almost a decade, had to be involved.

Posing as car owners in search of parts for a 1965 Ford Mustang, Frensley and Segarra visited Espudo's garage and wrecking yard. The owner was nowhere to be found, but young workers the federal agents assumed to be Espudo's sons or nephews allowed them to roam around. During the visit, the agents saw a large propane tank on the ground in the middle of the garage.

The investigation began to snowball. By September, Customs agents in Presidio began late-night meetings with an informant who had close ties to the Acosta organization. The informant would occasionally swim across the river to give his latest report, at the risk of getting caught by Mexican soldiers from the Ojinaga garrison who sometimes patrolled the river. The American agents would drive the man back to Presidio, and after debriefing him at length send him back across the Rio Grande.

This informant told the agents he saw Ismael Espudo at a ranch west of Ojinaga when a planeload of cocaine flew in. He witnessed the cocaine being buried in an underground tank, and saw it later dug up and transported with an escort of soldiers to a warehouse in Ojinaga, a facility owned by Pablo Acosta. The informant was also present when the cocaine was being stashed in propane tanks. He reported having witnessed other planeloads of cocaine landing at the Ojinaga municipal airport. He was also present at Pablo's recent going-away party at the Hotel Rohana for the outgoing *comandante* of the Directorate of Federal Security.

Every time some drug-related activity took place, Mexican soldiers or Mexican police officials were involved, the informant said.

It was one thing for an informant to see propane tanks being loaded up with kilo bricks of cocaine in Ojinaga, another to connect them with Henry Harrison Flores. The informant could not recall seeing anyone matching Harrison Flores' description. Nor could he recall the license plate numbers and other details of the trucks he saw in Pablo's high-walled compound that would indisputably link the Alamogordo, El Paso and Los Angeles cocaine loads to Pablo Acosta.

Even so, the DEA agents were confident that they finally had an overview of the smuggling operation.

Evidence revealed in federal court later showed that Henry Harrison Flores worked for a smuggling network that operated through El Paso run by a Mexican national named Audelio Arzola. At first, investigators thought that Arzola may have been dealing independently with Colombian cocaine producers and had his own corps of drug couriers. Later it became apparent that his role was as a subcontractor, undertaking the high-risk smuggling tasks for whoever had the Colombian connections.

The one with the connections was Pablo Acosta. He was a key link in a chain beginning in Colombia and ending at unknown delivery points in the United States.

It became clear that this was an enormous case with vast, disturbing implications. As much as five tons of cocaine a month were passing through Pablo's hands, meaning that 60 tons a year were coming into a small, nondescript Mexican border town with a name that was difficult to pronounce and that few people had ever heard of. Sixty tons of cocaine per year! Official DEA estimates put the annual U.S. cocaine consumption at the time at less than 100 tons a year, though unofficially DEA experts placed consumption at closer to 200 tons. Therefore possibly one-third of the cocaine entering the United States was coming through Ojinaga. And all of this apparently occurring under the protection of agents and agencies of the Mexican government.

Later, informants filled in the details: For a fee of $1,000 to $1,500 per kilogram, Pablo was warehousing and safeguarding the cocaine in Ojinaga for the Colombians, offering the security of his *plaza*, his governmental franchise. He was also providing the logistical support and technical facilities for independent smuggling operations like the one run by Audelio Arzola, whose organization was transporting about a ton of cocaine a month.

What was evident to DEA analysts when the extent of Pablo's Ojinaga operation became clear was that the Colombians had shifted much of their smuggling operations from south Florida to Mexico. The arid Chihuahua-Texas corridor had been transformed into a new south Florida, the new route of preference for smuggling cocaine into the United States. Border towns such as El Paso and their twin cities in Mexico stood to become centers of corruption and murder—the new Miamis of the drug war.

By the end of 1985 the investigation had become too massive for the two DEA agents assigned to it. Each fresh lead brought new gold mines of information about Acosta and hundreds of other people, from car thieves to heroin dealers, who had dealings with Pablo Acosta. Ernie Perez, the Cuban-born DEA chief in El Paso, conferred with the chief prosecutor at the U.S. Attorney's office in El Paso, Tom McHugh. They agreed that the time had come to turn the investigation into Acosta's operation into an Organized Crime Drug Enforcement Task Force (OCDETF) case.

In 1982, the Reagan administration created twelve regional OCDETFs with the goal of dismantling "high-level drug trafficking enterprises" through the investigation and prosecution of its most important members. Inspired by an earlier task force in south Florida, the idea was to combine narcotics investigators from various federal, state and local law enforcement agencies into a single investigative unit. West Texas, Pablo Acosta's frontyard, fell under the Gulf Coast Task Force, which was made up of Texas, Mississippi and Louisiana.

On February 14, 1986, a task force committee consisting of representatives of the DEA, the FBI, U.S. Customs, the Immigration and Naturalization Service, the Internal Revenue Service, the U.S. Attorney's office, the El Paso Police Department and the Texas Department of Public Safety jammed into the DEA's conference room in El Paso to discuss the Pablo Acosta organization. Copies of a five-page DEA assessment of Acosta's organization were passed around.

The draft read in part:

> The tentacles of this organization reach throughout the Mexican states of Chihuahua and Sonora, and in the United States in West Texas, northern Texas, southern and eastern New Mexico, and into areas of Kansas, California, Colorado, Oklahoma, Missouri, New York, New Jersey, Nevada, Idaho, North Carolina and Michigan. The current

assessment, by an analyst of the El Paso Intelligence Center, depicts the Acosta organization as a multi-faceted group of family members and well established associates of over 500 individuals.

Pablo Acosta has been well documented as an extremely dangerous and ruthless fugitive who has been responsible, either directly or indirectly, for in excess of twenty murders. Firearms are imported into Mexico from the United States by members of the Acosta organization. As with stolen vehicles, these firearms are most often exchanged for drugs.

Current intelligence indicates that numerous public officials throughout West Texas, which include sheriff's deputies, local police officers, state and local prosecutors, and other elected and appointed officials, are associates of the Acosta organization.

The last paragraph raised a few eyebrows among the agency representatives and their younger assistants. "Seven or eight" local officials and cops from El Paso, Culberson and Presidio counties were under suspicion, task force coordinator Chris Thompson told them.

The silver-haired Thompson, a senior DEA special agent in El Paso, outlined the investigation beginning with the arrest of Henry Harrison Flores in Alamogordo to the discovery of Pablo Acosta's cocaine depot in Ojinaga. He traced Acosta's criminal history from the Eunice heroin sting that caused Pablo to flee to Mexico up to the current intelligence on Pablo's marijuana, heroin and cocaine operations.

Each agency gave a briefing of its intelligence on Pablo.

The goal of the task force would be to break up all of the Acosta factions that had been identified in dozens of West Texas and New Mexico communities. They also wanted to arrest Acosta. Some reports indicated that he crossed the border to visit relatives in Odessa and other towns; if not, he would have to be lured across the border.

Pablo Acosta had been around for many years. Everyone in the room knew of him and nearly everyone had dreamed at one time or another of capturing him. After nearly three hours of reports and discussion, the committee voted. It was a unanimous show of hands. Pablo Acosta and his organization would be the next target for the task force.

"We'd known about the guy for a long time, and everyone felt that it was about time we went after him," one of the agents would later comment.

Chapter Twenty

MIMI'S MIRACLE RANCH

E ven before the task force targeting Pablo took form in
El Paso, a U.S. Customs narcotics agent based in the
Big Bend had been meeting monthly with Pablo Acosta in
Ojinaga in an attempt to develop him as an informant.

David Regela was a seasoned agent who had been sent to
Big Bend National Park in 1983 with orders to "disrupt the
Pablo Acosta organization." He had met Pablo several months
before Henry Harrison Flores was arrested in Alamogordo
and had continuing secret contacts with the Ojinaga drug lord.

Athletic, with a reddish-brown beard, light-blue eyes and
a passion for running the rapids of the Rio Grande in kayaks
and rafts, Regela ranked as one of the service's top narcotics
investigators. He had been recruited upon graduating from
the University of Illinois in 1971 for the Sky Marshal Program, created by the Customs Service to counter a rash of
airplane hijackings. With a firearm concealed under his business suit, Regela was eager to be the first cop ever to foil a
skyjacking at 30,000 feet. He never got the opportunity, but
he did nab some passengers who were smuggling narcotics
on their bodies or in their luggage.

When the Sky Marshall program was phased out with the
introduction of airport metal detectors and the X-raying of car-
ry-on baggage, Regela became a Customs narcotics investigator
and in 1973 was assigned to El Paso. He worked on and off in
the Texas Big Bend on temporary assignment from El Paso.
In 1983, when the Ojinaga gang wars had already claimed

numerous casualties and reports of barbaric murders were filtering in through informants, Regela was assigned there permanently to run a five-man enforcement station in Big Bend National Park at Panther Junction.

For him the investigative experience became the thrill of traveling backwards in time. Smugglers wearing sombreros and crisscross bandoleers studded with high-caliber cartridges used tactics their forefathers had employed even long before the Mexican Revolution to evade detection. It was not uncommon for Regela and his fellow agents to spot signal bonfires at night on distant mountain tops, or catch the glint of mirrors flashing messages in the daytime, or to track and fall upon mule caravans carrying contraband twenty miles or even thirty miles north of the Rio Grande.

His baptism by fire occurred in the Big Bend on a cold December night in 1976 when he and a small band of Customs agents waited to arrest what they thought would be a half-dozen smugglers crossing the Rio Grande with two tons of marijuana. Regela and two other agents were cooped up inside a camper, waiting for a signal from one of the undercover agents outside to jump out to make arrests. At first, only a few horsemen appeared out of the darkness, then some men on foot. The mounted smugglers were wearing sombreros and leather chaps and were armed with Winchesters and revolvers. A truck with the marijuana pulled up behind them, with more men sitting on top, singing country ballads as if they were on their way to a fiesta. More and more men kept arriving. Regela lost count at three dozen. The American agents began to sweat when they realized that they were surrounded by a small army of smugglers.

One of the riders trotted up to the camper and tried to look through the side window. When another of the smugglers demanded to look inside, the Americans had no choice but to take action. The undercover buyer banged loudly on the side of the camper. Regela and his fellow agents leaped out, shouting in Spanish to the dozens of startled smugglers that they were *all* under arrest. The Mexicans started shooting. The Americans fired back. They traded volleys of gunfire

before the troop of traffickers stampeded back across the river
with their dead and wounded. The San Vicente shootout, as
it was later tagged, was widely reported by the American
media. It was easily the biggest border gun battle since the
attack on Columbus, New Mexico, by Pancho Villa.

The American agent's most important investigation led
to the arrest of Pablo's uncle, Manuel Acosta. A large man
with thick callused hands who trained racehorses on his ranch
near Terlingua, Manuel smuggled about a thousand pounds
of marijuana a week to Dallas for Pablo Acosta. Regela
learned that Pablo's uncle was transporting the drug in recreational vehicles driven by American couples posing as
tourists. After a nine-month investigation, Regela and his
agents scored a major arrest when they stopped one of the
boxy RVs as it was heading out of the park with half a ton of
marijuana inside. One of the couriers, a pregnant Dallas
woman who eventually decided to cooperate, fingered Manuel Acosta. He was convicted of conspiracy and sentenced
to twenty years in the federal penitentiary.

Then, in January 1985, Regela arrested Armando Acosta,
one of Pablo's heroin-addled younger brothers, after a chase
through the canyons of Big Bend National Park. The Border
Patrol had tried to stop Armando and his girlfriend the day
before on a highway just north of park headquarters at Panther Junction. As soon as he saw the red lights behind him,
the Acosta brother skidded his El Camino off the road and
he and the girl fled on foot into the mesquite-covered desert
valley. Regela, called in to assist, found fifty pounds of marijuana in the back of the vehicle.

The manhunt was suspended when it got dark for fear of
an ambush, but at first light the next day a search plane spotted the couple walking into Dog Canyon, about six miles
southeast of the highway where the Border Patrol had stopped
them. If they got through the canyon, Regela knew, they could
easily reach the Rio Grande and escape into Mexico. The federal agents quickly blocked the canyon on three sides.
Armando was armed with a chrome-plated .38-caliber semiautomatic and could have made his capture difficult. But

when Regela and the other agents closed in, Armando pulled out a hypodermic needle from his shirt pocket. Just as Regela ran up to them, badge in one hand and pistol in the other, Pablo Acosta's brother pulled the plastic cover off the needle and jammed it into his forearm.

"He knew he was caught and all he could think of was getting in that one last fix," Regela later recalled.

To David Regela, Pablo Acosta was only a two-dimensional character. When he tried to visualize the notorious drug lord, his image was that of a Frito Bandido with drooping *bigotes* and smoking six-shooters. Pablo was the flamboyant bandit across the river with a reputation for ostentatious violence, the shadowy figure who controlled the flow of narcotics all along the Big Bend, a sinister character who thumbed his nose at American law enforcement from his Mexican sanctuary. As long as the Ojinaga drug lord remained in Mexico, he was untouchable.

Regela understood from his informants the franchise-like nature of organized crime in Mexico and knew from reams of intelligence reports that it was an institutional reality—the government there allowed people like Pablo Acosta to operate as an unofficial extension of governmental agencies. His informants told him of the protection Pablo enjoyed from federal authorities and from the army. He knew the army provided Acosta protection for his fields and his shipments. But it was not his job to tackle such a government, only to catch the catchable, to make cases against lawbreakers on the American side.

However, on one occasion he and other agents in the Presidio enforcement office were able to observe such protection first hand. American agents had detected a three-acre marijuana field on the Mexican side of the Rio Grande in Colorado Canyon, about midway between Presidio and Big Bend National Park. The field was on a three-acre ledge about fifty feet above the river, at the base of the sheer cliffs that towered on both sides of the canyon. Because of the elevation and the tall cane that grew along the riverbank, the field and the irrigation pipes were not visible from the river. But the operation could be seen through binoculars from the top of the towering cliffs on the American side. It was a sophisticated undertaking. The field had been terraced and had rows of young plants next to mature ones to allow for successive harvests. During their surveillances, the American agents noted the presence of soldiers. Information was passed on through Customs channels to authorities in Mexico City. In response, the Mexican government announced it was sending a special unit with orders to destroy the field. The Mexicans agreed to allow the Americans to lead them to it. However, hours before they were to leave, the Americans were told their assistance would not be needed. The next day, the Mexican government announced that the field had been located and destroyed and that arrests had been made.

Regela did not have any reason to disbelieve the report, but a week later he decided to see how thorough an eradication job the Mexicans had done. He and a girlfriend kayaked down the river. They climbed the slope and saw that the marijuana field was intact. Before even reaching the edge of the field they heard a gunshot. A bullet whizzed over their heads. Eight soldiers emerged out of nowhere demanding to know what they were doing there. Regela acted like a dumb tourist and explained they were searching for Indian ruins. The soldiers finally let them go.

During further surveillances from the American side of the river, the agents saw that soldiers were guarding the field in shifts that lasted three days at a time. During the daytime, they observed soldiers harvesting mature plants, loading the marijuana onto mules that were then led up a steep trail to the top of the cliff. When each three-day shift ended, the troops would leave in the dead of night. Three or four hours later, a replacement unit, rifles slung over their shoulders, would walk down the steep trail in single file.

During one of these shift changes, a group of off-duty American agents floated to the site on rafts. They quickly scaled the bluff. They worked feverishly to uproot all of the marijuana plants and destroy the irrigation system. Before leaving, they threw the plants and equipment into the river.

Street view of a radio station in Ojinaga owned by Malaquias Flores. He operated a private radio communication system for Pablo Acosta from this site. A former Ojinaga police chief, Flores became a liaison officer with the Mexican army ostensibly to handle public relations. But in fact he served as a go-between for the Mexican army garrison commander in Ojinaga and Pablo Acosta and played an important role in the protection the military gave the Ojinaga drug lord. (Photo by Terrence Poppa)

The task completed, the raiders made it back to their rafts and disappeared down the river.

When the next shift of soldiers arrived, they found a Texas flag planted in the middle of the demolished plantation.

When he first arrived in the Big Bend, Regela never thought the day would come when he would meet the drug lord face to face, much less that Pablo would one day offer to cooperate with him to develop cases against drug buyers. The opportunity to meet him came about in the middle of 1985, just as an airlift of turboprops from Colombia began landing near Ojinaga with phenomenal amounts of cocaine.

The meeting was arranged through Mimi Webb Miller, a niece by marriage of U.S. Senator John Tower and the owner of a three-thousand-acre mountain ranch in Mexico not far from Pablo Acosta's ranch near San Carlos. She had known Pablo Acosta as a neighbor for several years. A straw blonde in a land where dark hair, skin and eyes are the norm, Mimi definitely stood out. She raised goats, cattle, corn, apples and the blood pressure of Mexican ranchers who gallantly proposed marriage to her any time she ventured into San Carlos.

A university student during the late 1960s, Mimi developed an interest in art history at colleges in California and Texas. After earning a degree from Southern Methodist University she mounted exhibits for an art gallery in Houston. In her spare time she lectured on art history at Rice University. On a trip in 1977 to organize an exhibit in Lajitas, a Rio Grande tourist town fifty miles downstream from Presidio and Ojinaga, she fell in love with the Big Bend.

Lajitas was built to duplicate a Wild West shoot-'em-up town, with unpainted rough-wood storefronts, thick board sidewalks and dirt streets. Many tourists thrilled by the facsimile probably would not have come within a hundred miles of the border if they had known that in the adobe towns and villages just south of it, *real* gunslingers were stalking the dusty streets.

But Mimi sensed adventure; she accepted an invitation from the Lajitas developer to set up an artist-in-residence program. Before long, she was plowing across the river in a four-wheel drive and attending cockfights and raucous all-night *pachangas* in San Carlos. That was where she met a swarthy Mexican with curly black hair and the rugged, slim build of a *vaquero* who introduced her to the ways of the Mexican borderlands and who showed her the mountain property that became her ranch.

She called it *Rancho El Milagro*—Miracle Ranch. The ranch house was a stone building with two-foot-thick walls, a shaded patio, kerosene lamps, a wood-burning stove and an outhouse. The nearest telephone was at the Lajitas Trading Post, a seventeen-mile, two-hour drive north along a washed-out dirt road. The only running water was the forty-foot spring-fed waterfall that cascaded into a stream just behind the house. Most of the land consisted of steep slopes up the side of a towering mountain range, visible from Lajitas on a clear day. Mimi's *vaquero* friend became her common-law husband, and she put the property in the name of his half-brother since it was against Mexican law for non-citizens to own property within fifty miles of the border.

Pablo Acosta became a frequent visitor to Mimi's ranch, even before he took over the Ojinaga *plaza* and became the underworld power in the area. It turned out that Mimi's common-law husband had had dealings with Pablo, and in the course of those dealings had begun to shoot up heroin. The first time Pablo visited the ranch, it was with the usual display of weapons and the usual entourage of *pistoleros*. He and his men lounged around in the shade of the patio. Pablo looked like he hadn't washed for two weeks. His skin was blotchy, his teeth misaligned, his nose a real honker. He leered at her with his gold-filled mouth hanging open as she went back and forth serving beer and vittles to the guests.

She thought he was ugly.

Mimi never changed her opinion about his looks, but she became less intimidated as she came to know him. In conversations with him, she began to pick up on a keen mind. When he finally acquired the Ojinaga *plaza*, she saw what a powerful man this unwashed, poorly educated peasant actually was. They became friends, and Pablo helped her obtain visas for horseback tours she gave into hidden semitropical valleys southeast of San Carlos.

As time went on, Mimi's Miracle Ranch turned into an R&R center for Pablo and his people. Not long after moving in, Mimi had a stone livestock watering tank built with the dimensions of a small swimming pool. It was fed with pristine spring water from the stream out back. Mimi shooed away the cattle whenever she wanted to go for a swim. Pablo would drive out to her ranch with Pedro, Armando, Hector Manuel and an escort of gunmen and hold noisy poolside parties with plenty of beer and a freshly slaughtered goat for a barbecue.

Though sometimes strapped for money, Mimi refused Pablo's occasional offers to help her make payments on the property. But she did allow his assistance once in building a chapel. The brother of Mimi's *vaquero* had been suffering from a liver ailment and nobody expected him to live. Mimi and her husband vowed that if the brother recovered they would build a chapel to the Virgin of Guadalupe and always burn a candle there. When the brother survived, Pablo came out with a dozen of his gunmen and with cement, whitewash and other materials to build a small stone structure. They went to work in the morning erecting the chapel on a small pointed hill overlooking the ranch and were finished by late evening. Inside, they set up a large plaster statue of the Virgin of Guadalupe and lit votive candles.

By the beginning of 1985, however, Mimi's relationship with the swarthy Mexican was over. Even before becoming involved with Mimi, he was using heroin. It is said he acquired an addiction from absorption through his fingernails, while breaking down blocks of heroin for packaging prior to shipment. Then the addiction progressed. He quit using it and had been able to stay off the needle the first few years they were together. But the attraction was too powerful and he began using heroin again. After two more years of enduring his addiction, Mimi told him it was over.

She began dating other men and soon was seen frequently with David Regela. Like Mimi, Regela was on the rebound from a relationship that had gone sour. She spent time with the American officer in his quarters at Panther Junction; he spent his days off at her ranch, basking in the sun next to the pool or photographing and exploring ancient Indian camps and burial grounds located here and there on the ranchland. Both fond of white-water rafting, they often ran the rapids in Colorado Canyon together.

Theirs was not the sort of relationship that could be kept a secret for long in the sparsely populated borderlands. They made horseback trips across the mountains from her ranch to San Carlos. She introduced him to her friends and showed him around the quaint Mexican town, pointing out the places of interest there including the dancehall where Pablo's brother Juan was shot to death and the church where Shorty Lopez's funeral mass took place.

Pablo inevitably found out about the liaison. He knew Regela was the federal agent who had sent his uncle and brother to the penitentiary. Mimi's ranch was located right along a major smuggling route. Was Regela pumping Mimi for information about him and about these activities? Pablo visited Mimi's ranch one day when Regela was not there and demanded to know what was going on.

Mimi answered with her characteristic earthiness: "You don't have anything to worry about. All he wants is to get into my pants."

The answer seemed to satisfy Pablo, but a couple of months later he told Mimi he wanted to meet the American agent.

Regela thought it over. He was certain that Pablo Acosta knew he was the cop responsible for Manuel's arrest. The drug lord must also have known of Regela's role in Armando's capture and his testimony at the trial in Pecos. That put David Regela in a potentially dangerous situation. Could it be that Pablo was looking for revenge? But Mimi insisted Pablo was a man of honor. Pablo would guarantee Regela's safety.

Because Pablo was a fugitive, the meeting could not take place in the United States. Pablo suggested Malaquias Flores' radio station in Ojinaga. After they assembled at the station, Pablo posted some men outside while he and the American agent and Mimi went into Malaquias' small office.

A tall, dark-complexioned, balding man with bottle-thick glasses and heavy gold chains around his neck, Malaquias was at work behind an executive desk when they walked in, Pablo in the lead.

"We're going to use your office," Pablo said as he put a bottle of Mexican brandy on the table and plopped into Malaquias' comfortable swivel chair. "Go get me some glasses."

Over the years, Pablo had told Mimi about Malaquias and Mimi had repeated much to Regela. The American agent was already acquainted from other sources with Malaquias' role in the protection scheme that Pablo enjoyed with the military. A former police chief of Ojinaga, Malaquias had been given an honorary military title. It was his role to collect the *plaza* money and pass it on to the military.

Regela noted that Pablo did not seem to have much respect for Malaquias. After returning with three tumblers and some ice which he placed in front of Pablo, Malaquias bowed like a servant and walked backward out of the room. Pablo reached up and locked the door. A few minutes later someone knocked timidly. Regela heard Malaquias asking to be allowed back in.

"Not now, Malaquias," Pablo shouted impatiently. "Get lost!"

"Tell me about my brother," Pablo said to Regela, "and tell me about my uncle, Manuel."

The American agent told it just like it happened. He explained that Manuel had been his main target ever since Regela was sent to the Big Bend from El Paso. U.S. Customs had an open case on Manuel's smuggling operation out of Terlingua for several years, but nobody had been able to nail him. Regela went over the details of the case that had come up in the trial. He also explained how Armando Acosta, who had escaped from jail in Alpine three months before the Big Bend incident, got caught and described the chase through the Big Bend. He told Pablo about the hypodermic needle.

"To tell you the truth, we didn't even know it was your brother," Regela added, stroking his reddish beard and staring at Pablo with his light blue eyes. "He gave us a phony name and we didn't know who he really was until we took him to Alpine for booking. The jailer recognized him and said 'Mando! You've come back to us!'"

Pablo was actually pleased that Armando was behind bars. "My brother's a junkie and it will do him some good to spend time in jail. I have no problem with that. You did your job."

Over the next few hours they finished the brandy. Pablo drank more than half of it on his own. Throughout the conversation Pablo insisted that he trafficked only in marijuana and vehemently denied having anything to do with heroin or cocaine. At the time, Regela didn't have any reason to disbelieve him about the cocaine.

They told war stories. Pablo told him about his escape from the United States in 1976 and insisted that he had been set up. He thought he was going with Delfino Rendon to work out a marijuana deal.

Regela, in turn, told him about the shootout at San Vicente

that same year, describing what it was like to be inside a cramped camper surrounded by three dozen cutthroat bandits. He told Pablo he did not think they would have lived if it had not been for the fact they were armed with machine guns and had the advantage of surprise. Pablo remembered the incident. At the time he was working for Shorty Lopez and it was Shorty's marijuana that was seized. It had been fronted to Shorty's cousin for the San Vicente deal. Pablo himself had driven the marijuana downriver and delivered it to the cousin, Belen. That was Belen who demanded to see inside the camper, forcing the three agents to leap out, Pablo told Regela. Pablo's job on that deal was only to deliver the marijuana—the smuggling of it was not his concern and he was preparing to drive back to Ojinaga when he heard the thunderous gun battle across the river. He got back to the Rio Grande just in time to see the smugglers stampeding across the river, shooting with everything they had as they retreated.

Pablo told him that the Mexicans took heavy casualties that night. Four or five were killed and many more were wounded. But they learned from the experience. From then on, they sought to replace their antiquated weaponry with machine guns and semiautomatic pistols.

As the meeting in Malaquias' office progressed, Regela began to feel out Pablo as a potential source. He did not think there would be any harm in asking Pablo to help him make some cases. Like any other trafficker, Pablo had rivals he needed out of the way. "So why not work together?" Regela asked. "You have competitors, *gringos* coming down to the river to buy dope from other people. Help me out."

Regela saw a crafty look in Pablo's eyes, as if the drug lord was thinking about someone he would like to see arrested.

"I'll think about it," Pablo said.

They broke off the unusual meeting about midnight. Pablo found the American agent to be entertaining and possibly very useful. The American narcotics agent found the Mexican drug lord to be charming, friendly and potentially very useful. They did not specify when or where their next meeting would take place, but as they shook hands they agreed to work out the details through Mimi. Given Pablo's cutthroat reputation, Regela had been ready for anything, but the evening had turned out to be as enjoyable, casual and nonthreatening as a backyard barbecue among neighbors.

Once he was back out in the dirt street in front of the radio station, however, an absurd incident reminded him that he was operating behind enemy lines without any backup. He had driven down to Ojinaga from Panther Junction in an unmarked government sedan, and he had forgotten that the door on the driver's side would not open from the outside. As soon as he put his hand on the door handle, he remembered the problem and strode around to get in through the passenger door. Anywhere else the unexpected movement would not have meant anything. But just as he opened the door and stooped to slide in, Regela saw Pablo's brother and nephew step out from the dark shadows into the light of an amber streetlamp. The two gunmen had been hiding around a corner of a cinderblock wall that surrounded the radio station and apparently interpreted his unusual movement as hostile. They lifted their machine guns eloquently.

Perhaps they thought he was going for a bazooka? Or maybe a fragmentation grenade? Regela didn't know what was going through their minds. He waved his hands in the air and shouted, "Hey, the door's stuck. I gotta get in on the passenger's side."

He slid behind the wheel and got the hell out of there.

The meeting was the beginning of an unusual relationship between a Mexican drug lord and an American narcotics agent. They continued to meet for the next eighteen months even after Regela was transferred from the Big Bend back to the regional office in El Paso. He and Mimi had ended their relationship though they continued seeing one another as friends.

About once a month Regela made the 265-mile trip from El Paso to Ojinaga to meet with Pablo. Though these meetings mainly consisted of Pablo's monologues about his death-cheating exploits, ramblings about his views concerning drug trafficking, economics, the relations between the United States and Mexico and other subjects of little interest to the American, these contacts gave Regela the chance to observe the drug lord in his milieu, slowly gain his confidence and study the people surrounding him.

At one of these meetings, Regela got a glimpse of Pablo as family man when the drug lord of Ojinaga invited him and Mimi to his brick home on Calle Sexta. When they were let into the living room, they came upon the fearsome trafficker reading Snow White and the Seven Dwarfs to his daughter and several of her friends. As Pablo read, he altered his voice to sound like a dwarf, or the witch, or Snow White. When the reading was over, the girls left the living room and Pablo attended to his guests.

Always there were guards—sometimes two or three, sometimes as many as six. Pedro Ramirez Acosta, Pablo's nephew, was invariably present. Of all the people surrounding Pablo, Regela thought Pedro was the spookiest. Pedro rarely said anything more than "Hello." Regela never once saw him smile. The nephew always stood around with a machine gun, smoking customized Marlboros while Pablo, Regela and Mimi talked.

Regela felt that if anything were ever to go wrong and he had to defend himself, he would have to take out Pedro first. Pedro was truly the dangerous one.

With Pablo's knowledge, Regela always wore a concealed weapon to these meetings. Mimi later told Regela that it was a rare honor. In all the time she had known Pablo, he had always had his men search visitors for weapons before allowing them into his presence. Only Pablo's inner circle of relatives and friends and his personal bodyguards were allowed to keep their weapons around him.

At first Regela was as puzzled about the meetings with Pablo as Clayton McKinney, the Texas Ranger, had been about his earlier contacts. Regela could not put his finger on what Pablo wanted from him. Gradually he came to the same conclusion the Texas Ranger had reached: that Pablo wanted to keep the door to the United States open in case it got too hot for him in Mexico. And if it came to giving himself up, he wanted to be able to hand himself over to someone he already knew, someone who could smooth the way for him.

Nothing much came of the meetings until early 1986. By then, the investigation stemming from the Alamogordo propane-tank bust had broadened and Regela had read all of the investigative reports. He began looking at Pablo with even greater interest.

Following the ambush in front of the *supermercado* and Pablo's suspicions that Lupe Arevalo was behind it, Pablo saw how the American agent could be of use to him. A month after that ferocious gun battle, Pablo asked Mimi to set up another meeting with Regela. They met again in Malaquias Flores' office.

Pablo had told Regela many times about the blood feud between the two families: how it started, the casualties on each side, the shootout with Fermin and myriad other details about the bloody struggle for control of Ojinaga. He told Regela that Lupe Arevalo was now living in Chihuahua City and was running heroin through his territory without his authorization. He told Regela he wanted to get Lupe out of the way. He offered to help the American agent get Lupe busted in the United States.

"Why don't you just take care of him yourself if he's such a problem for you?" Regela said.

"If I do anything to him, it will just continue the feud. But if you arrest him, nobody is going to know that I helped you."

Lupe Arevalo would be a good target, Regela agreed. American authorities knew that the Arevalo faction was dealing in heroin and they suspected that Lupe, the eldest male of the clan, was in charge. He was considered a major heroin violator, capable of dealing in multi-kilogram quantities.

Out of fear of Pablo, Lupe Arevalo had gone to Chihuahua City after recovering from the gunshot wounds from the 1982 ambush in front of the ice cream parlor. When he made trips to Ojinaga to visit his mother and sisters and to arrange deals, Lupe always traveled in a truck with tinted windows, arriving late at night.

For about a month, Pablo passed information on to Regela by phone regarding Lupe's activities. Arevalo family members, Pablo claimed, were taping ounce packages of heroin that Lupe provided to their bodies and were walking across the international bridge with the drug. Regela relayed the information to the inspectors and immigration officers. But Pablo's tip-offs either came too late, or the information was incorrect, or the inspectors missed it during their searches, because they never caught any of the Arevalos with heroin. And they never once saw Lupe.

If Pablo really wanted Lupe, he and Regela were going to have to figure out a way to lure him to the United States, Regela told Pablo. Lupe himself rarely if ever set foot in the United States, but perhaps he could be lured there if convinced he could make a major drug deal? Say for a couple of pounds of heroin? Regela was either going to have to pose as a drug dealer or get someone else to pose as one.

The American agent suggested using one of his informants. Ever since the early 1970s, Regela had worked successfully with an informant from Ciudad Juarez, on the other side of the river from El Paso. His informant had helped him bust some big dealers in El Paso. Let the informant make contact with Lupe, Regela suggested. After gaining Lupe's confidence, the informant could lure Lupe to the United States with the prospect of a big heroin deal; Regela would then arrest Lupe in possession of the heroin. If they did it right, the informant could probably also help take down other members of the Arevalo faction.

The idea appealed to Pablo.

Regela brought the informant, who went by the nickname Gene the Bean, to see Pablo at Malaquias Flores' office. It was a hush-hush meeting of Pablo, Regela and Gene; not even Mimi was present. Pablo told the informant what he wanted him to do and left it up to him to find a way to get to Lupe.

Because he was not authorized to work cases directly in Mexico, Regela left the informant's actions to be worked out between him and Pablo. But it amounted to a plan to have Gene the Bean pose as a heroin buyer and make a series of purchases from Lupe to establish himself as a reliable outlet. Pablo promised the informant all the money he would need to buy heroin. Once Lupe had enough confidence in his new buyer, they would then get Lupe to the United States for a really big sale.

Obviously, Pablo could not introduce the informant to anyone in the Arevalo faction, but Gene proved to be very resourceful. A few days after the meeting with Pablo Acosta the informant struck up a friendship with a shoeshine boy outside of one of the hotels in downtown Ojinaga. The boy said he had been rooting for Fermin Arevalo after Lili was killed. The informant took the shoeshine boy with him in a taxicab to point out the home of Fermin Arevalo's widow.

The informant went back later and knocked on the door. Antonia let him in. Gene the Bean had a good line: he had been in the federal pen for the last ten years for heroin. He used to buy from Manuel Carrasco, *La Vibora*. He was told he could get in touch again with *La Vibora* through Fermin Arevalo. He had some big buyers lined up in the United States through his prison contacts, and they were eager to start dealing.

Antonia told him that Fermin was dead and she did not know anything about Manuel Carrasco. He had been gone from the area a long time. Without flinching, the informant said he had been advised that if he could not get in touch with *La Vibora* to talk to Pablo Acosta. Could Antonia put please put him in touch with Pablo Acosta?

As expected, Antonia got upset. "You stay away from Pablo Acosta. He's no good. He's the one trying to control everything in town and he's the one who killed my husband!"

Briefing Pablo and Regela later, the informant said that Antonia had asked him a lot of clever questions to see if she could trip him up about any of his claims. She even asked about the prison where he said he had been, and, having been there himself once, he described it satisfactorily, down to the cellblock, the visiting room and other details only a former inmate could know. Finally, Antonia suggested Gene get in touch with her son Lupe in Chihuahua City. Antonia promised to arrange a meeting.

When he learned of the progress, Pablo was happier than he had been in a long time. His chief nemesis was soon to become history. He instructed the informant to go ahead with the meeting and to buy a couple of ounces of heroin from Lupe.

Later, the informant could continue buying further ounce quantities to demonstrate to Lupe that he was a serious buyer with good connections in the United States. When he had Lupe's complete trust, then they could set Lupe Arevalo up in the United States.

In the meantime, Pablo took a much-needed break. He flew down to Cancun, where he stayed for two months. He told everyone in Ojinaga he was going to the famed Mexican beach resort for rest and relaxation. But David Regela, Mimi and others close to Pablo knew the real reason. Pablo's addiction to cocaine had worsened to the point where even he had to acknowledge that it was a serious problem. He went down to Cancun to get away from Ojinaga and its tons and tons of tempting cocaine. He wanted to dry out and kick the cocaine habit once and for all.

While in Cancun, Pablo sometimes practiced his English by posing as a bellhop in some of the tourist hotels where Americans stayed. The tourists gratefully tipped him, little suspecting that this funny, chatty, helpful person with the gold-lined teeth and a face full of scars was in fact one of the most feared drug traffickers in northern Mexico. Pablo got a big kick out of being the only one in on the joke.

Through sheer willpower and distracting play with tourists, he managed to stay off cocaine for two months.

Part Three

Death
of a
Drug Lord

*A*costa was reportedly shot in the head in 1983 during a skirmish during which Fermin Arevalo was killed. He received a serious eye injury and was wearing an eye patch. However, recent reports indicate that his appearance has changed considerably, as he now weighs between 185 to 195 pounds. His hair is turning grey and he has had plastic surgery to repair the bullet wound. He is allegedly experiencing problems with the Mexican federal judicial police in Chihuahua, and with other trafficking elements in the Ojinaga area. Varying reports give Acosta's current whereabouts as Ciudad Juarez, Nogales, and Ojinaga.

Information was received in May 1985 that he was purportedly trying to get out of the drug business and was planning to leave "La Plaza" in Ojinaga to a subject identified only as Armadad, while Acosta moved deeper into Mexico. In June 1985, information was received that Amado Carrillo Fuentes may be the head of Mexican organized crime in the Ojinaga area and superior to Acosta. Carrillo has been in the Ojinaga area approximately three months and owns Rancho La Perla in Manuel Buenavides, Chihuahua.

Carrillo was reportedly from the Guadalajara area and worked for the Mexican federal government in an unknown capacity for the last five years. Allegedly, Carrillo is extremely well connected, including links to the comandante of Ojinaga and possibly to the infamous Rafael Caro Quintero, a major narcotics trafficker from Guadalajara. The possibility exists that Amado Carrillo Fuentes is the same as Armadad.

On July 13, 1985, a shipment of 265 pounds of cocaine was seized at Alamogordo, New Mexico, and on July 17, 1985, a shipment of 263 pounds of cocaine was seized in El Paso, Texas. The cocaine was concealed inside propane tanks placed on pickup trucks. This cocaine is believed to have been destined for Los Angeles, California, and reportedly was part of a shipment of 850 kilograms sent by aircraft from Medellin, Colombia, to Ojinaga.

From the introduction to a confidential 223-page U.S. Drug Enforcement Administration report, *The Pablo Acosta Organization*, April 1986

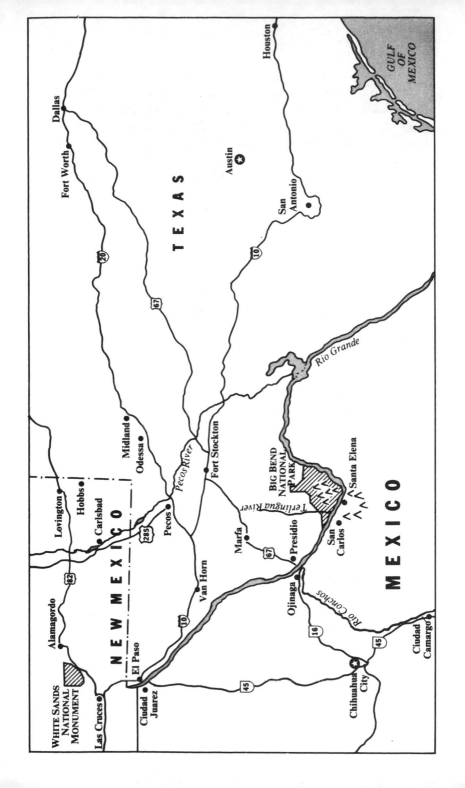

Chapter Twenty-One

WHITE GODDESS

"Traeme dos novias vestidas de blanco."

Pablo had been using cocaine off and on for some time, but until 1984 he had only snorted it. Though he was by then a big league marijuana and heroin trafficker, even he at times had trouble getting enough cocaine for personal use. That is when he used to call Sammy Garcia from Ojinaga with a coded message that help was needed. *"Traeme dos novias vestidas de blanco*—Bring me a couple of brides dressed in white" meant for them to supply him with two ounces of cocaine. Becky had her own source in El Paso, so getting Pablo what he wanted was never impossible provided Pablo was willing to wait a couple of days.

In 1984, one of Pablo's brothers introduced him to crack cocaine smoked *a la mexicana.* That consisted of pulling the strands of tobacco from the end of the filtered cigarette, then using the tip as a shovel to scoop up a fraction of a gram of powdered crack. After twisting the end into a wick, Pablo would pass a butane lighter underneath the cigarette to vaporize the cocaine and then take a long draw. Within seconds the drug was circulating in his brain, bringing with it the feelings of supra-humanity he had begun to crave.

Cocaine hydrochloride, the drug produced by the Colombian cartels, has a high melting point and cannot be smoked easily. Cocaine stripped of the hydrochloride molecule, however, is easy to vaporize. And so it is smokable. "Cooking" cocaine, the traffickers' expression for eliminating the hydrochloride from the formula and lowering its vaporization temperature, was a ritual Pedro Ramirez Acosta, Pablo's inseparable nephew, carried out with the reverence of a priest consecrating bread and wine.

Pedro had two ways of preparing it. One was the crude way, melting a mixture of cocaine and baking soda together over a flame. Any big spoon and a sustained flame would do for small amounts. Any pot and an oven would do for preparing larger quantities. Next Pedro scraped and scraped the solidified rock until all of it was reduced to fine, smokable powder. This was the technique Pablo and his entourage generally used to prepare crack, putting up with the impurities that were the disadvantage of the method.

The more sophisticated way consisted of dissolving baking soda in water, bringing it to a boil, then adding cocaine. As the solution cooled, the insoluble cocaine base floated to the top in an oily film and coalesced in the center. The impurities, meanwhile, remained in solution. When the coalescence solidified, Pedro would then mortar or scrape it into a fine powder.

It was the myrrh and incense of the traffickers' credo.

Over time, Pablo became obsessed with anything having to do with the subject of cocaine and cocaine trafficking. *Scarface,* the film about a slick Marielito trafficker who eventually got rubbed out in Miami by a small army of Colombian gunmen, became a big hit in Pablo's home on Calle Sexta. Not long after Becky Garcia first drove down to Ojinaga to work for Pablo, she was waiting at Pablo's brick house for people to arrive to discuss some deal that Pablo had going.

"You wanna watch a movie?" Pablo asked.

"Sure, why not?"

Pablo slid a videocassette of *Scarface* into the VCR.

"I've been wanting to watch this one," Becky said as she snuggled into the sofa.

"Oh, it's great, great! Wait till you see it."

Just about everybody in Pablo's inner circle had seen it again and again. A group of Pablo's people would be meeting somewhere, at Becky's apartment, at the apartment up behind Malaquias Flores' radio station, at Pablo's brick home on

Calle Sexta or at Pedro Ramirez Acosta's home downtown. Pablo would send someone for a VCR and the videocassette and they would all sit around snorting cocaine or doing free-base while watching the De Palma flick.

Once, a few days after everyone had viewed *Scarface* for the umpteenth time, the small group of Pablo's most intimate circle—Marco, Becky, Pedro and a couple of Marco's brothers—were sitting around a table in Becky's apartment on one of the side streets near the downtown plaza, weighing ounces of cocaine on a scale. In front of them were three or four pounds of cocaine in several plastic bags. One of the bags contained an entire kilo. Pablo picked it up and opened it. He rolled back the top and with a clever smile looked around the table. "Watch this!" he said. Mimicking Al Pacino in one of the more bizarre scenes of *Scarface*, Pablo let his head fall into the bag. When he raised it, there was cocaine all over his face—in his moustache, on his high Indian cheekbones, on his big nose, in his nostrils and all over his chin.

His gold-lined teeth sparkled through the powdery mask. "What's left in life?" he asked.

It was not just the cocaine that drew him to the film. Pablo identified with the shootouts, the murder attempts, the traf-ficker's rise to power, the bloody hits, the flash of dollars, the lavish living, the feeling of being number one.

He never watched *Scarface* from beginning to end, perhaps not really wanting to see how it all turned out. Instead he would tell Becky or someone else to rewind it or advance it to the parts of the movie he really wanted to see.

"You remember that part where ...? It was just like when ..."

The Scarface of the movie was Cuban, and Pablo talked about going to Cuba one day because the Cubans were into trafficking cocaine too. Or to Colombia. But no, if he went to Colombia he would get too big, bigger than those "sons-a-beeches" he had begun warehousing and smuggling cocaine for, and somebody would try to kill him. It really did not mat-ter how big the castle, just as long as you were king of it. Better just to stay in little old Ojinaga.

Here he was the lord.

Just how bad Pablo's addiction had become was already evident by late 1985. He could go days on end—he had to—just to keep everything running: the drugs coming in, the buyers supplied, the authorities appeased, and his gunmen, runners, pilots, packagers, suppliers, pot-farm workers and intelligence sources paid. By snorting cocaine or smoking crack he could get by on an hour or two of sleep a day. He had girlfriends all over the place and kept some women lodged at the hotels and motels—a habit, along with the cocaine, that eventually alienated his wife. He would go to one of the rooms and just zonk out. Half an hour, an hour, two hours later he was back on his feet. But eventually the pace would catch up with him.

Marco and Becky knew how to recognize the symptoms. First he would start to forget things, important things, like a meeting in the afternoon that he had set up with somebody that very same morning. Or he would lose track of what he was saying, or suddenly switch subjects and start talking about how they blew away Fermin at El Salto, or how he and Pedro had machine-gunned that punk kid who tried to kill him at the intersection near Motel Ojinaga. His command of English would start to deteriorate, and even in Spanish he would not make sense.

"Huh? What did you say?" Marco or Becky would ask him, looking at each other.

On one occasion in the autumn of 1985, following one of these stressed out and coked out episodes, they drove Pablo downstream to the village of Santa Elena, his birthplace, to force him to dry out enough to start functioning again. They had driven to this out-of-the way adobe village numerous times for one reason or another, more often than not to smuggle drugs. This trip would be the last that Pablo, Marco and Becky would ever make to Santa Elena together.

On previous trips, Pablo had been entertaining, talking knowledgeably about the history of the village. But on this trip, Pablo kept mumbling and rambling on like a drunk. It was driving his companions crazy. They had to take the uneven dirt road through San Carlos, then on to Providencia, then down the tricky mountain road from the top of the Sierra

Ponce to the river—a long, bone-jarring drive. The only customized cigarettes they had were the ones Pablo brought with him in his shirt pocket. He always prepared an entire pack to smoke when he was on the road. By the time they got to Santa Elena, the pack was all smoked and there was not any cocaine in the village.

That was why Marco and Becky were bringing him there—to dry him out.

They drove up in midafternoon in front of Pablo's adobe, about 100 yards from the Rio Grande, followed by the gunmen. The *pistoleros* went to scout around the village and to take up their usual positions. Marco and Becky helped an unsteady Pablo inside. They sat him down on the edge of a bed in one of the small bedrooms inside the U-shaped building that was practically all bedrooms, with the living room, dining room and kitchen merged together in the front by the lack of partitioning walls. Pablo had fortified the adobe with heavy metal doors and window shutters thick enough to stop bullets. The doors had slits wide enough to stick the muzzle of a gun through. The walls were nearly two feet thick. The adobe housed an arsenal of semiautomatic and automatic weaponry and a stockpile of ammunition. In other village homes were further stockpiles of ammunition.

After they sat him down on the bed, Pablo started asking for his *gon*. Marco and Becky had confiscated his rifle and pistols as a precaution. Whenever he got superstoned Pablo frequently would get into a Wild-West mood and shoot at walls or in the air like a drunken gunslinger. As he felt around his belt for his .45 and in his boot for the smaller pistol he usually kept there, he suddenly realized that he had been stripped of his weapons. Then he saw he was out of crack-laced cigarettes and that there wasn't any cocaine to make more of the cigarettes with. Like a true addict, he started throwing a tantrum:

"You dumb motherfuckers!" Pablo screamed. "Let's go, let's go get some. I know where to go. Come on, let's go get some." He ordered them to drive him all the way back to Ojinaga to get more cocaine.

"Okay, listen," Marco said. "We'll go back and get some if you take a nap. Lie down and rest for just a few minutes. And then we'll go back, I promise."

"All right, all right," Pablo mumbled.

He lay down. Becky gave him some milk with ice. He drank it like a docile child. Soon he started drifting off, mumbling to himself. One of Marco's brothers who had been sent to scout around the village came back to the adobe after making the rounds. Everything okay, everything *tranquilo*—quiet, he told Marco. The brother joined Marco and Becky at the kitchen table playing cards. Finally Pablo dozed off. They knew he would wake up in an hour or so without a tranquilizer, but Marco was prepared. He pulled a syringe from a carrying case and sat next to Pablo on the bed. It was a sedative he had gotten from a doctor in Ojinaga. Marco skillfully slid the needle into Pablo's arm, taking care not to hurt him. Becky was always amazed at Marco's tender side, given all the brutal things she had seen him do. After giving the injection, Marco pulled Pablo's boots off, undressed him, and pulled a bedsheet up to his neck.

There was not much to do in an adobe village in one of the most isolated, inhospitable regions of North America. After tiring of cards, Marco and Becky walked around the village, then strolled down to the edge of the Rio Grande to watched the yellow-brown water flow by. On the American side, a good stone's throw across, Becky could see a wide sandbar that ended where a jungle of tall mesquite and ancient cottonwoods began. The thick vegetation grew in the river floodplain for about half a mile inland. On the other side of the thicket, a two-lane asphalt road led up a hill to the U.S. ranger station. The station, its American flag flapping above, was visible from Santa Elena.

Marco sent someone across in the rowboat to buy up all the cigarettes at the park store. The villagers used the boat to ferry back and forth across the Rio Grande; some with border-crossing cards even kept their pickup trucks on the American side. They could drive to Presidio and cross over to Ojinaga in less than two hours using the highway on the

American side. On the Mexican side it was a six- or seven-hour ride up through the mountains over the crude roads Marco and Becky had used earlier that day.

As they sat there watching the swirling water, Marco and Becky were reminded of the history of the village Pablo had told them again and again during their past stays there. Pablo had always loved the primitive Santa Elena valley, hemmed in on one side by the river, on the other by the escarpments of the Sierra Ponce. Pablo liked to boast to them about the exploits of his father when he smuggled candelilla wax with Macario Vazquez, the most famous of all the wax smugglers, and about their shootout with the *forestales* in the hills above Santa Elena. Or he would get historical and talk about the successive waves of settlers who cleared the land and worked it against all the odds.

Pablo had heard the pioneer stories from his father and aunts and uncles: how settlers had originally come in the 1930s from the Juarez agricultural valley to create an *ejido*—a communal farm—at Santa Elena, but the farming venture failed and most of the settlers headed north. Policarpo Alonzo, one of the original settlers, set out to establish another *ejido* at Santa Elena in 1950 by recruiting sixty families from the Juarez agricultural valley. They obtained communal title to the land, a loan from the rural bank to buy seed, fertilizer, picks, shovels, tractors and a pump to draw water from the river. In the beginning, while waiting for the loan money, they had little food and went into the mountains to hunt wild burros they killed by chasing over cliffs or by cornering in box canyons and clubbing to death. In the first year, Pablo recounted, the settlers cleared seventy hectares of boulders and tenacious mesquite roots and planted cotton to repay the rural bank. As usual, some of the men worked more than others, some not at all, even though the loan money and the land had to be divided up in equal shares. Pablo described how the settlers made adobe bricks for their shelters and gathered ocotillo stalks for the roofing and felled cottonwoods for the beams. They erected adobes on what they thought was high ground, but at the first big rain the water cascaded off the top of the Sierra Ponce and turned the nascent village into a depressing muckbath. Then in 1958, the Rio Grande flooded and wiped out much of the labor of eight years. Many of the families saw that there was not any future for them in Santa Elena, working land that could never really be theirs: both nature and a government claimed it. They eventually migrated north.

The stories about communal Santa Elena usually went over Becky's head. How do you explain an *ejido* to an American? But Marco understood.

Much later, Pablo and his gunmen would sometimes run into some of the people he had known back in those early days of poverty and struggle. They would cross paths on the dusty road between San Carlos and Ojinaga, or in one of the sunbaked mud villages here or there in the desert. Some of these former acquaintances had been caught up in evangelical movements and went about the desert preaching *la palabra de Dios*—the word of God. They would give Pablo a copy of the New Testament printed in large type. These old acquaintances now had the pushy insistence of converts, but Pablo was troubled for another reason. One of these preachers would later tell about one of these desert encounters and how Pablo said to the preacher, earnestly, "Please pray for me," and, "Don't forget me in your prayers."

The next morning Pablo woke with an excruciating headache. It was not caused only by the withdrawals; for the most part his headaches were the consequence of the many bullet wounds to his head. One bullet that had grazed Pablo just above an eyebrow had somehow affected a nerve. That eyelid continually drooped, particularly when one of his headaches raged. He asked Becky for some aspirin and swallowed a handful. Still half-stoned, he was also groggy from the sedative. Marco fixed him a breakfast, then cooked up another meal when he said he was still hungry. After that, Pablo smoked some regular cigarettes and went back to bed. He slept soundly for another 24 hours.

Marco and Becky had some business to take care of in

Ojinaga. They drove back that day, leaving some of the *pistoleros* to watch over Pablo. When they came back the following morning, Pablo was already up and was showered, shaved and fresh looking. Instead of the stoned, irrational half-man of the last couple of days who had been ready to shoot up everything with his semiautomatic weaponry, here was the bright, intelligent and alert Pablo that Marco and Becky had always admired.

They were back in Ojinaga later that day and Pablo was back on top of the world, eager to start moving again.

Chapter Twenty-Two

INFORMANT

The agents assigned to the Organized Crime Drug Enforcement Task Force in El Paso would have preferred working the Acosta organization in secret, but news about their target soon came out. In April 1986, two months after the task force meeting in the DEA conference room, newspapers in El Paso and Albuquerque published lengthy stories about Pablo Acosta and his "alleged chief enforcer," Marco De-Haro, who at the time was being held in Eddy County jail in Carlsbad. The stories linked Pablo Acosta with the two cocaine seizures in Alamogordo and El Paso.

Citing a Mexican underworld source in Sinaloa, one of the news accounts rated Pablo Acosta one of the top seven narcotics godfathers in Mexico.

The DEA divisional director in Dallas, Phil Jordan, whose jurisdiction covered West Texas, conceded to newsmen that an organized crime task force had indeed targeted Pablo Acosta, though he refused to provide any details about the investigation. Jordan characterized Acosta as a "vicious, extremely dangerous person with little regard for human life." One of the news stories alleged that Pablo Acosta had a barbaric ritual of dragging the bodies of his victims through the desert behind his Bronco.

Other than the Ojinaga weeklies that had been intimidated into silence, this was the first time Pablo's name had appeared in a newspaper since the shooting in Lovington in 1964 in front of La Poblanita. At first, Pablo derived a narcissistic pleasure from the notoriety; then he became angered by the portrait drawn of him. It was all a distortion, Pablo raged to Mimi Webb Miller and David Regela.

Whether or not that was the case, the fact that stories were coming out about him was not a favorable sign. The publicity had blown his relative anonymity. He had been essentially unknown outside of the Ojinaga area except by law enforcement and the drug underworld on both sides of the border. Now his name had gone international, and he realized it was going to cost him.

People close to him knew that publicity was not his most serious problem. When Pablo came back from Cancun in the late spring of 1986, he was able to stay off of cocaine for a few more weeks. But the temptation in Ojinaga was too strong: practically the entire criminal underworld Pablo dealt with was using it. There was just too much of it everywhere, in barrels, in crates, in cardboard boxes, in storage tanks. Staying away from it was like trying to avoid sand in the Sahara.

David Regela, who resumed his visits to Ojinaga after Pablo came back from the beach resort, was amazed by the amounts of cocaine and brandy Pablo was starting to consume. He had been told that Pablo's inner circle could go through an entire kilogram of cocaine in a week. When he saw Pablo chain-smoking crack cigarettes that summer, Regela believed it. It was as though Pablo were making up for his two months on the wagon while in Cancun.

As their meetings continued, the American Customs agent noted that Pablo was becoming increasingly obsessed with getting rid of Lupe Arevalo, as if Lupe were the source of all of his problems. The murder attempt against Pablo earlier in the year, Regela believed, could have been the work of any of dozens of people: the Ojinaga *plaza* was now one of the most important on the border, given its role as a cocaine depot and smuggling hub. It was reasonable to assume that more groups than just the Arevalo faction wanted to gain control of it.

As far as Pablo was concerned, the only person who wanted to get him out of the way was Lupe Arevalo.

Since that *supermercado* ambush, Pablo lived in fear of another attempt on his life. The drug lord took such precautions that Regela complained how hard it was to find him. Pablo was constantly on the move. He never slept in the same place two nights in a row. He reduced the number of bodyguards to two or three so as not to draw attention to himself. He rode in different vehicles, sometimes even switching cars and trucks several times just to go from one side of Ojinaga to the other. Usually, Pablo let only Hector Manuel and Pedro Ramirez Acosta, both blood relatives, accompany him. If a situation merited additional protection, Pablo had another carload of gunmen follow him at a distance.

Pablo became more cautious about his meeting sites with the American agent too. When Regela first began visiting him in Ojinaga, he and Pablo would talk at leisure in a room at one of the hotels or in the office at Malaquias' radio station. But after the bloody ambush in front of the market, they began meeting mostly at Mimi's isolated ranch near San Carlos or at Pedro's house near downtown Ojinaga. Whenever they met at Pedro's house, Pablo and his visitor talked in one of the stuffy, windowless back rooms while Pedro kept his cold eyes on the street through the wrought-iron fence in front of the house.

If there was any bright spot in Pablo's increasingly gloomy horizon, it was that Regela's informant, Gene the Bean, appeared to be making progress with Lupe Arevalo.

While Pablo was in Cancun, the informant managed an introduction to Lupe Arevalo through Lupe's mother, Antonia. Lupe was short, thin, with an adolescent face even though he was pushing thirty. After repeating the story he had given Antonia, Gene told Lupe he desired to do regular business. To show that he was earnest, the informant purchased a few ounces of heroin. Over the summer, he bought heroin from Lupe Arevalo several more times, each time about three ounces, with money Pablo had given him.

By August, Gene had convinced Lupe that he could arrange a really big buy in El Paso, that he had some clients who wanted a kilogram of heroin immediately. Regela's informant made it sound as though this could be the Big One for Lupe, the ultimate connection that could give Lupe an outlet for dozens of kilograms of heroin a year. The only problem related to this transaction, Gene explained, was that his clients did not trust Mexican police and did not want to do any deals in Mexico. The deal had to take place in the United States.

To boost his confidence, Gene invited Lupe to Ciudad Juarez where they stayed for a few days at the classy El Presidente Hotel on Avenida Lincoln. He took Lupe to chic restaurants and to some trafficker-owned discos and introduced him to his underworld friends. Some of those friends were big names, recognizable throughout Chihuahua. Lupe was duly impressed. To both Pablo and Regela, it looked as if they were going to be able to lure the Arevalo across the border and fairly soon.

When Regela filled the Ojinaga drug lord in on the most recent developments, Pablo appeared pleased.

About the end of August 1986, Pablo startled Regela by telling him that he wanted to use the informant to make some other busts as well.

"Who do you have in mind?" Regela asked, expecting him to name some low-level marijuana traffickers or heroin dealers from Odessa who had been encroaching on Pablo's territory.

Pablo looked at him calmly and said, "I want to get the Colombians out of Ojinaga"

Regela sat forward, heart pounding. Pablo had always denied any involvement with cocaine smuggling, though Regela knew that a lot of cocaine was coming through the small border town and he clearly understood the implications of Pablo's *plaza* franchise. After his return from Cancun that spring, Pablo himself began making vague references about the Colombians during his meetings with the American agent, though without admitting any participation.

Without spelling out his warehousing and smuggling role, Pablo finally admitted that he had allowed the Colombians to come into Ojinaga. He was making good money off the arrangement, more money than he could ever spend in a lifetime, but now he regretted it. The Colombians were taking over, both in Ojinaga and in other parts of Mexico. Their presence was bringing lots of heat from the Americans. If he had just stuck to marijuana smuggling and had kept Ojinaga clean of cocaine, there probably would not have been an American task force out to get him.

Pablo had other reasons he did not discuss with Regela but that were common knowledge in the Ojinaga drug underworld. Many of the rank-and-file smugglers, the hundreds of men up and down the river who bought small quantities of marijuana—five, ten, twenty pounds—from Pablo or who found employment in some branch of the marijuana or heroin business, were also beginning to grumble about the South American presence. Life was getting real tough for them, they complained. Because of the Colombians, there were now more cops patrolling the American side of the Rio Grande than ever before, and it was getting harder to get a load of drugs across without getting caught. It was getting tougher to make a living to support their families. And the worst was still to come: The *gringos* were already talking of calling out the National Guard to patrol the border. They blamed Pablo because he was the one who allowed the Colombians into Ojinaga in the first place.

Pablo therefore wanted to drive the Colombians out; he wanted to get the Americans off his back; he wanted to return Ojinaga to the good old days.

Pablo had already thought it through. Regela's informant was the key, he explained. He could get Gene on the inside of the Colombians' operations on the border. Then the informant could make the American agent all the drug busts he had ever dreamed of—big busts of hundreds or thousands of kilograms of pure cocaine. There was something in it for the informant too—the reward money the United States paid. Gene could make a fortune.

The next time Regela's informant was in town, Pablo took him around and introduced him to his Colombian contacts as a personal friend, a man who could be trusted and who was in a position to broker some big cocaine deals with his own connections in the United States.

Among other people, the informant was introduced to Amado Carrillo Fuentes and Ismael Espudo. Amado, who at the time was barely a blip on the American intelligence screens but who eventually was to become the most powerful trafficker in all of Mexico, had been a fixture in Ojinaga since 1985. He lived in a gorgeous three-story home on a hill near downtown Ojinaga that overlooked the United States. Whenever he was in town, guards with machine guns were posted at the front gate. According to U.S. drug intelligence, Amado was a young, well-educated, slick-dressing trafficker who had been some kind of federal official in Guadalajara. Customs intelligence had picked up reports Amado had been a DFS agent for five years prior to his arrival in the border town. He was thought to represent powerful Guadalajara traffickers for whom Pablo also warehoused cocaine.

Ismael Espudo, the former Culberson County commissioner, fearing an arrest warrant was out for him in the United States, stayed in Ojinaga or on his ranch farther south near the village of Cuchillo Parado. Espudo was a frequent guest at Amado's house.

Among the Colombians the Customs informant may have been introduced to in Ojinaga was Carlos Lehder Rivas, one of the most important of the Colombian cocaine traffickers who was known to visit Mexico on occasion. The person Gene described to the American agent called himself Carlos Rivas—a Lehder alias. He fit the physical description of the half-Colombian, half-German Medellin Cartel figure who was finally arrested in Colombia in 1987 and extradited to the United States.

Regela was acquainted with Amado Carrillo Fuentes from conversations with Mimi and others, and from Customs intelligence reports. But Pablo's associate was still an enigma.

After introducing the informant to the inner circle of Mexican and Colombian traffickers, Pablo arranged for Regela to meet Amado too. Pablo brought Regela and the informant

to breakfast with Amado on two occasions at downtown
Ojinaga restaurants. Not knowing anything about the American, Amado was cool and reserved. Conversation never
went beyond small talk. Regela, meanwhile, was limited to
absorbing impressions. During the first meeting, Regela noted
that Pablo's bodyguards sat at separate tables from Amado's crew of gunmen. He sensed a tension between the two
traffickers. There was a coolness in the tone of their conversation that could not be attributed to Regela's presence.
When the breakfast was over, Regela and Gene were leaving first, but they were still within earshot when Pablo began
speaking to Amado in a low but firm voice. Regela had dif-
ficulty following rapidly spoken Spanish, but he caught the
inflections and body language. Pablo's face had a look of
sternness. Amado's reply was crisp.

Once outside, the informant explained the conversation.
The traffickers had a stash site for cocaine somewhere in the
desert, in an underground storage tank. Somehow the DEA
had learned about it. Somehow Amado found out that the DEA
had found out. Amado and Pablo were both greatly concerned about a security leak. But Amado had taken the matter
into his own hands. Without Pablo's knowledge, he had six
people who had some involvement with the stash site kidnapped, tortured and killed. Because of the thoroughness of
the interrogation, Amado was satisfied that none of the men
was the leak. None of them even suspected an informant
had been in their midst. Pablo was furious when he learned
of Amado's action. He still had not gotten over his anger
when he, Amado, Regela and Gene met for breakfast.

At the restaurant, Pablo was demanding an explanation,
calling the killings a waste.

"What have you done?" Pablo said. "You've killed six people and what have you accomplished by it?"

Amado replied coolly, in a tone that did not invite any further discussion: "It is better for six innocent men to die than
for one guilty man to go unpunished."

Chapter Twenty-Three

PABLO TALKS

About the time he decided to attempt to sabotage the Colombian presence in Ojinaga, Pablo became involved
with Mimi Webb Miller. His addiction to cocaine had alienated
him from his wife Olivia who kept warning him to get off the
stuff. But the addiction was so advanced that it was no longer
possible.

Pablo got Mimi an apartment in Ojinaga with a telephone,
and she began spending more time there than at her Miracle
Ranch. Her apartment became one of Pablo's safe houses and
she became his confidante.

As a result, David Regela became preoccupied with Mimi's
safety. Amid scheming and intrigue, plots and counterplots,
murders and attempted murders, she was naive and trusting.
Regela could see that the blond Texas senator's niece had become enamored with the border drug baron. Regela wondered
if she really knew who she was getting involved with. Pablo
was a walking target. Any day somebody could ambush him
and if Mimi were with him, she could get blown away too. The
American narcotics officer often cautioned her: "Pablo isn't
going to last another year. You need to disassociate yourself
from him and go back to giving tours. Or, even better, go
back to your family in Wichita Falls and wait until this settles
down."

Instead of retreating to a prudent distance, Mimi seemed to
have taken up Pablo as a cause. The Pablo she knew did not
square with the DEA's characterization of him as a "vicious,

extremely dangerous person with little regard for human life." Her view of Pablo was the one he wanted to project, the only side he allowed her to see: that of a champion of the poor, a man of honor who filled in for a rapacious government that was only interested in perpetuating and enriching itself at the expense of the people. He did wrong, Pablo admitted to her, but he did so to raise money to repair schools, to pay hospital bills for the indigent, to provide jobs for people. He gave while everyone else with power took.

Regela understood that Pablo was careful to keep the darker side of his activities from both of them. Mimi never knew of the early morning kidnappings, the barbaric torture sessions, of people vanishing forever, of the hits ordered in Mexico and in the United States.

She wanted other people to see Pablo the way she saw him. American law enforcement misunderstood Pablo. He was doing good for his community, despite everything. And things could be a lot worse if someone else came to power in Ojinaga, she warned.

Mimi began promoting Pablo even before his control over Ojinaga started to slip. In the summer of 1985 she arranged for him to meet a journalist from Arizona who was traveling from the Gulf of Mexico to the Pacific Ocean to document the clash of cultures along the U.S.-Mexican border. Mimi came across the journalist, Alan Weisman, in Lajitas. Weisman had questions about the Mexican Mafia and had heard the blond woman had some of the answers. Mimi told him she could put him in touch with the Mafia's controlling hand, the man with *all* the answers.

Granting an interview would be a good way for Pablo to cultivate his image and counter rumors about him, Mimi argued to Pablo. Pablo agreed, reluctantly, and spent three hours with a tense Weisman in Malaquias Flores' office. Throughout the interview, Pablo minimized his importance in the drug world. Though airplanes with 1,800-pound loads of cocaine were flying into Ojinaga with the regularity of a shuttle service, Pablo claimed that he only trafficked in marijuana; and even then not in big volume.

"People think I am a rich man, that I make my money lying down. They are mistaken. Mistaken. I don't even have a carport," Pablo told Weisman, then rambled on about how he helped the poor with his money.

Then a journalist writing for *The Washington Post's* Sunday magazine about the so-called Terlingua rape briefly met Pablo through Mimi. Walt Harrington was preparing an article about how a Mexican accused of raping a Terlingua woman had been broken out of jail in San Carlos one night by three masked men wearing army camouflage and carrying assault rifles. The rape had occurred in Terlingua, on the American side, and the rapist, who had been jailed in Mexico after being accused of the crime, was hauled back to Texas and tied stark naked at a rest stop near Alpine for the sheriff of Brewster County to find.

More than a few people thought Pablo had something to do with the jailbreak because the Terlingua rape victim was a close friend of Mimi's—and due to the fact that nothing seemed to happen down there without Pablo's consent. It became a highly publicized international incident, this violation of Mexico's sovereignty, but no one ever identified the three armed "midnight extraditers," as Harrington later tagged the kidnappers.

Mimi brought the Washington journalist to Ojinaga. They waited for Pablo to show up outside Malaquias' radio station. Having heard the legends about the Ojinaga Mafia chief from people less sold on Pablo's virtue than Mimi, Harrington was in an emotional state verging on panic by the time Pablo drove up in a dusty Ford pickup. Pablo pulled up next to Mimi. He was all tequilaed up, he told her, and did not feel like talking to anybody.

"I didn't have anything to do with it," he shouted to the journalist from the truck. "I hear four *gringos* did it." And he sped away.

Regela began joking with Pablo that Mimi had now taken over public relations duties for him. It seemed almost true when Mimi trooped a couple of FBI agents from Midland down to Ojinaga to check out rumors Libyan terrorists were sneaking into the United States through the Big Bend and of terrorist training camps hidden in the canyons of northern Chihuahua. Pablo told the FBI agents he hadn't heard about such camps. His people would have informed him of their existence. The only terrorists he had ever heard of in northern Mexico were the Soviet-backed urban and rural guerrilla groups of the 1960s and 1970s, but they had been wiped out by the government.

To the astonishment of the FBI agents, Pablo volunteered to fight the terrorists if indeed there were any preparing to attack America. He did not want anything to happen to the United States. He owed everything he had to the United States and would be willing to fight Arab terrorists *for free*. Pablo did everything but pull out an American flag and snap a salute.

The FBI agents later wrote back to Mimi that meeting Pablo had been one of the "high points" of their long careers.

Then in late October 1986 a reporter from an El Paso newspaper, which had previously published articles about Pablo, left a message for Mimi at the Lajitas Trading Post. "Would Pablo Acosta be willing to talk about the claims being made about him?"

Pablo agreed to a meeting, but when Mimi told Regela and Regela's informant about the upcoming interview they tried to talk Pablo out of it. Regela argued that any publicity was going to hurt Pablo, and if he was hurt, their efforts to burn the Colombians were going to be hurt too.

"Regardless of how the article comes out, if you get your name in the paper, the Mexican government will decide it can't afford you," Regela told Pablo.

Regela's informant thought it would be a mistake too. He pointed out that the entire state of Chihuahua was in political turmoil over controversial state elections that had taken place in July. Allegations were flying that the government, despite the promise of clean elections, had once again rigged it in favor of the ruling party. Mexican protesters were making front page news all over the United States by blockading the international bridges for days at a time between Ciudad Juarez and El Paso. The timing just wasn't right for an interview with the American press, Gene said. If the Mexican government was embarrassed by anything Pablo said, Pablo was going to pay for it.

Nevertheless, Pablo went ahead with the interview. He believed that it could benefit him by allowing him to give his version of things, and give him a forum to deny American police claims that he had allied himself with the Colombians.

The meeting was set for noon on October 27, but when the reporter arrived at the Motel Ojinaga and met with Mimi, he was told that Pablo would not be immediately available. Mimi explained that the drug lord was moving from safehouse to safehouse around town to avoid a squad of Mexican federal police that was in town with a kilogram of seized heroin. The authorities claimed the heroin was Pablo's, that he hadn't paid to clear the shipment, and they wanted money from him. Pablo, however, told them through intermediaries that the drug was not his and refused to pay tribute. The reporter and Mimi waited in a motel room for seven hours until clearance finally came by telephone.

They drove in an old pickup truck through dusty streets to Malaquias' radio station. They were let through a series of metal doors into a dark courtyard. Across the courtyard, on a landing at the entrance to a second-floor apartment, was Pablo Acosta, pacing back and forth while smoking. He was dressed in jeans, a dark blue cowboy shirt, a black leather vest, wearing cowboy boots and a large oval belt buckle. A .45-caliber semiautomatic pistol was stuffed in his belt.

When the American arrived at the top of the landing, the *padrino* asked in a raspy voice about how to get a twenty-pound watermelon inside a five-gallon water bottle. Mimi had earlier relayed the question to the reporter, saying that the drug lord had been toying with the idea of exporting such things to France to sell as a novelty. It was Pablo's idea of a joke. When the reporter concluded the watermelons would have to be *grown* inside the bottles, Pablo broke into a broad smile and escorted his guests into a sparsely furnished living room. "Come in," he said, "I like talking to an intelligent man." The drug lord opened one of the pint bottles of El Presidente brandy the reporter had brought, placing it on a long table in the middle of the room. Loaded machine-gun clips were scattered across the table, and ashtrays overflowed with cigarette butts. There were no gunmen in sight, but leaning against the wall, within arm's reach of Pablo, was an assault rifle with the trigger and grip facing forward.

Only Mimi was with them, interpreting occasionally and reminding Pablo of things to say.

Pablo usually had people searched before allowing them into his presence, but had not done so with the reporter. He leaned back in his chair, relaxed, but scrutinizing the American and watching his hands. People didn't understand him, he began. The border is a rumor mill, and untrue stories had been told about him. Yes, he killed, but he never shot first. Yes, he was a drug trafficker wanted in the United States, but he only dealt in marijuana and only to fill a demand as any entrepreneur would. Yes, his *pistoleros* killed Lili Arevalo, but not on his orders.

Squinting, he obligingly went over a list the reporter had brought of twenty-six murders attributed to him. Pablo disclaimed responsibility for all but the ones in which he acted in self-defense. He explained how many of the others had come about. He spoke at length of the killings between the Acosta and Arevalo factions that led to a showdown finally at Fermin's ranch. Acosta insisted that he had taken his men to the ranch to put and end to the warfare.

At one point, describing his plea to Antonia to stop the fighting, Pablo whipped out his .45 semiautomatic and handed it to the reporter, showing him how he had given the same weapon to Antonia that fateful day.

"I told her, if this will bring Lili back, then shoot me and get it over with," Pablo said.

As he had done countless times with Regela, Mimi, Becky and numerous others, Pablo described Fermin's failed ambush at the cattle guard. As if to overcome doubts about how close he had come to death, Pablo lowered his head, parted his black hair, and placed the reporter's forefinger on the long scar across the top of his skull.

"Feel that," he said. "That is where Fermin's bullet hit me."

His role in drug trafficking was greatly overstated by the DEA, he insisted; he didn't have an "army" of 500 people working for him, just a few people to help him when he smuggled small loads of marijuana up the river, between Lajitas and Santa Elena; he didn't deal in heroin because there wasn't any money to be made in it. As for cocaine, *ni modo*—no way. Being a small-timer, he didn't have the money to finance loads of cocaine. The cocaine that he did have was for his own consumption, he insisted.

While talking, Pablo pulled out a plastic bag full of white powder and a box of baking soda. He demonstrated how his entourage prepared crack cocaine: three-quarters cocaine and one-quarter baking soda. He mixed the two together, then scooped some up with a large aluminum spoon and held it over a candle. The mixture melted and fused together, bubbling slightly before Pablo removed it from the flame. When it cooled, Pablo dumped the small block onto the table. While he talked with the reporter, he scraped it vigorously with the worn blade of a jackknife, reducing the crack to powder. He scooped up some of the white powder with the tip of a Marlboro cigarette after pulling out some of the tobacco. He tapped the cigarette and made a wick of the end. He held the cigarette under a butane lighter then inhaled, his body leaning backwards as if to expand his lungs to accommodate all the smoke.

He went on about the ambushes and shootouts. They were unfortunate but they were to be expected in his business. He had cheated death so many times that it seemed to him God had mandated his survival so he could continue helping the poor and the struggling Ojinaga community. For every $20 he earned trafficking, he retained only one. All the rest went to helping people, he said.

The reporter was curious about the payoffs, about reports that Pablo was paying $100,000 a month for protection from the authorities.

"I would like to see that kind of money," he scoffed. But

he acknowledged that the federal police were part of the overhead: "There isn't any contract. If I make some money, I give them something for them to eat well and so forth. I give them as much as they want. The government doesn't give them cars. They need a car, I give them one. If you're a federal policeman, you're never going to make enough money to send your kids to school. So you've got to get money from somewhere. I don't blame them, I blame the government."

He planted marijuana once with permission from the army, he admitted. "I grew a little bit, but I was doing it for the schools."

The conversation was interrupted at one point by an unexpected visitor. A short, stocky man in the uniform of a Mexican army officer rapped stiffly on the front door. Pablo walked out to the landing and talked in his low gravelly voice for about a minute with the visitor. Then Pablo said loudly, "I have company. Come back tomorrow."

"*Un amigo de borachera*—a drinking buddy," Pablo explained.

About midnight, Acosta glanced at the $4,000 solid-gold watch on his wrist—a gift from Amado Carrillo Fuentes, as was the one-ounce Credit Suisse gold ingot that dangled from his neck. Pablo announced he wanted to pay a visit to a blind girl. She was proof of his philanthropy: he was arranging to have a cornea transplant so she could see again. As they were leaving the apartment, Pablo grabbed the machine gun that was leaning against the wall, jammed a full magazine clip into it, shoved another into his ostrich-skin cowboy boot, and picked up a third clip from the table.

"If there's another ambush, I will protect you," he said matter-of-factly.

His mood had varied from humble to cocky throughout the evening. He was cocky as he picked up the AR-15 and swept the room with it with his right arm, as if shooting. He liked AR-15s because they were lightweight, in contrast to the banana-clip Kalashnikovs popular with traffickers in other parts of Mexico. He showed the reporter how two years before he had held the same AR-15 out the passenger side of his truck and shot Jesus Munoz twice in the back of the head as he and Pedro Ramirez Acosta chased after him down by the railroad station.

Munoz, a young man with curly black hair, had been hired by someone in Odessa to kill him, Pablo explained. The gunman was in a pickup truck and shot six times while Pablo and his nephew were waiting for the light to change at an intersection near the international bridge. The gunman missed and sped away, with Pedro and Pablo right behind. "I could have shot him then, but we were on a residential street and I was afraid of hitting some kids," Pablo went on, taking a drag from a modified Marlboro. He described how the gunman raced down a road leading to the train station. The road ended at the railroad tracks, but Munoz bounced over the tracks and onto a rutted dirt road on the other side. Pedro bounced over the tracks too, and chased the shooter's truck almost bumper to bumper. Pablo showed how he leaned out of the window to get a clear shot, holding the assault rifle with one arm. "It was bumpy, but I never miss," he said, squinting as if taking aim.

Pablo, Mimi and the reporter were walking down the wooden stairway to the courtyard. Pablo was just warming up to the story. He described how Munoz was hit in the back of the head and crashed into a ditch. Two bullets had penetrated the sides of his neck and had come out of his chin. They thought he was dead or mortally wounded. But just as Pablo and Pedro jumped out of their truck, Munoz popped up from behind his crashed pickup and fired six more rounds.

"He had another revolver. I counted one, two three all the way to six. And when he used up his ammunition, I said to Pedro, 'Let's get him.' Pedro ran around one side, I ran around the other side. The pickup was in a ditch and the gunman was lying against the seat trying to reload, but we didn't give him a chance."

Pablo showed the reporter how he and Pedro aimed their rifles and fired into the hitman's back until they ran out of ammunition.

He recalled how Munoz's hands were shaking severely as he frantically tried to reload the pistol.

"I don't like any of this," he said, waving a machine-gun clip above his head as he led his visitors through the court-yard and out to the street. "I don't like killing people. I have to carry this since all of the killing started and I don't like it. I used to be able to walk around Ojinaga in shorts, without carrying a gun."

Mexican border towns are ringed with eroded adobe shacks. The blind girl and her seventy-year-old mother lived in one of them. Elva Fernandez, her eyes bandaged from some preliminary treatment she had received prior to going to Chihuahua City for a cornea transplant, groped for Acosta's hand and kissed it when he sat next to her on the bed. Her mother stood off to one side, smiling warmly at their benefactor. Pablo rested the machine gun on his knee and explained that Elva's mother had mistaken hydrogen per-oxide for eyedrops when the girl was only a few months old. Elva had been blind ever since. The girl was difficult to un-derstand. She had fallen on her face so many times while out begging in the streets of Ojinaga that she had lost her front teeth. Her nose and forehead were disfigured from a life-time of such headlong falls.

An hour later, after Pablo, Mimi and the reporter stum-bled out into the dark, unpaved street, Pablo said, with a voice slurred by all the crack he had been smoking: "There were people before in Ojinaga who made money traffick-ing. How come they didn't do anything for these people? I don't love money so much as I love people. I do what I do for people."

The next day, the drug lord gave the reporter the grand tour of Pablo's Ojinaga, that part of the border town he wanted an outsider to see: the old people's home he was build-ing one block from Amado Carrillo Fuentes' swank home; the schools he had refurbished; the shootout sites that had formed the basis for Pablo's legendary durability.

The tour ended in one of Pablo's safe houses. Shortly af-ter they arrived, Amado Carrillo Fuentes dropped by. He was tall, polite, reserved, dressed in expensive Western garb. At Pablo's request, he had brought over a VCR. He and Pablo discussed some business in a backroom, then Amado left.

After Amado's departure, Pablo left his guests watching a videotape filmed the preceding winter on Pablo's ranch near San Carlos: it featured Pablo, Pedro, Amado, Hector Manuel and several other men on horseback. All of them were smoking modified Marlboros. They took turns whirling ropes in awkward attempts to lasso calves released from a makeshift chute. The men, high, laughed uproariously at one another whenever someone came close to falling from a horse. Every once in a while one of them managed to get a rope around the neck of a calf.

While the video played, Pablo was in the kitchen, "cooking." The smell filled the air and soon the entire house was thick with the odor of cocaine fusing with bicarbonate of soda. He must have been brewing an entire kilogram back there. The reporter began to feel his head throbbing and, after half an hour, a wave of nausea. He announced that he had to leave.

Mimi informed Pablo. Pablo came out of the kitchen and seemed surprised and disappointed. It was only seven o'clock. The night was just beginning and he was just warming up! But the reporter insisted and politely gathered up his belongings. Pablo escorted him to the front porch. The drug lord threw his arm around the visitor with a customary Mexican *abrazo*, thumping him twice on the back before shaking his hand.

"Come back any time," he said warmly. "Ojinaga is yours."

Chapter Twenty-Four

SURRENDER?

Pablo's days as the drug lord of Ojinaga were numbered, the result chiefly of his worsening cocaine addiction. He spent twelve to fourteen hours each day smoking modified Marlboros and drinking brandy or whiskey. People who had to do business with him could only take care of it between noon, when he usually got up, and three in the afternoon. After that, serious negotiating or important decision making was out of the question. Sometimes by midnight he was hardly coherent. When David Regela briefed the organized crime task force members in El Paso, he told them his belief that cocaine would finish off Pablo before they could ever get their hands on him.

Many of Pablo's associates were losing confidence in him and were deserting, Mimi told Regela. They could see he was no longer mentally or physically capable of running a complex trafficking organization. Even the low-ranking *pistoleros* seemed to be jumping ship. Regela recalled that in the recent past he had always seen the same faces. Now, the only ones he recognized were Pedro and Hector Manuel. The others were newcomers, youngsters thrilled at the idea of working for a famous drug lord.

The first indication Regela got that Pablo also understood his control of Ojinaga was drawing to a close came during a conversation he had with Pablo shortly after the informant was introduced to the Colombian organization. Pablo and Regela met at Pedro's home to discuss the informant's progress with Lupe and the Colombians. After Regela brought Pablo up to date concerning the informant's activities, Pablo unexpectedly began questioning him about a way to give himself up. Was there any sort of deal that could be worked out with the Americans, he asked Regela?

Back in El Paso, Regela relayed the question to Tom McHugh, the assistant U.S. attorney who handled OCDETF prosecutions, informing him that Pablo might be willing to surrender on the international bridge in Presidio or El Paso provided certain conditions were met. Namely, Pablo wanted to bring his family and all his cash with him to the United States. In exchange, he would shut down his drug operation.

McHugh, a thin, scholarly-looking attorney who had prosecuted major drug cases in Florida before going to El Paso, found this to be an intriguing development. He had arranged plea bargains, but Pablo's offer was unacceptable. He made it clear that were Pablo to give up he would have to serve time for the heroin indictment still outstanding in Albuquerque, handed down after Pablo fled to Mexico ten years earlier. Pablo would have to go to Albuquerque to face those charges after surrendering.

On a return trip to Ojinaga, Regela explained the assistant U.S. prosecutor's position and discussed options. He told Pablo that some kind of deal was always possible and that it was worth exploring further. On the next trip back to El Paso, Regela passed on Pablo's message: He wanted to talk to the American federal prosecutor about surrendering, but such discussions would have to take place in Mexico. Pablo would guarantee McHugh's security while the American prosecutor was south of the border. High among Pablo's concerns, Regela told McHugh, was his citizenship status in the United States. Pablo wanted a federal promise that no attempt would be made to deport him back to Mexico after he had served time. If he was going back to the United States, he wanted to *stay* in the United States.

Regela cautioned the American prosecutor that Ojinaga was another world: "There are going to be people with machine guns around and people smoking dope."

McHugh thought it over. He had followed the investigation into Acosta's organization even before the task force
case had been created earlier that year. Everything the task
force knew about Pablo Acosta, he knew. To him, Pablo Acosta seemed by far the most sinister person he had ever come
across in his years as a prosecutor. This was one adversary
he wanted to meet face to face. But caution prevailed when
he started asking himself what he might be getting himself
into. Regela insisted that the Ojinaga crime boss was a man
of his word. But what if Pablo had an ulterior motive,
McHugh pondered? What if, for example, he intended to have
someone take a photograph of them together? If that was
his intention, did Pablo think he could then manipulate a
federal prosecutor and the U.S. government with an embar-
rassing photograph?

After considering Pablo's offer, McHugh called David
Regela into his third-story office at the federal courthouse in
downtown El Paso to inform him of his decision: "Tell Pablo
Acosta that if we're going to talk, it will be after he gives up,
not before."

At their next meeting, Pablo only shrugged when Regela
passed on McHugh's message.

Regela left the door to surrendering open. "You know
they want you to give up. If you do it through me, I'll make
sure you get fair treatment."

By October, months after Regela had introduced Gene
the Bean to Pablo, the informant still had not provided much
useful intelligence to the American agent. He was only just
beginning to become accepted inside the Colombian organization. Nor had he made much progress regarding Pablo's
chief obsession: getting rid of Lupe Arevalo. Pablo was becoming angry and suspicious. If the informant had not gotten
his archrival arrested yet, it was because he was pocketing
the money given him to buy heroin from Lupe. Gene was
feeding Pablo a lot of "boolsheet" stories, as Pablo pro-
nounced it. Regela was boolsheeting him too. *Everybody* was
boolsheeting him.

That wasn't true, Regela said. Lupe Arevalo was mistrustful, and with good reason: he had already been in jail in the United States and did not want to go back. He was cautious. After the trip Gene and Lupe made together to Ciudad Juarez, Lupe kept putting the informant off. Finally, Lupe said outright that he did not want to handle the deal. The whole thing just didn't "feel right" to Lupe, Regela told Pablo.

Gene had shrugged when he told Regela about the defeat, saying, "About the only way to get that guy to the United States is to kidnap him."

It was clear that getting Lupe was going to take a fresh approach. Regela paid a visit to the federal police *comandante* in Ciudad Juarez, Guillermo Gonzalez Calderoni, to ask for his help in getting Lupe arrested in Mexico. When Regela returned several days later to inquire about progress, the *comandante* told him coolly it wasn't going to be possible: "He's got protection, the best kind, and there's no way I can touch him."

Regela explained the situation to Pablo and defended his informant. The American agent pointed out that it was in Gene's interest to get Lupe because he would collect reward money from the United States government, up to $25,000, if they could nab Lupe with a couple of kilograms of heroin. And he would be the one to collect reward money for other busts Pablo would help them make, particularly if the Americans could catch some big loads of cocaine and make arrests.

"It's not in his interest to screw you," Regela told Pablo.

Even so, Pablo was getting more and more impatient about Lupe. It seemed that the more Pablo's world contracted, the more he focused on Lupe.

Regela realized just how much of an obsession his rival had become when Pablo solicited him for murder. He offered Regela $500,000 to kill Lupe in Mexico.

"You won't have to worry about money for the rest of your life," Pablo told him.

Regela looked at him incredulously.

"Get off it, Pablo," he said. "Murdering people isn't in my

job description. I'm interested in busting him with dope and I still think we can do it."

A month later, Pablo, increasingly believing that Regela's informant was deceiving him, telephoned Gene at a home in El Paso. Pablo let loose his coca-fanned suspicions and threatened, "I've killed motherfuckers like you for less."

Regela's informant had lived and breathed and survived in the border underworld for three decades. "You mother-fucking wetback Mexican bastard," Gene shouted back. "We're from the same country but I'll show you what I can do to you."

"Well, you can come down here and we'll see how big of a badass you are," Pablo retorted.

Regela tried to reassure Pablo through Mimi Webb Miller, who was now closer to Pablo than just about anybody. Through Mimi, Regela arranged to accompany his informant to Mimi's Miracle Ranch to meet Pablo, to smooth things out and reconcile Pablo and Gene. Regela wanted to be there to make sure that Pablo didn't try to kill his informant in a fit of paranoid rage. The American agent also wanted to meet with Pablo to press him about making him some cases.

Regela learned later that he himself had reason to worry about his own safety. The day of the meeting Pablo asked Mimi if she had ever seen Regela or his informant with hand grenades. Pablo was convinced the American agent had access to fragmentation grenades and was certain Regela was plotting to kill him: "It'd be easy for him to kill me," he told Mimi. "All he'd have to do is toss a grenade into the Bronco when I drive up to your ranch."

In late November Regela and Gene crossed the Rio Grande in a small rowboat at a river crossing at Lajitas, the tiny American tourist town due north of Mimi's ranch. Mimi was waiting for them on the Mexican side. They drove south to her ranch and sat in the shaded patio, tensely waiting for Pablo to show up. An hour after he was due to arrive, they saw a Ford Bronco coming up the road in a swirl of dust. Several hundred yards from the ranch entrance, in a dip where the road went through an arroyo, the Bronco mysteriously stopped. All they could see was the roof of the Bronco and the heads of a couple of men running away from the vehicle and up a creekbed that led to the rear of the ranch house.

"What's Pablo doing? Surrounding the house?" asked Regela.

The Bronco finally drove up to Mimi's ranch house. Hector Manuel Acosta and two other men jumped out with machine guns. Pablo was not with them. One of the men with Hector was called the "young Pablo" and the other neither Mimi nor Regela recognized. Hector coolly told Mimi he wanted to check all the rooms in the house. The gunmen stepped into the two-story stone building and searched all the rooms. When they came back they sat quietly in the shaded patio with their machine guns between their legs. Mimi offered them beer.

Twenty minutes later, Pablo arrived with his trusted nephew, Pedro. Pedro was armed with an assault rifle, and Pablo had his chrome-plated .45 stuffed in his belt. Pablo was not smiling. He didn't offer his hand to Regela or Gene.

Pablo motioned to some chairs and he and Regela's informant sat down face to face, knee to knee. They launched into a long animated talk in Spanish that Regela couldn't follow. Regela assumed that Gene was giving Pablo an accounting of his actions. The two men talked for about half an hour while Pablo's nephew stood sullenly with the muzzle of his the AR-15 pointing at the ground.

These people were getting spookier all the time, Regela thought. With all the crack they were doing, it seemed that Pablo could do a flip-flop at any time, from charming friend to deadly enemy. One snap of the finger from Pablo, Regela imagined, and Pedro could lift that AR-15 and blow Gene and him away.

But Pablo warmed up the more he talked with the informant and by the end seemed positively happy. Evidently they resolved the problem between them because the drug kingpin threw his arms impulsively around Gene and Regela and said with feeling, "God, it's good to see you both again."

The Rio Grande cuts through the Big Bend, forming the international line, as seen here upstream from Boquillas near the Chihuahua-Coahuila state line. Villages such as Boquillas, Santa Elena, San Vicente and others that dot the Mexican side of the river were originally founded as agricultural hamlets, but now have become chiefly staging sites for smuggling activities. (Photo by Terrence Poppa)

Despite the sudden burst of emotion, Regela noted a haunted, distracted look in Pablo's eyes. It was as if he was making an effort of will to focus his mind on what was happening around him, that the Ojinaga drug lord was preoccupied with troubling thoughts.

Following the embraces, Pablo snapped his finger. Pedro, machine gun in hand, went to fetch a stock of customized cigarettes. Pablo lit up, Pedro lit up, Gene lit up.

Regela knew from the beginning that cultivating Pablo as an informant was going to be a long, arduous task. Now he feared that just as he was gaining Pablo's confidence Pablo seemed to be losing it everywhere else: with his drug suppliers, with his patrons in the Mexican federal police and the Mexican army and wherever else he was getting protection. Pablo lately had in fact passed on information to Regela through Gene about planeloads of cocaine coming into West Texas in the area of Lomas de Arena. U.S. Customs had staked out the landing sites and sent up pursuit aircraft, but the loads never came through. Either they were too early, too late, the loads got delivered somewhere else, or the clandestine flights had been postponed. Whatever the reason, the Americans did not get their busts. Regela was getting impatient. They may not have been able to get Lupe Arevalo busted yet. But at the same time, Regela emphasized, Pablo had not been a very big help with the Colombians either.

"You've got to make me a case," Regela said. "I've spent too much time with all this and I don't have anything to show for it. And you know, I'm making some effort so you need to make an effort too."

Pablo took a long drag on a customized Marlboro. "I'll see what I can set up for you."

After reflecting a minute, Pablo told the American agent of his intentions. He had been thinking for a long time of getting out of the drug business altogether. It had been a good life, he said. He had made more money than he could ever spend. Now, however, it was time to retire. As a way of wrapping up his career and satisfying Regela too, the drug lord promised to call all of his main marijuana customers and sell them his entire stockpile of pot. When he did, he would tip Regela off and Customs could pop them as they came back across the river with their loads.

"What about right now? There's no time like the present. If you call them now, I won't leave. I can get some manpower sent down from Presidio and El Paso."

Pablo shook his head. "We've had a lot of rain south of here, up in the mountains. I'd do it right now for you, but I can't get my trucks down there to bring it up here."

He promised to arrange it as soon as possible.

Later that evening Mimi drove Regela and Gene back to the Rio Grande crossing at Lajitas. The sun had already set, and it was twilight when the two men crossed the muddy water in a rowboat to the American side.

Before they stepped into the boat, Regela again pleaded with Mimi to distance herself from Pablo before it was too late. "I wish you would get out of this, Mimi, and get out of this fast. You're going to get hurt." He waved goodbye to Mimi as she stood on the riverbank on the Mexican side against the fading light. Her blond hair was tied back in a bun, and Regela thought how soft and vulnerable she looked.

During the drive back to El Paso on Interstate 10, Regela said to his informant "You know what? I think Pablo knows he's gonna die soon."

"How do you know when a man knows he's gonna die?" asked the informant.

"It was a look in his eyes," Regela said, recalling Pablo's flat, lusterless, haunted eyes. "He just looks like he knows he's not going to live long."

Gene agreed that it was a possibility. His death, they realized, would have implications for both of them. The informant had been able to further his contacts with the Colombians on his own, but he was still working under Pablo's umbrella. Sooner or later the informant would be able to establish himself with the Colombians to the point where he no longer needed Pablo's assistance. But was Pablo going to be around long enough for that to happen?

Chapter Twenty-Five

COMANDANTE CALDERONI

Regela's concern that the newspaper interview could backfire on Pablo proved justified.

One month after the interview with the American reporter, the first of a three-part series about Pablo Acosta was published in the *El Paso Herald-Post* with a front-page photograph of the Ojinaga *padrino* sitting on a bed in the adobe hovel with his arm around Elva Fernandez, the blind girl. The headline read, PABLO ACOSTA. HE SAYS HE IS A MINOR DRUG SMUGGLER WITH A DESIRE TO HELP OTHERS. BUT OFFICIALS CHARGE HE IS A KEY PLAYER IN THE BORDER DRUG TRADE, A MEXICAN GODFATHER.

The stories quoted Pablo about payoffs to the Mexican federal police and his admission to having planted a marijuana field with the permission of the military. The series gave vivid accounts of some of the drug slayings Acosta had been involved in. The stories were distributed by wire services in the United States. In Mexico, the pro-government newspaper chain *Organización Editorial Mexicana* also distributed the reports, but with all references to police and military participation deleted.

DEA officials in Dallas and El Paso and agents assigned to the Organized Crime Drug Enforcement Task Force began taking bets that Pablo would soon be arrested or killed.

The reaction in Mexico came almost immediately. On the third day of the El Paso newspaper series, an FBI agent who worked as a liaison officer between the El Paso bureau and

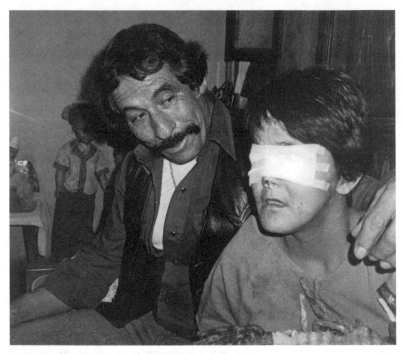

Pablo Acosta enjoyed his role as *padrino* and insisted that he gave most of the money he made from drug trafficking to the poor. Here he comforts an Ojinaga blind girl, Elva Fernandez, who was soon to undergo a cornea transplant in Chihuahua City thanks to Acosta's generosity. The photo was taken during an interview with the author. At first, Acosta would not allow photographs. Then he changed his mind, saying, "Well, if they're going to get me they're going to get me with photos or without photos." (Photo by Terrence Poppa)

the Mexican federal police in Ciudad Juarez happened to be in the office of the federal commander when orders came from Mexico City to go after Pablo. Authorities in Mexico City had unearthed three federal warrants, one several years old that had been issued by a federal judge in the state of Michoacan, for the arrest of Pablo for drug violations. The attorney general's office also ordered jurisdictional changes, giving the Juarez commander authority over Ojinaga. The orders were to take Pablo Acosta dead or alive.

Guillermo Gonzalez Calderoni, the Juarez *comandante*, rushed a squad of fourteen men to Ojinaga via Chihuahua

City. But Pablo had already fled, as well as Amado Carrillo Fuentes, Ismael Espudo and other important traffickers. The federal police searched some homes, set up roadblocks and arrested small-time dealers who had not gotten word of the raid. Pablo was nowhere to be found.

A former rancher, newspaper owner and federal administrator, Gonzalez Calderoni was unlike most Mexican federal commanders of the time. Whereas many of his colleagues were from poor backgrounds, his father had held an important post in Pemex, Mexico's nationalized oil company, and he was said to be independently wealthy. His mother was Italian-American, he was educated in private schools, and he spoke English and French well. People on both sides of the border referred to him by his mother's last name, Calderoni, rather than his father's last name, Gonzalez. Though he had only been a federal policeman for three years before his Ciudad Juarez assignment, the oval-faced, wavy-haired commander had earned a reputation as a town-tamer in rowdy border communities near the Gulf Coast.

At the time of Calderoni's assignment to Ciudad Juarez, American agencies greatly mistrusted Mexican police, particularly the federal agencies. U.S. intelligence files were nothing if not massive compilations of informant information and other intelligence about the involvement of the Mexican federal police system and personnel in protection for organized crime. The Mexican Federal Judicial Police and the Directorate of Federal Security had been implicated all along the border, time and time again, not only in protection for drug traffickers, but for automobile theft rings that preyed on the United States and for *coyote* rings—alien smuggling organizations. It was learned through numerous informants and insiders that the *comandancias* were routinely purchased like franchises from the PGR—the Office of the Mexican Attorney General—by influential and wealthy *comandante*-gangsters for fees ranging into the millions of dollars; then once a position was acquired, the *comandante* remitted a monthly *plaza* fee to his patrons, an amount determined by the volume of revenues derived from criminal enterprises in any given zone.

For American law enforcement agencies, requesting co-operation or passing any information to Mexican police, therefore, was like dealing directly with the Mafia itself. Many in the United States were beginning to question if there were any longer a distinction to be made.

Mexican federal police, conversely, greatly mistrusted and feared the American police.

Calderoni, however, at first seemed to be cut from a different cloth. When he had been in command in Matamoros and Reynosa, American police in the Rio Grande towns of McAllen, Laredo and Brownsville found they could sometimes get useful assistance from the Mexican official. Now Calderoni was ordered into Juarez two days after Gilberto Ontiveros, the most notorious of the Ciudad Juarez traffickers, kidnapped and tortured an El Paso freelance photographer and threatened to kill an El Paso journalist who had written about him. The *comandante's* first official act reportedly was to give his predecessor "twenty-four hours to clear out of town." His second was to kick in the door of Ontiveros' mansion and arrest him and twelve of his henchmen—after getting past the trafficker's pet tiger, boa constrictors and alligators.

Following the jailing of the trafficker, American police officials from the various narcotics enforcement agencies in El Paso invited the new Juarez federal police commander to lunch at a Mexican restaurant in El Paso. Calderoni accepted and entertained his hosts with stories about his exploits up and down the Rio Grande Valley. He told them of the arrest of Ontiveros, of putting the muzzle of his machine gun into the trafficker's mouth to force him to stand up while his men handcuffed him. Fascinated by the exploits, the American police pretended not to notice the pistol strapped to the *comandante's* boot.

He had been sent, Calderoni told them, to clean up Ciudad Juarez, the sprawling city of more than two million people across the Rio Grande from El Paso. Big-time traffickers, some of them top-ranking federal officials like Rafael Aguilar Guajardo, had operated there with impunity for years.

Ciudad Juarez was a town badly in need of housecleaning. The state district attorney there was shown to be running his own marijuana-smuggling operation with a handful of Chihuahua state policemen. Testimony in the federal district court in El Paso at the drug trafficking trial of Cesar Ontiveros, the brother of Gilberto Ontiveros, revealed that the federal and state police stationed in Ciudad Juarez were collecting $12 to $17 from protected traffickers for each pound of marijuana coming through town. These were often loads of 10 tons or more trucked in from large plantations in the mountains of southern Chihuahua. American newspaper investigations showed that auto theft rings that preyed on towns in West Texas and New Mexico were controlled from the state and federal police headquarters. The Chihuahua attorney general, his son and ranking Chihuahua officials had been caught driving automobiles stolen in the United States by these rings.

Important state elections were nearing and public outrage in Chihuahua over worsening economic conditions and blatant corruption was becoming politically dangerous. Many people feared outbreaks of violence, if not outright revolt. Given the political context and the arrests Calderoni was able to make, some in U.S. law enforcement speculated that Calderoni represented a reformist wing of the administration of Miguel de la Madrid, then president of Mexico. Subsequent events disproved the theory, but it gained credibility because of the commander's bold police actions and his adeptness at public relations.

Pablo Acosta, however, was going to be harder to catch than an out-of-control Juarez trafficker. If Pablo went back to Ojinaga at all, it was under the cover of darkness. After an unsuccessful weeklong search, Calderoni left several of his agents in Ojinaga and launched a manhunt for Pablo throughout Mexico. Reports said that the fugitive trafficker was hiding in Chihuahua City, Torreon, Guadalajara, Toluca and Puerto Vallarta. Calderoni followed up each of the leads, but by the end of January 1987 he was still no closer to capturing Pablo than he had been two months earlier.

While on the run, Pablo's problems continued to pile up. The arrest warrant issued three years earlier for the murder of Fermin Arevalo was resurrected. New accusations were surfacing. Two weeks after Pablo fled Ojinaga, Chihuahua newspapers began publishing reports of the murder of a Chihuahua City telephone operator in which Pablo Acosta and a federal security police agent were implicated. The murder took place on October 30, two days after Ojinaga drug lord gave the interview to the El Paso reporter. The badly beaten body of the telephone operator, the mistress of a former DFS agent in Chihuahua City with whom Pablo had had dealings, was found off a highway near Ojinaga.

Mexican police arrested Hugo Lozano, the son of the DFS chief in Ojinaga, and charged him with kidnapping and homicide. In a signed confession he claimed that Pablo Acosta had paid him $10,000 to lure the woman from her home in Chihuahua City and hand her over to Acosta's men. According to the confession, Pablo had some unspecified "accounts" to settle with a former DFS agent, Alfredo Sandoval. Sandoval had refused to meet with Pablo to resolve the problem. So Pablo sent his nephew Pedro, Lozano and a trafficker named El Mudo—The Mute, to kidnap the DFS agent's girlfriend and bring her to Ojinaga as a hostage. But she was beaten to death between Ojinaga and Chihuahua City and her body was dumped by the side of the road.

In the confession, Lozano said he had left the woman in the hands of Pedro and El Mudo, and did not try to pick up the $10,000 from Pablo when he learned the woman had been murdered. Lozano later recanted, saying he was forced to sign a fabricated confession under coercion: the state police threatened to arrest his wife and father if he refused. Nevertheless, a judge issued an arrest warrant for Pablo and his nephew, charging them with the murder.

Despite the frustration of having Pablo slip through his fingers, Calderoni zealously directed the pursuit from his small office at the penitentiary in Ciudad Juarez. The first real break came when his agents captured Pablo's nephew while he was in Ojinaga looking for some heroin.

According to Mexican court records, Pablo and Pedro had been staying at the El Presidente Hotel in Torreon. They had gone to the home of a Torreon attorney with Amado Carrillo Fuentes and Amado's brother Cipriano, where they were drinking and smoking crack-laced cigarettes. Pedro left the party alone and tried unsuccessfully to obtain some heroin to bring himself down from the heart-racing effects of the cocaine, but he did not have any heroin connections in Torreon. Without telling Pablo, he drove his truck back to Ojinaga in an all-night, four-hundred-mile trip north, snorting cocaine along the way to stay awake. He got to Ojinaga about eleven in the morning and called Pablo.

Pablo had been pacing the hotel room wondering what had happened to his nephew. He was furious when Pedro's call finally came through. "You idiot!" he shouted. "Get out of Ojinaga this very minute. Calderoni's men are all over town. If they catch you, they're gonna kill you."

Pedro promised he would leave immediately after taking care of a "few things," avoiding any mention of the heroin he craved so badly. Then he went looking for heroin. He left a message at the home of a pusher that he would be waiting at Samborn's Restaurant. While he was there, someone called the federal police to alert Calderoni's men. They sped up the Chihuahua Highway to the restaurant. By then Pedro was getting back into his truck. He spotted the Mexfeds and managed to escape.

The frustrated federal police went back to headquarters. Several hours later, an anonymous caller told them that Pedro was driving on the main street downtown. After a chase, the agents stopped him in front of a grammar school. Pedro reached for a gun, but the Mexfeds pulled him out of the truck and pummeled him. They took him to federal police headquarters for interrogation.

Twenty-four hours later Pedro was dead.

According to the federal police report Pedro admitted having participated in the killing of Lili Arevalo, Fermin Arevalo, Olga Gutierrez and others. Throughout the interrogation, Pedro acted like a wild animal, the official report stated.

When he wasn't threatening shrilly that "Pablo's people" were going to kill the Mexfeds, he was beating his head against the desk or the wall, the Mexican agents said.

According to the report, the agents called Calderoni to find out what to do with Pablo's nephew. In Chihuahua City for a meeting with high-level federal authorities, Calderoni ordered them to bring Pedro to him in the state capital. The federal police later claimed Pedro died of a heart attack on the way, presumably from all the cocaine and heroin he had consumed. They gave Pedro mouth-to-mouth resuscitation in an unsuccessful attempt to revive him, the official report said. An autopsy performed that same day in Chihuahua City listed the "principal cause" of death as cardiac arrest.

But another trafficker who had been arrested in Ojinaga and brought to Chihuahua City with Pedro told Mexican newspapers later that Pedro was alive when they got to the capital. If he died in custody, he died at the federal *comandancia*. Following the burial a few days later on a hill above the village of Tecolote just south of Ojinaga, Pedro's widow claimed to reporters that Pedro had been beaten to death. His ribs had been broken and he died from a blow to the head. An American policeman who later saw photographs of the body said it looked like one side of Pedro's skull had been caved in with a blow from a rifle butt.

During the fatal interrogation, Pedro told the federal police where he and Pablo had been staying in Torreon. Calderoni rushed to Torreon and the Mexfeds staked out the hotel. But Pablo had already fled. He had learned of his nephew's capture and was out of the hotel minutes later.

The Mexican police were certain he was still hiding out somewhere in the big industrial city. The federal *comandante* in Torreon predicted Pablo would be arrested "any time now." The optimism proved groundless: Pablo had already slipped out of Torreon and disappeared into the rugged Chihuahuan desert, one of the most arid and sparsely inhabited regions of Mexico. After the failed capture attempt, the chief federal prosecutor in Chihuahua called on every police agency in Mexico to assist in capturing Pablo Acosta.

After years of impunity, Pablo Acosta was now the most wanted man in Mexico.

David Regela had not entirely lost contact with the fugitive drug lord. During the early days of Pablo's flight, prior to Pedro's death, Regela had been able to get telephone messages to him through Mimi. Only a week or ten days after Pablo fled Ojinaga, Mimi called Regela in El Paso. Regela could hear Pablo's voice in the background telling her what to say or answering questions Regela had posed. Mimi didn't explain where they were calling from, nor did Regela ask.

Pablo thought he could still work things out and said that he thought he would probably be able to return to Ojinaga soon to take over the *plaza* again. Then they could resume their collaboration. The newspaper interviews had complicated his problems, he said, calling the interviews an "error in judgment." But he didn't think the damage was irreparable.

Regela reminded Pablo of his promise to set up a case for him. "Tell him I need something right now," he said to Mimi. "I spent a lot of time and effort and I need to show something for it."

Two days later, Pablo finally came through. Regela got a call in El Paso from his informant. Wherever he was in Mexico, Pablo knew that a kilogram or more of cocaine was coming across the Rio Grande in El Paso that night near the Asarco copper refinery. Regela and other Customs and Border Patrol agents staked out the river. They spotted a man wade across and get into a van. The American police chased the van down the river highway a couple of miles, and saw the driver jump out while the vehicle was still moving. The van crashed into a building while the smuggler took off on foot. Regela jumped out of his car and chased him. The smuggler dove into a deep canal on the American side of the river and disappeared under the swift current. Regela thought he had drowned, but the smuggler popped up about two hundred yards farther down—right into the arms of a couple of border patrolmen who were waiting for him to come back to the surface. The smuggler fought his way clear and sprinted down to the Rio Grande. One of the patrolmen, a strapping six-foot, four-inch rookie, splashed into the river and grabbed him. But after a few more furious punches were exchanged, the smuggler escaped to the other side, to the safety of Mexico.

Back in the smuggler's van, the U.S. Customs agents found three pounds of cocaine. It was not a large amount compared to the major loads Regela knew were being smuggled through the region, but it showed what Pablo could do if he wanted to—even while he was on the run from the Mexican police.

Regela still retained some hope that Pablo could smooth out his problems in Mexico and return to Ojinaga. Mimi had arranged for Gene to meet with Pablo. At that meeting, Pablo told the informant that he had already made a $100,000 "down payment" on a settlement with the Mexfeds to get them off his back. Things should soon be back to normal, Pablo predicted.

But after Pedro died, Regela realized that it was soon going to be all over for Pablo too.

After learning of Pedro's death, Mimi called Regela. She related to him one of the versions of the death then circulating in Ojinaga—that the Mexfeds had not been content with beating Pedro; they had also chopped some of his fingers off with a bolt-cutter while interrogating him concerning Pablo's whereabouts, a rumor later denied by the family after they had retrieved the body for burial.

But Pablo believed the rumors and had fallen into a deep depression. Pedro was the son of one of his sisters, the son he had never had. Now he had helped bring about Pedro's death. And if they had killed Pedro that way, surely they intended to do the same to him.

When Pablo was not immobilized by depression, he was flying into a rage. He wasn't even thinking any longer about giving himself up to the Americans. He wanted to revenge himself on the Mexfeds for the way they killed his nephew, he told Mimi. He wanted to kill as many of them as he could, even if it meant dying himself.

Rumors later circulated that Pablo even called Calderoni at his office in Ciudad Juarez and challenged him to a *mano-a-mano*, a duel to the death just between the two of them. "You leave your men in Ciudad Juarez, I'll leave mine in Ojinaga," Pablo supposedly said.

The *comandante*, the rumor goes, laughed at Pablo.

From Torreon, Pablo had fled through the northern desert to Santa Elena, the Rio Grande village where he was born.

It was an ideal hideout, on the other side of the river from the United States and the barren, rugged, almost uninhabited Big Bend National Park. The Mexican police could not come for him from that direction without violating American sovereignty. Directly behind the village and for miles to the east and west were the 1,800-foot cliffs of the Sierra Ponce, a limestone mass that had surged from the ground in some tectonic cataclysm eons ago. Five miles upstream, the Rio Grande flowed out of a canyon and meandered into the river valley. Except by daredevils in rubber rafts, the village of Santa Elena was not approachable through the canyon. And if the police tried that route, they would be sitting ducks as they floated down the river. For a police assault, that only left the narrow river valley downstream, a fertile swathe between the river and the massive cliffs. Yet, despite Pablo's problems with the government, many of the *campesinos* in villages downriver or up on the plateau of the Sierra Ponce were loyal to him. He would get word of any unusual movements of people coming from the south long before an enemy could reach him in Santa Elena.

Pablo set about recruiting young men for a standoff. Some of his younger cousins stood guard, and at all times Pablo had at least half a dozen men under arms. He kept weapons stashed inside the adobe, and boxes of ammunition. In the back of the building was a stone storage shed with a thick wooden door that held an arsenal of automatic weapons and ammunition.

In addition to the *pistoleros*, Pablo was said to have brought duffel bags of cash with him, possibly more than a million dollars, that he kept stashed inside the adobe. He kept the cash flowing to make sure his needs were met. People brought Pablo supplies, including a ration of cocaine, either through the mountain-pass road to San Carlos and Providencia or from the United States.

It was easy to get to Santa Elena through Big Bend National Park. Several hundred yards down the two-lane highway from the Castolon Ranger Station was a rutted unpaved road that cut directly south to the river. The dirt road went through a half-mile of mesquite, salt cedar and cottonwood trees that grew densely along the Rio Grande floodplain and ended at a sandy clearing next to the river. Directly across the river was Santa Elena, up on a bluff that jutted out into the Rio Grande, creating a bend where the river was narrow, deep and swift. Visitors to the village of about three hundred people crossed in a rowboat from the American side, then climbed the steep, thirty-foot bank to arrive at the plateau upon which the village was built. Pablo's adobe was a hundred yards south of the river, in front of a cement basketball court that served as the town square.

Following the *padrino* tradition, Pablo was attentive to the needs of the locals. In March of that year, some of the villagers came to him, straw hats in hand, and told him the roof of the three-room grammar school leaked. He sent some of his men to Ojinaga for supplies. The following day they returned with rolls of black roofing paper, lumber, blocks of tar, five-gallon buckets of whitewash, paintbrushes and tar mops. After the supplies came in, Pablo told the villagers to organize a work brigade. The drug lord rolled up his sleeves to supervise the repairs.

A fugitive, Pablo could have disguised his presence in the river village for a few days but not for a month. By the beginning of April 1987, park rangers were reasonably certain from the activity across the river that Pablo was in Santa Elena. Among indicators was the fact that in the past, every time Pablo had been in Santa Elena, someone had always come across in the rowboat and bought up all of the cartons of cigarettes at the park store. Now, every time the store got a supply of cigarettes, someone would invariably come by the next day and buy up all the cartons.

Another giveaway lay in the loud street fiestas with accordion and guitar music and the falsetto cries that accompany *norteño* music. Normally, parties in Santa Elena consisted of small groups of men sitting under the mesquite bushes next to the river drinking beer, but these recent parties were boisterous *pachangas* that took place at all hours of the day and night. The rangers could hear the ruckus from their prefab residences just up the road from the ranger station.

In the middle of the second week of April, five-man teams consisting of Border Patrol and Customs agents began staying in the area to discreetly monitor the region. They remained until the twentieth of April and left as quietly as they had come, never explaining to any of the park rangers the reason for their visit.

Calderoni, meanwhile, got a lead on Pablo's hideout through the wiretapping of telephones of people close to Pablo, including the telephone of his wife Olivia. Based on the wiretaps, Calderoni brought two people in for questioning. From them, the *comandante* learned that Pablo had been staying in Santa Elena and would probably remain there through the following Sunday. Convinced by Calderoni there were no options other than cooperation, one of them drew a map of the village to show where Pablo's adobe was in relation to the rest of the village, and even drew a floor plan of the U-shaped adobe. Through the informant, Calderoni now knew how many gunmen Pablo had at his disposal, the location of other homes where hostile fire could come from, and Pablo's habits from the time he got up to the time, stoned on crack, he went to bed.

Yet the police commander was unable to move against Pablo for the same reason the drug lord had chosen the river village as a hideout. Pablo would be able to flee before Calderoni and his men could get close. If Calderoni flew in by helicopter, he would have to position jet-fuel tankers along the way. And even in the desert Pablo had eyes and ears every-where, people equipped with CB radios who would alert him quickly if helicopters were on the way. If the police came in by land, Pablo would learn of it just as readily. To capture Pablo in Santa Elena, Calderoni understood that he needed the element of surprise. He needed to fly in, but it wasn't possible from the Mexican side. The only solution was to fly into the village from the U.S. side of the river, to avoid Pab-lo's intelligence network.

To do that, he needed the cooperation of the Americans. The Mexican *comandante* looked over the maps and sketch-es spread out on his desk. He picked up the telephone. He dialed the international code and then an El Paso number. When a female voice answered in English, he asked to talk to Bernardo 'Mat' Perez, acting agent in charge of the Fed-eral Bureau of Investigation in the American border town.

At the same time Calderoni in Ciudad Juarez was con-tacting the FBI in El Paso, three-hundred miles downstream Mimi stepped into a rowboat to cross the narrow but deep Rio Grande to Santa Elena. The boatman strained against the current and a minute later the boat touched the other side. She paid the boatman a dollar and climbed the high embankment to the village and walked down the dirt road to Pablo's adobe.

Like many other people still loyal to Pablo, Mimi had been going back and forth, visiting him in Santa Elena even though he had warned her repeatedly of the danger. She was a tar-get because of their close relationship, Pablo told her. After Pedro was killed, she had become more and more afraid to return to her Rancho El Milagro home. Now she was stay-ing with friends in Lajitas.

To Mimi, Pablo looked very ill and extremely depressed, worse than she had ever seen him before. Since the time she saw him last, his stomach had swollen like a pregnant wom-an's. He looked ten years older. Perhaps it was the effect of the cocaine on his kidneys and liver. They didn't know. Pab-lo could not bring in a doctor to Santa Elena for consultation;

nor could he go to Chihuahua City or anywhere else to seek medical help.

They spent that afternoon and night together. Pablo alternated between spates of weeping and calmer moments full of memories of better days. He predicted he was not going to live another two weeks. Either he was going to die from whatever illness he was suffering or he was going to be killed. He could always run again, but he was tired of running. He was going to stand his ground this time and fight.

He told Mimi what he had told other people: under no circumstances were the *judiciales* going to take him alive. He was certain that if captured he would be tortured to death, and in a manner much worse than he believed had befallen his nephew.

Mimi spent all of Thursday morning with Pablo, and a part of the early afternoon, talking in the modest kitchen-dining room-living room in the front of the mudbrick house. Two of Pablo's nephews, half-brothers of Pedro's from Odessa, hung around in the kitchen as Pablo's personal bodyguards.

They talked about the strange things that had been happening at Mimi's ranch. Someone had driven by recently and machine-gunned the ranch house while no one was there. Then it was rumored that a criminal complaint had been filed in Chihuahua City accusing Pablo of the shooting. The complaint allegedly contained Mimi's signature. If it were true that such a document existed, it was absurd. Pablo theorized that someone wanted to kill Mimi and blame it on him. The fabricated complaint would serve as a pretext for accusing him. Pablo pleaded with Mimi to leave the borderlands entirely, to go back to Wichita Falls where she was born and where her family lived.

"If you stay around here, they'll kill you and they'll kill you bad," he said.

"What do you mean by 'kill bad,'" Mimi asked.

He shrugged his shoulders. "They'll make you hurt before they kill you."

Mimi turned to one of Pablo's nephews and asked him to

tell her in plain English what Pablo meant. The nephew described graphically what he thought they would do to her, first as an attractive woman in the hands of a group of brutal men and then as someone they wanted to die a slow and painful death.

"You don't have to say any more," Mimi said, turning pale.

About two in the afternoon Pablo told Mimi she had to leave. Someone was coming to see him and he did not want that person to see Mimi there with him. They bade one another a tearful goodbye. One of the gunmen escorted her down to the river and stood on the riverbank as the boatman rowed her back across the Rio Grande.

Mimi had to walk up the dirt road to get to her car. She turned around before entering the thicket of mesquite trees and looked back at the river and at the high bluff on the other side that hid the village from view. She had a feeling that she was never going to see him again.

Prior to Mimi's visit, Pablo had again considered the option of giving up. Several days before her visit, he sent someone to talk to the sheriff of Presidio County about it. He made similar overtures to the sheriff of neighboring Brewster County and to the Customs Office of Enforcement in Presidio. A customs officer later said the drug lord actually set up a meeting at the river. But he failed to show up.

While Mimi was with him, Pablo had not discussed these overtures. If he had, she would have understood from his face why he hadn't already handed himself over to the Americans. As she walked up the dirt road to get back to her car, Mimi understood that Pablo had lost the will to live.

After arranging a meeting with the FBI's Mat Perez, Calderoni asked for help to organize a raid on Pablo's river stronghold through West Texas. Perez relayed the request to FBI headquarters in Washington, along with Calderoni's conditions: he wanted control of the operation even while in American territory. And the Mexican *comandante* wanted to keep any word of the pending attack from the DEA,

Customs, the Border Patrol and from state and local agencies. He feared a leak could jeopardize the raid.

"If anybody else other than the FBI shows up, I'll call it off," Calderoni warned.

Perez, at the time the highest-ranking Hispanic in the FBI, quickly received the green light to lead the secret mission. Not even the State Department was going to be notified until after the action. Another agent, Leo Gonzalez, a former Marine Corps infantry officer who had done two tours in Vietnam, accompanied Perez to Ciudad Juarez to help Calderoni plan the attack.

The plan was straightforward: take the village by surprise by swooping in from the American side. The FBI would escort him through U.S. territory. He and his agents would fly into the village in their own helicopters while the Americans landed on the U.S. side to block the river in case Acosta and his men attempted to flee north.

The Mexican federal commander arranged for two blue-and-white Bell 212 helicopters belonging to the Office of the Mexican Attorney General to fly to Ciudad Juarez from Sinaloa. The helicopters, each with a squad of well-armed agents dressed in street clothes, arrived at the Juarez International Airport before daybreak. A tanker truck filled with jet fuel was readied in Ciudad Juarez. As a security measure, only two or three men in the Mexican federal police and only Perez and the liaison officer of the FBI and their superiors in Washington knew about the coming raid.

The night before the raid, Perez telephoned fourteen agents in El Paso and four others in Midland, Texas. He ordered them to report for duty at six the next morning. "Get a good night's sleep," he told them. "You will receive instructions in the morning."

Early the next morning, the FBI agents drove to Biggs Army Airfield at Fort Bliss, on the east side of El Paso. An army helicopter with an FBI pilot was supposed to be waiting for them for an early departure. But permission to use an Army chopper had hit some bureaucratic snags, and authorization still had not been obtained. Perez and other

FBI agents in Washington ended up on the telephone with the Pentagon for several hours before getting a helicopter released.

Meanwhile, at the Juarez International Airport, about fifteen miles south of the huge American military base, seventeen unshaven Mexican federal agents, for the most part men in their twenties or early thirties, gathered around Calderoni in front of the two blue and white PGR helicopters, to hear last minute instructions from him and from Leo Gonzalez, the FBI liaison officer. Gonzalez had driven across the border before dawn and made use of some of the time to instruct the agents in combat tactics. A decorated Vietnam vet, the FBI agent had seen plenty of combat as captain of a Marine Corps rifle company. He was to fly in one of the Mexican helicopters.

The Mexican commander was wearing fancy cowboy boots, gray stretch Levis and a tan flack jacket. He was holding a Kalashnikov assault rifle and wore a Colt .45 semi-automatic pistol in a belt holster. Calderoni's informant, a short, thin man about thirty years old, was standing to one side in handcuffs, his eyes cast to the ground. The luckless informant was being forced to accompany the assault team to point out Pablo's house when they reached the village—or he was going to be thrown out of the helicopter, he had been warned.

After explaining the purpose of the mission, Calderoni gave last minute instructions: "The most important aspect of this operation is your safety. I want Pablo Acosta taken alive. But not if your safety is jeopardized."

Seventeen men had to take an entire village of three hundred people in which every male villager old enough to carry a gun was a possible Acosta sympathizer or outright *pistolero*. They had to secure the village, round up all the men they could, eliminate any snipers and isolate Pablo Acosta. Their only advantage was surprise. It was going to be dangerous, and there could be casualties.

The Mexican agents were dressed in faded blue jeans and wore bulletproof vests. All were armed with AR-15s and

Kalashnikovs. None of them gave any sign of wavering. To the FBI liaison, Calderoni's men seemed well trained and well disciplined. Every time Calderoni addressed them, they snapped to attention: "*Sí, mi comandante*," or "*No, mi comandante.*"

Drawing on his combat experience in the jungle villages of Vietnam, the FBI agent discussed airborne assault and insertion tactics with the two Mexican pilots: circle the village with the door at an angle towards the target; let one of the choppers descend for the agents to jump out and secure a perimeter while the other circles above for cover, then repeat the maneuver to allow the second chopper to descend.

Calderoni waited impatiently for word from Mat Perez, who was still frustrated trying to get an Army helicopter. Calderoni, who had hoped to leave just after dawn, was concerned their mere presence at the airport could compromise the operation. Though parked at the far end of the airport runway, the two blue and white PGR helicopters stood out.

When word from the American side finally came, the assault team climbed aboard the helicopters, putting the handcuffed informant in the lead helicopter with Calderoni. Ten minutes later, the two blue-and-white aircraft were whirling over the Rio Grande. A few minutes later, they joined up with the olive-drab Huey carrying the FBI agents. Bristling with machine guns, the three choppers flew two hundred miles southeast to the Border Patrol airfield at Marfa, where they refueled under the quizzical stares of the airfield workers.

On the way down, the Mexican agents were getting restive and trigger happy. At one point, the FBI liaison radioed frantically from Calderoni's chopper that the Mexfeds wanted to fly low to shoot some big horn sheep they had spotted on a mountainside for target practice.

"Tell them they can't do that!" Perez radioed.

"I'm trying to!" the FBI liaison radioed back.

After refueling, the assault force flew another hundred miles southeast and landed in an isolated valley ten miles from the Big Bend Park Headquarters at Panther Junction. There, a park ranger, the four FBI agents from Midland

and a van full of supplies that had been driven out from El
Paso joined up with the three helicopters. An FBI spotter
plane circling overhead at 15,000 feet had coordinated the
rendezvous.

The ranger was needed as a guide though the mountainous Big Bend to Santa Elena. The FBI also needed to
exchange some gear. As the assault force flew down, the
FBI liaison and the Mexican commander concluded that the
bulletproof vests the Mexfeds had been outfitted with would
not be worth much against machine-gun fire. They were designed for protection against handguns. The FBI agents, on
the other hand, had brought along combat vests lined with
50 pounds of armor plating. These vests were surplus equipment that had once been favored by helicopter crews in
Vietnam because of the thick armor plates and the high ar-
mored collars. The FBI agents pulled these heavy vests out
of the supply van and gave them to the Mexican agents.

The sun was going to set in about half an hour, nearly the
time it would take to reach Santa Elena. At the most, they
could count on forty-five minutes of light to pull off the attack. None of the helicopters had landing lights. Perez
suggested they wait until the next morning, but Calderoni
looked at the sky, then at the helicopters and at his men.

"If we wait until tomorrow, somebody is going to get word
to Pablo and he'll be gone before we get there. My men are
ready, so let's just go ahead and do it."

Everyone scrambled back into the helicopters. The park
ranger joined the American helicopter. With the ranger to
show the way, the FBI helicopter was to lead the Mexican
choppers as far as the river, twenty-five miles to the south.
At the Rio Grande, the American chopper would set down
on the wide sandbar opposite the Mexican village. The FBI
agents were to fan out along the river.

Simultaneously, the Mexican assault force would swoop
directly into the village and take out Pablo Acosta.

Chapter Twenty-Six

SANTA ELENA

When the three helicopters took off from Panther Junction, in Santa Elena the older village women were at their chores, expecting their husbands and sons back from the fields any minute.

Several homes away from Pablo's adobe, under a tall cottonwood tree on the other side of the street, two dozen boisterous men were standing around an open fire roasting a calf that had been impaled on a long iron rod. April 24 was the birthday of Fidel, one of Pedro Ramirez Acosta's half-brothers and one of Acosta's bodyguards. The entire village had been invited to the fiesta. Men in straw cowboy hats and western dress were crowding around the firepit or were pulling bottles of Carta Blanca or cans of Tecate from coolers. A few of the drug lord's hired guns were there, conspicuous because of their machine guns; the rest of the men had either returned early from the fields or were among a growing number of village youth who were much too ambitious for farm labor any more.

Pablo was not present at the little fiesta. Earlier that day, two women had come to visit him, and now they were returning to the river accompanied by Pablo and a brown mongrel dog Pablo had adopted. Enedina Ortega, the wife of the mayor, watched Acosta and the two women walk by her modest adobe house, followed by the dog. She ran a two-table restaurant from the patio of her home, which lay between the river and Pablo Acosta's adobe. Anyone going to and from the river had to pass by her home. Some of Acosta's visitors occasionally stopped at her shaded patio for a soda or a meal of tacos and beans that she prepared in her kitchen. A lot of visitors from the other side had paid calls on Acosta during the last two months, but she had never seen the two women before.

"*Buenas tardes, señora,*" Pablo said to her as he and his companions passed in front of her home.

"*Buenas tardes, don Pablo,*" she replied, using the title of respect.

Having a man like Pablo Acosta for a neighbor was not easy on the nerves. For years Pablo Acosta had come and gone, and there had never been any trouble. Now rumors were flying that he was being chased by the *judiciales* and he was preparing for a standoff. His adobe was only three houses away from hers. She looked at her children who were quietly going about their business in the house. The thought of what could happen, of bullets flying and people being shot to death, made her pray that Pablo and his men would find some other place for a showdown.

Enedina watched Pablo and his guests stroll to the edge of the bluff a hundred yards further down the road, where the village ended and the swift-moving river began. They disappeared down the path, heading for the rowboat operated by her son.

Ten minutes later Pablo returned from the river, this time with only the dog in tow, heading back to his adobe. She saw some of the men at the fiesta wave their beer bottles and whistle for drug lord to join them, but he waved back and continued toward his house.

It was at that moment helicopters arrived, with a terrifying *whump-whump-whump* of rotor blades. One landed on the American side; two others screamed into the village and circled at a sharp angle just over the rooftops.

The men around the open fire scattered. A man with a machine gun ran out of Pablo's adobe and took aim at a helicopter that was hovering low while dropping men onto nearby rooftops and into the street behind where the fiesta had been underway.

Pablo recognized the informant, who was leaning out of the helicopter to point out Pablo's house. Pablo shook his fist and shouted, "Traitor!" He and the other man sprinted into the door of Pablo's adobe.

Enedina Ortega saw one of the helicopters hover fifty yards behind her home above the recently planted corn field, the blast of air flattening the young plants and raising clouds of dust. Men armed with machine guns jumped into the field even before the chopper touched ground. Ducking their heads, the Mexican federal agents fanned out as they ran toward the slope leading up to the village.

Her eldest son was still at the river with the rowboat. Her husband had not yet returned from the fields. She ran into the house and latched the screen door with trembling hands. Just as she was doing so, a young man wearing a heavy bulletproof vest and holding a machine gun appeared in the doorway. *"Judicial federal!"* he shouted. The federal policeman could not have been much older than her eldest son, but there was a toughness in his eyes and in his mouth she hoped she would never see in her son.

"Who lives here?" the agent demanded.

"The mayor. I am his wife."

"Who else lives here?"

"My sons."

"Open up!"

She unlatched the door, her hands still shaking. Her youngest daughter clung to her legs and burst into tears. The young, unshaven Mexfed stepped into the kitchen, his machine gun at the ready. He looked quickly to the right and left, searching for any hint of a gun barrel or for someone trying to hide. He took a step toward the bedroom. Just as he did, the terrified mother ran in front of him, bumping against the barrel of his machine gun. "They are just boys! They have nothing to do with those people," she pleaded.

The agent looked at her. "Nothing's going to happen to any of you, *señora*. Get your children down on the floor and stay on the floor and you will be safe."

He turned and ran out the door.

She could hear sporadic machine-gun fire and the roar of a helicopter as it swept back and forth over the village. Her adolescent sons were in the bedroom lying flat on the concrete floor below the level of the windows, behind the protection of the thick mudbrick wall.

The raid was so sudden that Pablo's gunmen, caught out in the open, had abandoned their weapons in panic and tried to make a dash for it with some of the young villagers who had been partying with them. But the blue-and-white helicopters quickly herded the fleeing men back into the village by shooting in front of them. Several pickup trucks full of men barreled down the main road towards the action, but sped away when the helicopter swooped down and fired at them.

The men from Calderoni's chopper had run up the hill from the cornfield to assist other agents in rounding up villagers and in searching homes. They herded every male villager they could find into a street several houses away from Pablo's adobe. The villagers were made to lie facedown with their hands and legs spread apart. In all, there were about three dozen captives.

Other of Calderoni's men simultaneously searched all of the homes in the vicinity and warned the frightened residents to get under cover. Several men were pulled out and made to join the other prisoners.

It had taken less than ten minutes to secure the village, miraculously without a single casualty. By radio, Calderoni kept his FBI counterpart up to date on the progress of raid.

With the first sweep of Calderoni's helicopter into the village, the informant had seen Pablo run into the adobe and had pointed the U-shaped home out to the Mexican commander. After rounding up all the male villagers the agents could find, Calderoni ordered his men to surround the drug lord's home on three sides. All the shutters and doors were shut. Above, one of the helicopters ranged back and forth across the village looking for snipers.

His Colt .45 drawn, the Mexican police commander shouted

Two views of Pablo Acosta's adobe hideout in Santa Elena after the shootout and fire. The exterior view shows the front of the house, where much of the gunfire was concentrated. Inside, two village girls examine the ruins of what had been the kitchen and living room. (Top photo by Terrence Poppa. Bottom photo courtesy of Carolyn Cole)

through a bullhorn. "This is *Comandante* Guillermo Gonzalez Calderoni of the Federal Judicial Police. We have you surrounded, Pablo. Give up!"

He repeated the order several times.

While the search of neighboring homes and the roundup of possible gunmen and sympathizers progressed, Pablo had jammed magazine clips into each of the semiautomatic rifles in his arsenal. He piled loaded clips beneath the windows throughout the adobe. He strapped a bulletproof vest on over his dark-blue cowboy shirt, which he found difficult to do because of his swollen belly. He had armed at least a half-dozen men but now only two were in the house with him at the critical moment and he realized the others were not going to be of help. He did not know their fate. They had been either captured or killed. Some of his other men were out of Santa Elena on errands.

He had been vilely tricked. Who would have thought the Mexican police would come from the American side? One of the two remaining men was his nephew, Fidel, from Odessa, the one who had run out of the adobe, taken aim at the helicopter, then sprinted back; the other man was Jesus, a peasant from the Ojinaga region who had arrived in Santa Elena that morning to deliver a large amount of pesos to Pablo.

After Pablo and Fidel ran back into the building, Pablo shouted to them, "We're screwed. They've got us surrounded. I don't know about you, but they're not going to take me alive." He told Fidel and Jesus they could give up if they wanted to; there was no point in them dying too. Then Pablo ran into a back room and began preparing his weapons.

Fidel and Jesus stared in confused and frightened silence at the kitchen floor. They decided to fight.

The moment Calderoni identified himself and shouted for them to come out, Pablo and the two remaining gunmen stuck their rifles through windows and began shooting. About a dozen of Calderoni's men opened fire simultaneously with their assault rifles to cover the *comandante* and two of his men as they ran up to the front of the house. One of the agents,

Ranulfo Galindo, kicked in a door. The moment he stepped into the room, the Mexican agent saw Pablo aiming a machine gun at him from the doorway of one of the rooms. Pablo fired two bursts and hit Galindo four times. Three rounds hit the armor plating of the vest; one of the bullets tore through the Mexican agent's upper left arm. The impact knocked him to the ground. But as he fell backwards, the wounded agent squeezed the trigger of his automatic rifle and managed to fire a dozen rounds through the door at Pablo.

Calderoni and another agent grabbed Galindo by the jacket to pull him to his feet. Crouching, they sprinted to the wall of a neighboring house to get out of the line of fire. Blood was pouring down the wounded agent's arm and dripping in a continuous stream from his fingertips. The *comandante* ordered his men to keep firing on the house and radioed to Mat Perez.

Calderoni shouted into the radio: "I've got a man down. I'm sending him across by helicopter."

The wounded agent was helped aboard one of the Mexfed choppers and taken to the U.S. side, where the FBI agents stanched the bleeding and flew him to a road nearby where the FBI spotter plane had landed. The plane flew the injured agent to a hospital in Alpine.

Meanwhile, two of Calderoni's agents kicked in the door to the kitchen. Fidel, alone in the room, threw his hands in the air. The agents pulled him out of the building and pushed him face down with the rest of the captives.

When the helicopter returned from the American side, Calderoni ordered the firing to stop and in an instant the deafening gunbattle gave way to utter stillness. The adobe fortress had been hit by hundreds of rounds. Broad sheets of plaster had fallen wherever the bullets had gouged into the structure, forming white piles of debris at the foot of the walls. Many of the wooden shutters had been shot to pieces.

Bullhorn in hand, Calderoni shouted: "Pablo, you don't have a chance. Come out with your hands up."

The bullhorn carried across the river and the FBI agents along the river could hear the Mexican commander clearly.

Pablo and his remaining gunman answered with more

bursts of machine-gun fire. Though he had appeared listless and ill before, Pablo was now a dynamo of adrenaline-fueled and hate-filled action. He fired first from one window, then another, from one side of the adobe to the other side. Both he and his remaining gunman held their machine guns by one hand and fired blindly over the windowsills.

Return fire ripped through what was left of the shutters and struck the plaster-covered walls behind them. As long as they kept their heads below the level of the window frames, they were safe: bullets don't ricochet easily off mudbricks.

The Mexican police had reached the village shortly after six o'clock. By 6:30, they had rounded up every potential sympathizer and surrounded Pablo's adobe. For the next hour the Mexfeds and the drug lord of Ojinaga shot back and forth in furious exchanges. Calderoni periodically let up on the shooting to give the besieged trafficker the opportunity to give up. Each time Pablo shot back, starting another round of intense gunfire.

The only time anyone heard Pablo say anything was at about 7:30, when the village was completely dark. The drug don shouted back from behind one of windows: "Go fuck your mother, Calderoni! You're not going to take me alive! If you want me, come in and get me!"

On the American side of the river, the FBI agents had heard the Mexican commander at various times threaten to lob smoke grenades, tear gas cannisters, ram the building with a truck or burn him out. Making good on the threats, the Mexicans lobbed smoke grenades and tear gas into the abode, but Pablo still would not surrender. The two-foot thick adobe walls held firm when an agent, ducking behind the dash board, tried to ram in one of the walls. On Calderoni's orders, he backed up the truck out of range and several of the agents pumped gasoline out of it into buckets. One of the agents ran up to the side of the adobe and threw gasoline onto the roof; another threw a torch onto the roof. The dry ocotillo branches that formed the base of the roof quickly caught fire and flames spread. An explosion of bullets, too rapid for even ten men to fire, suddenly came from one of the rooms where crates of ammunition were stored. Bullets expoded like strings of firecrackers. The burning rounds continued to go off for several minutes.

"Hold your fire!" shouted the remaining gunman, Jesus, from another part of the adobe, as he came running out with his hands up. The Mexfeds grabbed him and pulled him away, leaving only Pablo Acosta alone inside.

Calderoni waited a few more minutes. They heard a few more bullets going off inside the adobe. Calderoni signaled to one of his men to look through a window from which they believed Acosta had been shooting. While others provided cover, the agent ran bent over up to a wall. Straining his neck, he looked in. The agent could see someone lying slightly propped up on a bed. It looked like his eyes were half open, but he wasn't moving. He was holding an automatic rifle and a pistol. "I see him. I think he's still alive!"

The flames were quickly spreading to that part of the adobe. Jesus, the gunman, was brought before Calderoni. He said he thought Pablo was dead, that Pablo had been wounded earlier and was lying on a bed in the back of one of the building's wings. He had been bleeding and may have bled to death. Calderoni ordered the agent, who had his back to the wall of the adobe with his machine gun held tightly against his chest, to look again. The agent breathed deeply, then shoved his machine gun through the window and cautiously peered farther in than he had before. Acosta still hadn't moved.

"He's dead!"

The agent motioned to Calderoni, who ran up to the window shouting orders to pull Pablo's body out before the entire building went up in flames and the body burned beyond recognition.

One of the agents jumped in through the window while two others ran in through a back door. A *bandido* to the very end, Pablo was still clutching a machine gun in one hand and his .45-caliber semiautomatic pistol in the other.

He died while waiting to shoot anyone who came through the door.

They dragged his body out of the smoke-filled adobe and

into the dirt street. He was still clutching the .45. One of the agents pried it loose from his hand and gave it to the *comandante*. In the light of the flames, which had spread through the house and were now shooting through the roof on one side, Calderoni unstrapped Pablo's bulletproof vest. The only wound was in the back of the head. There were several bruises on his chest, evidently caused by the impact of bullets against the vest. Except for the trickle of blood above an eyebrow, Acosta looked like he was sleeping.

Calderoni pressed the transmitter button of his portable radio. "I need your help over here," he said to Perez.

The FBI agent radioed back that he was not authorized to become involved in a gunbattle in Mexico.

"*Pablo ya está muerto*—Pablo's dead," Calderoni said. "It's all over. I think he killed himself."

The Mexican police commander repeated several times, as he pressed down on the transmitter button: "*Acosta ya está muerto.*"

The FBI helicopter still had not returned from its task of ferrying the wounded Mexican agent. Calderoni therefore sent his own helicopter to fetch the FBI agent. Perez saw flames shooting from from the roof of Pablo's adobe as the chopper rose above the river. After the helicopter landed on the basketball court opposite the house, Perez leaped out and saw a line of men leaning with outspread arms against the wall of a nearby building. Other men, perhaps two dozen, were lying face down further down the road in two rows, head to head. A Mexican stood guard over them with orders from Calderoni "to shoot the entire line if any one of them tried to get up."

Three teenage boys had been sitting the entire time on a doorstep not far from the action with assault rifles across their laps. All three were in a state of shock. When it was all over, someone noticed them, grabbed the weapons and made them join the line of prisoners.

Calderoni wanted to take all of the captives back to Ciudad Juarez the same way the assault force had come. But the FBI agent told him it would not be possible to do so through the United States. The men had not committed any crimes in the United States and there would not be any legal way to hold them once they crossed the river. Calderoni had all the prisoners photographed with a Polaroid camera and later released all but three: Fidel, Jesus, and a third, older man nicknamed El Perro—The Dog—for his long jowls. El Perro had been captured in front of Acosta's adobe just after the Mexfeds landed.

The three prisoners were hogtied and thrown into the back of pickup trucks that Calderoni commandeered. He ordered three of his men to drive them back to Ciudad Juarez on the Mexican side. The agents left with the prisoner but returned shortly. Up the road, the agents were warned of a possible ambush and came back to ask for the American bullet-proof vests again. After Pablo Acosta was killed, everyone had taken the heavy vests off; but now these agents thought it prudent to don them again until they were clear of the village and high into the mountains.

One of the Mexican agents took Polaroids of Pablo's sprawled body while other *judiciales* searched the center of the village for weapons. They found four thousand rounds of ammunition in a house across the square from Acosta's and smaller quantities of ammunition and some weaponry in other buildings. Because of the darkness, they didn't dare venture far beyond the center.

Calderoni and Perez examined the body. It did seem that the drug lord had killed himself, but it would take an autopsy to confirm the cause of death. Perez noted some bullet impacts on the backside of the Pablo's bulletproof vest, and questioned why there were not any bruises on the drug lord's back.

One of the Mexican agents explained the likely reason for the bullet marks: in Mexico it is not unusual for someone to shoot a few rounds of various caliber at a bulletproof vest before ever wearing it "to see if it works."

Both Calderoni and the American FBI agent were concerned about their vulnerability. Sooner or later, the shock of the assault would wear off and villagers sympathetic to the fallen drug lord could start sniping at them. Pablo's body was carried to Calderoni's helicopter, which was sitting on the concrete basketball court. Mat Perez climbed aboard and lifted Pablo from under the arms while Mexican agents on the ground pushed the body in. The FBI agent was struck by the strong odor of tobacco coming from the dead drug trafficker.

Once all the seized weapons and ammunition were loaded aboard, the Mexican helicopters with their assault team lifted off. They flew to the American side and were joined by the FBI helicopter.

Pablo's body had been placed next to the passenger seats parallel to the door. Orange peels and crumpled paper lunch bags littered the floor. As the helicopter maneuvered out of Santa Elena, the body kept rolling back and forth. The weary agents put their feet on the body to keep it from rolling around and banging into the wall.

It was pitch black outside and none of the helicopters had landing lights. Perez arranged by radio for a landing site. Every available automobile was brought into action, including the personal vehicles of the rangers living in a clutch of homes near the park station, a couple of miles from the river. On a field across from the ranger homes, the vehicles formed a large circle, illuminating the night for all three helicopters to land.

The FBI agents, still wearing combat gear and camouflage overalls, crowded around to look at the body of Pablo Acosta while it was still inside the helicopter. An agent from Midland, one of the two American agents who had visited Acosta in Ojinaga eight months earlier to question him about the rumors concerning Libyan terrorists, leaned down and took a close look at the face. Acosta had shaved off his mustache, but there was no mistaking the gold dental work, the high cheekbones and all the scars.

"Yeah, that's Pablo Acosta all right," he said.

Other FBI agents identified him from the few photos that existed—including the ones that had been published five months earlier by an El Paso newspaper. Some of the Mexfeds

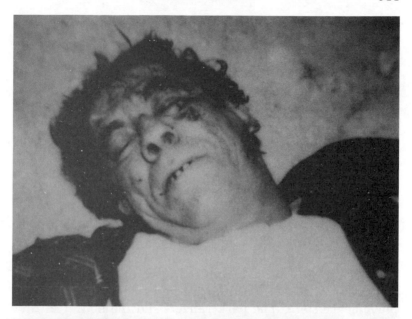

An hour after Mexican federal police helicopters flew into Santa Elena and trapped him in his adobe with two gunmen, Pablo Acosta was dead. His body was dragged out of the blazing home, which the Mexican police had torched. His last words were: "You'll never take me alive!" (Photo courtesy of the DEA)

also acknowledged that it was Acosta, as did the informant, brought up to the helicopter in handcuffs to examine the body.

Some of the Mexican agents repeated that they thought Acosta had killed himself. One of the park rangers and one of the FBI agents pried open Acosta's mouth and looked inside with a flashlight. The roof of his mouth appeared blackened, but they could not find a hole in the back that would explain the wound at the base of skull. It looked like he had been hit from the side. Later, Perez learned that the blackening was very likely the result of years of smoking crack.

While the Mexican and American agents milled around the helicopters, one of the park rangers went to fetch a body bag from the ranger station, where a supply was always kept for the inevitable auto accidents and river drownings. Another ranger returned from the town of Study Butte, an hour away, with $27 worth of ice he had purchased from a convenience store. The park rangers slid the body feet first into the bag from the floor of the helicopter, packed the bag with ice, and left it zipped up under one of the Mexican helicopters. Park rangers armed with M-16s stood guard over Pablo's body and the three helicopters overnight.

The debate about how Pablo Acosta died continued at a restaurant in Study Butte where the FBI and Mexican federal agents were taken to eat and to stay the night. The consensus later was that Galindo, the wounded Mexican agent, may have hit Acosta early in the battle or that the drug trafficker was hit later, but before the fire started. Acosta continued fighting until he was too weak from the loss of blood. Then he lay down on the bed but kept shooting through the window until he bled to death. The agents who found his body noticed hundreds of expended shells next to the bed.

Though the autopsy results later performed in Ciudad Juarez were never released, sources close to the coroner's office there said that both the angle of entry and the absence of gunpowder burns near the wound ruled out suicide.

The next day, Calderoni wanted to fly back to Ciudad Juarez early with Acosta's body, but the return was delayed

Guillermo Gonzalez Calderoni (fifth from left) poses with Mat Perez of the FBI (right of Calderoni) and with some of the Mexican agents who took part in the attack on Santa Elena. Pablo Acosta's body, inside a body bag provided by the U.S. Park Service, is lying on the ground next to the helicopter. Several years later, Calderoni defected to the United States and provided the U.S. government with detailed information of the high-level involvement of the Mexican government in drug trafficking. (Photograph courtesy of Bernardo 'Mat' Perez)

by a string of frustrations. The tanker truck from Ciudad Juarez had broken down repeatedly after leaving El Paso, for the last time at Maverick Junction, near the Study Butte entrance on the west side of the national park. The three helicopters flew from the ranger station to the junction for refueling, and had landed in single file on a dirt road that led south to the river. The tanker truck fuel pump failed; when they at last got it going, the nozzle started spewing mud. The FBI radioed to Marfa to get a Border Patrol tanker sent down. Once the helicopters were finally fueled, the motor of Calderoni's helicopter would not start. His agents had to jump-start it using jumper cables one of the park rangers had in a truck and the battery from the other blue-and-white helicopter

By afternoon the temperature was nearing 100 degrees. One of the rangers was again dispatched to Study Butte for more ice to replenish the body bag, which lay in the *comandante's* helicopter like a crumpled traveling bag.

While they waited for the fuel truck to arrive from Marfa, Mimi Webb Miller and Acosta's daughter Karen drove up to the FBI helicopter in the red checker cab that Mimi kept in Lajitas. Mimi had stayed in the tourist town the night before and had quickly learned about the shootout in Santa Elena. The news had quickly spread throughout the region. The American and Mexican commanders watched with curiosity as the two women walked up to them. Mimi introduced herself and Pablo Acosta's daughter. Both had been weeping.

"We want to know if you have Acosta, if he's been killed," Mimi said.

Calderoni nodded and walked away.

"We want to know if we can claim the body," she said to the FBI agent.

"I'm sorry," Perez said, trying to sound both compassionate and firm. "You'll have to go to Juarez and work that out with the authorities down there."

"But he was an American citizen," Acosta's daughter protested.

The FBI agent shook his head. It did not matter. The body was in the hands of the Mexican authorities and they were the ones who would make the decision to release it.

Not long after the women left, the Border Patrol fuel truck arrived from Marfa. By three in the afternoon the international strike force was on its way home—the FBI to El Paso and the Mexican federal police to Ciudad Juarez.

Like a trophy, Acosta's body lay at the feet of the *comandante* all the way back to Mexico.

Acosta's funeral was held on April 28, 1987, in a village south of Ojinaga. It was crowded and was grimly festive, with mariachi and *norteño* groups singing *corridos* in memory of the fallen trafficker.

One went:
>The czar of traffickers is dead.
>Truly the Mafia king,
>He always won respect
>In the villages and towns around.
>Everywhere else he went
>Even the bravest shook with fear.

Another:
>Gone is Pablito, friend of the poor,
>Killed by the government
>In a world that shows no mercy
>For people like that.
>And the gringos,
>Laughing on their side of the river,
>Prayed for Pablito to die.
>Yet he had done nothing more
>Than give them what they wanted.

The mass was held in a chapel in La Esmeralda, an *ejido* next to the Rio Grande five miles upstream from Ojinaga. At first the Roman Catholic parish priest had refused to hold a Catholic funeral—at the downtown church or anywhere else. But the cleric relented after one of the dead drug lord's uncles reminded him that only God could pass judgment on Pablo Acosta and that the priest was not God. Though the body lay in an open coffin in the aisle of the small village chapel, the priest never once mentioned the trafficker by name during the service.

A funeral procession consisting of hundreds of trucks and cars, many with Texas and New Mexico license plates, drove from the river village through the streets of Ojinaga, then continued slowly south on the Chihuahua Highway to the village of Tecolote for the burial. Another thousand people were waiting in silence at a small cemetery on a hill overlooking the village.

Because of the publicity about the death, a rush of reporters and photographers from Chihuahua City, Ciudad

Juarez and Mexico City crowded into the village, waiting for the funeral cortege to arrive. The media presence was exclusively Mexican despite the extensive coverage given to his death in Texas and New Mexico. Reporters there feared the American media was getting the blame by the Ojinaga underworld for drug lord's death. But even Mexican reporters and photographers were threatened and shoved for getting too close as the pallbearers carried the coffin up the hill. One newspaper photographer was punched in the mouth.

Pablo's coffin was placed under a tent where a hole had been dug through the hard caliche two yards from the grave of Pedro Ramirez Acosta, Pablo's nephew, who had been buried there two months before. Pablo's mother and his widow Olivia decided to open the upper half of the casket to allow whoever wanted to view Pablo for the last time. A long line of people quickly formed.

Meanwhile, a mariachi and a *norteño* group took turns singing popular ballads with nostalgic and heroic themes, followed by extemporaneous *corridos* about Pablo's reign as drug lord of Ojinaga.

Finally, Acosta's body was lowered into the ground.

The sequel to Pablo Acosta's death at first held out promise that things were changing, at least in Ojinaga. Following Acosta's burial, the Mexican government cracked down. The state police *comandante* and several of his agents were arrested and taken to Chihuahua City. Hector Manuel, one of Pablo's younger brothers, was arrested for his participation in the killing of Fermin Arevalo and was jailed in Chihuahua City. Important traffickers associated with Acosta, such as Amado Carrillo Fuentes and Ismael Espudo, disappeared.

When a new general was assigned to command the Ojinaga garrison, word quickly spread that this brigadier was not like the ones who had come before him. He was refined and polite. He treated the citizenry respectfully. His wife started a finishing school to upgrade the manners of Ojinaga girls. Malaquias Flores was reportedly thrown out of the general's home after proposing a deal.

It was speculated in Ojinaga that such a general would not last long. The speculation proved correct. Three months later a new garrison commander arrived, bringing with him old ways. By the end of 1987, Customs agents in Presidio began hearing through informants that the Mexican army was again involved in protection. Around November 1987, barely six months after Pablo Acosta's death, the general's troops burned a field of marijuana near El Chapo. Photographs and stories appeared in Chihuahua newspapers. However, reliable informants said the disposal of the drug was a ruse: the troops had brought a truckload of used tires out to the field, covered them with alfalfa, and burned the tires rather than the *mota*. The pot had already been harvested and the soldiers trucked it to town following the rubbery bonfire. Backing up the information were further reports of soldiers boasting about the subterfuge in Ojinaga *cantinas*.

Informants reported that the airlifting of cocaine to Ojinaga from Colombia resumed not long after Pablo died. One of the dirt runways reportedly used for a landing was near the village of Tecolote, within view of the hill where Pablo Acosta was buried.

Ojinaga remained under the jurisdiction of the Mexican Federal Judicial Police in Ciudad Juarez, but the fact that the MFJP was still deeply involved in protection became indisputable after Calderoni was reassigned. Soon after the death of Acosta, Calderoni was promoted to coordinate special anti-narcotics operations from Mexico City. Upon leaving Ciudad Juarez, he stated to the Mexican news media that the city would find his replacement to be a "pleasant surprise." A new group of Mexfeds under the command of Salvador Joaquin Galvan, formerly stationed in Matamoros, across from Brownsville, Texas, replaced Calderoni.

Galvan's criminal activities were soon revealed through a DEA wiretap that had targeted a Mexican marijuana trafficker operating out of El Paso. The wiretap picked up a conversation between a marijuana trafficker and *Comandante* Galvan regarding the arrest of two of the trafficker's drug runners and their 330-pound load of marijuana. Galvan had telephoned the trafficker to demand $70,000 for the release of the runners, the vehicles and the *mota*. American feds later videotaped one of Galvan's men paying a visit to the trafficker's residence in El Paso. The wiretap lead to Galvan's indictment in January 1988 in the federal district court in El Paso along with the El Paso trafficker.

The court action caused strained relations between the Juarez MFJP and American federal police agencies in El Paso. According to informant information received by the DEA, Customs and the Border Patrol, Galvan put up a $25,000 reward to anyone who could point out the vehicle of an American federal agent in Ciudad Juarez so the Mexfeds could plant drugs in it and arrest the American officer for possession. All of the American agencies put out an alert warning their agents from venturing into Ciudad Juarez, even during off-duty hours.

Galvan and his Ojinaga subgroup remained in charge until July 1988 when a Juarez television anchorwoman, Linda Bejarano, her mother-in-law and a third person were machine-gunned to death in their car by ten of Galvan's men at an intersection in a Juarez residential district. For lack of a better excuse, the *comandante* lamely explained that his men mistook her car for that of a vehicle used by a group of cocaine smugglers and thought it necessary to take the action he took. The anchorwoman's husband had a different explanation: Galvan believed the reporter had gathered proof about his involvement in drug trafficking and was fearful she was about to go public with it. Galvan was then reassigned.

Pablo Acosta's memory lived on.

Not long after his burial, he joined the pantheon of the famous dead who are still alive. A thousand people had viewed his body before the casket was sealed and lowered into the ground. Yet rumors soon circulated that it was not really the body of Pablo in the casket. The real Pablo Acosta was still alive. He had cut a deal with American authorities and had been secreted across the border and was now living under the witness protection program. Or, it was rumored he had undergone plastic surgery and was living on a ranch in Sinaloa, or Coahuila or Sonora. Rumors circulated that he had been spotted, alive and well, in Odessa, Chihuahua City, Hobbs and other towns on both sides of the border.

For months after his burial in Tecolote, *corridos* to him remained popular among the peasants. When the projectionist at the Cine Armida, a theater that showed ribald Mexican films, played Pablo Acosta ballads over the loudspeaker at intermission, the audience jumped to its feet and cheered and clapped uproariously.

Nevertheless, what many in Ojinaga recall in the days after Pablo Acosta was killed was a certain buoyancy to the air, as if a tremendous weight had finally been removed from the border. It did not take much to understand why. Gone at last were the terror days of street warfare, midnight kidnappings and murders in broad daylight.

Pablo's death had cleansed the city of its fear.

Ever since Manuel Carrasco, *La Vibora*, murdered Domingo Aranda and transformed the border town into a major drug conduit, Ojinaga has had a recognizable drug lord. But two years after Pablo's death, the question, "*¿Quién está manejando la plaza?—*Who's got the *plaza?*" was still being answered by a shrug of the shoulder and another question: "*¿Quién sabe?—*Who knows?"

A lot of names were discussed: Amado Carrillo Fuentes, the cocaine trafficker from Guadalajara and Pablo's partner in Ojinaga, or one of his many brothers; Lorenzo Hinojos, alias The Mute, one of the suspects in the murder of the telephone operator; Ismael Espudo, the former county commissioner of Van Horn. Manuel Carrasco himself was supposedly seen staying at the Hotel Rohana. Had *La Vibora* finally returned to take back the *plaza* that was once his?

So far, no one has stepped forward to claim it.

At least, not publicly.

EPILOGUE

Pablo Acosta was not succeeded. He was superseded. Amado Carrillo Fuentes, Pablo Acosta's partner for a time in Ojinaga, disappeared when Acosta was on the run. When he reappeared, Carrillo Fuentes was already one of the most powerful crime figure this hemisphere has ever known. From his original base of operations in Ojinaga, he succeeded in creating a zone of control reaching through the entire central Mexico corridor.

What is distinctive about organized crime in the Mexico of the 1990s is how the government-trafficker combines carved up the country into mega-zones to manage the delivery of drugs originating in Mexico, Colombia and other countries to the United States. Under this broad arrangement, Juan Garcia Abrego controlled the Gulf Coast zone, which came to be called the Gulf Cartel. The west coast of Mexico saw the emergence of the Arrellano Felix brothers, the trafficking family behind the Tijuana Cartel. Carrillo Fuentes' organization, which based its far-reaching operations in Ciudad Juarez, came to be known as the Juarez Cartel and operated through central Mexico. It is believed that Malaquias Flores, the former military liaison and radio station owner, eventually gained control of the Ojinaga *plaza,* but answered to Carrillo.

Carrillo learned from Pablo Acosta's failures. It was clear to him that high profile as much as Acosta's own excesses led to his predecessor's end. Thus Carrillo kept in the shadows, expanding his influence quietly, building on his Guadalajara and Ojinaga connections and on his relationship with his jailed uncle, Ernesto Fonseca Carrillo. He underwent periodic surgery to alter his appearance.

The rise of Amado Carrillo Fuentes, drug lord, is essentially the same story as the rise of Pablo Acosta. It is a history of murder, treachery and complicity with authority. It is the numbers associated with Carrillo that fascinate the most: the volume of cocaine he transported through Mexico for the Colombians; the number of aircraft he owned through front businesses; the size of the airplanes and their cargo; the number of people he killed or had killed; the amount of money he paid for protection. American analysts peg the payoff budget between $500 million and $800 million a year flowing to his protectors in government. He was transporting up to eight tons of cocaine at a time in older, converted Boeing 727s or French Caravelles. Four hundred murders are attributed to him and his faction.

Despite Carrillo's cultivated low profile, American intelligence was able to keep track of him. The cocaine smuggling operations in the desert ranches outside of Ojinaga quickly resumed after Pablo's death, but Carrillo eventually shifted his landing and warehousing activities to Ciudad Juarez. He left operations to his brother, Vicente, while he maneuvered in and out of the tangled web of drug interests in different parts of Mexico. He formed a personal relationship with the Cali Cartel leader, Miguel Rodriquez Orejuela. At one point, he spoke with the Colombian on a daily basis by cellular telephone.

In the early 1990s, Ciudad Juarez *plaza* was believed to be under the control of Rafael Aguilar Guajardo, a former DFS commander and top-level trafficker who was related through marriage to a prominent Juarez industrial family. Aguilar was the product of a previous generation, of the 1970s when the Mexican federal secret police organized protection on a national scale, then divided up the nation into zones under the control of regional commanders like Aguilar. But the DFS was disbanded in 1985 following the murder of DEA agent Enrique Camarena. From then on Aguilar fended for himself just like any other trafficker, working out protection arrangements with whoever had the power to make such deals.

Carrillo's control over Ciudad Juarez was sealed with Aguilar's murder. U.S. intelligence picked up information that Aguilar had been complaining to his protectors about all of the money that he was being forced to pay. He was tired of paying. He threatened to go public with information about the Who's Who of protection if he was not left alone. His end came in 1993, two days after making the threat, when he was machine-gunned to death in broad daylight while on vacation in Cancun. Eight of his Juarez lieutenants were simultaneously kidnapped and murdered. American intelligence analysts believe it was Carrillo who arranged the killings on behalf of the authorities. It is also thought that the murder benefited both Carrillo and his narco-political allies: Carrillo's control over Ciudad Juarez was firmed up, and much of Aguilar's estimated $800 million in assets, which included resort hotels, became the private property of members of the Salinas administration or their associates.

Carrillo's low profile did not make him immune from attempts on his own life, but his cult of invisibility saved him. In early 1994, several hitmen entered a Mexico City restaurant where he and several associates were dining. Two of his top aides were riddled with bullets, apparently because the gunmen mistook one of them for Carrillo. Amid the confusion, Carrillo had ducked under the table.

Despite the often deadly rivalry, Carrillo was able to patch together a *modus vivendi* with other trafficking groups, brokering deals with the Colombians for them, arranging for delivery to them in Mexico using his formidable private air force for transportation. For lack of a better term, but to put a label on the growing power, organization and interconnectivity of Mexican trafficking groups, Americans began calling the loose association the Mexican Federation, with Amado Carrillo Fuentes in charge.

The 1990s was an era of unbelievable levels of murder. Like Ojinaga under Pablo Acosta, every Mexican border town became a killing field. Ciudad Juarez, Carrillo's base of operations, was statistically pre-eminent, with more drug-related murders committed there than anywhere else. This fact was a reflection of Carrillo's propensity for ordering the killing of people at the slightest suspicion they were informants—a sociopathic trait which revolted even Pablo Acosta, himself no slacker when it came to murder.

Carrillo enunciated his murder policy in 1986, within earshot of the Customs undercover agent, David Regela, when he said: "It is better for six innocent men to die than for one guilty person to live," referring to his torture-murder of six men to find an informant who had been passing information to the DEA about an underground cocaine stash site. Any time a drug load was seized, therefore, Carrillo assumed a leak, and people involved were tortured for information and then killed. At one point in 1995, Carrillo was believed to have obtained a list of informants on the U.S. payroll. The list had reached the MFJP in accordance with an information-sharing arrangement between the United States and the Mexican Attorney General's Office. Over the next few months body after tortured body was turning up in Ciudad Juarez, as many as sixty men and women.

At his height, through murder, cozy relationship with authority, direct dealings with Colombian cocaine producers, Carrillo Fuentes was bringing $200 million every week into Mexico from the sale of cocaine, more than $10 billion per year, the DEA estimates.

The sum of protection money being channeled to authority was evidence that the power system had reached dizzying levels of criminality. This was confirmed by a series of internecine political assassinations that occurred in quick succession in 1994. The hand-picked successor of Mexican President Carlos Salinas de Gortari, Luis Donaldo Colosio, was shot to death at a campaign rally in Tijuana in March. Then Jose Francisco Ruiz Massieu, leader of the PRI and an ex-brother in law of the president, was murdered. A PRI congressman was also slain.

After a new president took over in December 1994,

investigations into these high-profile killings led right to the Salinas family. The former president fled to Ireland, a country without an extradition treaty with Mexico. Raul Salinas de Gortari, the brother of the president, was arrested for supposedly masterminding the Ruiz Massieu murder. Investigators uncovered a Swiss bank account with $120 million in it, property of Raul Salinas. Allegations surfaced that the president's brother was the Grand Protector of Juan Garcia Abrego, the Gulf Cartel leader and that protection money was the source of the funds in the account. Garcia Abrego, in turn, was linked to the murder of the presidential candidate.

A further scandal broke out in February 1997 when the Mexican government announced the arrest of Gen. Jesus Gutierrez Rebollo, the Mexican Army general who had been appointed drug czar only two months earlier. He was accused of accepting bribes from drug traffickers, and living in a luxury apartment in Mexico City provided by Carrillo Fuentes.

The arrest of the Mexican army general needs interpretation. He was not *suddenly* found out. He was not arrested because he had committed crimes by protecting drug traffickers. He had been involved in protection for years while commander of a key military zone based in Guadalajara. The power elite had benefited from his efforts. He was part of a long-standing mechanism involving both the military and the MFJP to ensure Mexican skies were safe for Carrillo Fuente's drug shipments, and that the drug trafficker's landing sites in northern Mexico were secure. The general was selected for offering as a sacrificial lamb to neutralize the revulsion within Mexico of the now too obvious PRI-government connection with organized crime. And it was intended also to placate an equally revolted United States Congress, which was likely to decertify Mexico's cooperation with the United States in combating drug trafficking.

Gutierrez Rebollo was appointed drug czar by his superiors with the intention of sacrificing him several months later. A month prior to the U.S. Congressional debate regarding certification, therefore, the general was called to a meeting with the Mexican defense minister where he was informed of his sacrificial status. It was reported that Gutierrez Rebollo suffered a mild heart attack upon hearing the news.

The U.S. media, from newspapers to TV networks, jumped on the story, particularly relishing photos of the Mexican general together with the U.S. drug czar Barry McCaffrey, himself a former general, who two months earlier had called his Mexican counterpart a "guy of absolute, unquestionable integrity." This bland assurance easily ranks as one of the most regretted character references in history. It was also a chilling revelation of the depth of incomprehension in Washington of what has been transpiring for decades in Mexico.

Gutierrez Rebollo's connections to Amado Carrillo Fuentes were revealed, along with the fact that the U.S. government had passed on sensitive information to the general about Carrillo Fuentes. The general then presumably revealed to Carrillo what the Americans knew. These public revelations of military complicity with his operations overnight blew Carrillo's still relative anonymity and undermined his military sponsorhip, clearing the way for his arrest. Photos that had been taken of him years earlier were published throughout the world.

Carrillo reacted. He attempted to make a $60 million payment to the military to forestall the collapse of his empire. But it was rejected. Using a phony passport, he began traveling abroad, particularly to Chile where he purchased properties, set up front businesses and appeared to lay the ground for a vanishing act. Part of the disappearance involved further changes to his appearance. On July 3, 1997, he checked into a clinic in Mexico City where three surgeons, one of them a friend who had accompanied him on his trips to Chile, performed extensive facial surgery and liposuction. A radically new Amado was to emerge from the knife, but his heart, weakened from a decade of cocaine abuse, did not withstand the intense, sustained surgery. Amado Carrillo Fuentes died the next day.

Photos of a body in a casket, with a face ghoulishly deformed by unhealed surgery, were published worldwide. It was the inward brought outward, an indelible image of the Mexico of today.

The story of Pablo Acosta was also intimately tied up with the life of another: Guillermo Gonzalez Calderoni, the Mexican federal police commander who killed Acosta at Santa Elena. The *comandante's* success in tracking down and disposing of the doomed Ojinaga drug lord boosted his career within the Mexican federal police and enhanced his image abroad.

The son of a Pemex official, fluent in English and French, intelligent and polished, Calderoni had money and social standing even before entering the Mexican federal police in 1983 as a group commander. He boasted of a personal friendship with Florentino Ventura, then head of the MFJP, who sponsored Calderoni's early career. He told some of his FBI contacts that the operation against Pablo Acosta "made his

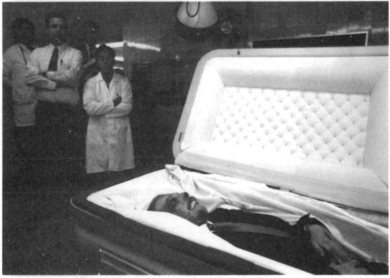

Amado Carrillo Fuentes lies in a casket three days after his freakish death while undergoing plastic surgery and liposuction to alter his appearance. Both the government of Mexico and the U.S. Drug Enforcement Administration affirmed it was the body of Carrillo Fuentes. Looking on are pathologists at the Federal Judicial Police Morgue in Mexico City. (Photo by Andrew Winning/Reuters/Archive photo)

career" in the MFJP. From Ciudad Juarez, he was promoted to Mexico City to handle special anti-narcotics operations. He arrested a number of high-profile traffickers, the most important of whom was Miguel Angel Felix Gallardo, the Guadalajara kingpin. He made himself useful to the PRI-system in other ways. In later interviews with American newspapers, Calderoni revealed a systems-maintenance function when he admitted using his wiretapping expertise to record the campaign conversations of an opposition presidential candidate, Cuauhtemoc Cardenas, during the 1988 presidential race. Such intelligence was of great assistance to Carlos Salinas de Gortari, the PRI candidate who became president of Mexico in December 1988. Salinas was not elected by the people of Mexico, but by the PRI-system that controlled and engineered the outcome—to some extent thanks to the help provided by the *comandante*.

Calderoni's bold, surgical actions against established border traffickers did seem like authentic law enforcement. Americans at first speculated that he represented a reformist wave within the Mexican government. When he burst upon the scene in Ciudad Juarez, he swiftly took down an out-of-control drug trafficker, Gilberto Ontiveros, who had kidnapped and tortured an American news photographer and threatened the life of an American journalist. Within a year of his arrival in the sprawling border town, the *comandante* was flying back to Juarez with the body of Pablo Acosta at his feet.

Calderoni made it known that he was sent "to clean up" the border town, like a sheriff sent to face off desperados at high noon. Impressed by his record, the FBI invited him to a conference in Chicago where the *comandante* was asked to speak about the Mexican police system. Calderoni acknowledged to his FBI audience that problems of corruption existed in Mexico. But he likened those problems to the Chicago of an earlier era, the Chicago of Prohibition and Al Capone. "Mexico is going through a phase in its development," he told the FBI agents.

The Chicago speech showed Calderoni as the quintessential man of the Mexican system. He was a smooth-talking public relations expert, adept at creating confusion about the true nature of his activities. His police actions in Mexico in fact had nothing to do with law enforcement, only with control. This is a distinction that has always been difficult for Americans to grasp. He created the illusion of law enforcement while in fact helping to set up new protection arrangements. Like Gen. Gutierrez Rebollo, Calderoni was an instrument of the system which at that time was using the MFJP and the military to carve out broader protection schemes than ever before, with new players.

Calderoni's role indeed was to clean up, but it was more like a corporate restructuring where some executives get the ax and new officers are brought in.

It should be kept in mind that MFJP *comandantes* were cash conduits for the PRI system. They often bought their positions from their sponsors in the attorney general's office, and had to pay a monthly quota to their bosses for the right to run a zone. They could not pocket all of the money. They were mid-level managers, controlling and regulating organized crime within their jurisdictions. They were obligated to forward proceeds up the chain of command. Though profiting handsomely from these arrangements, Calderoni was only carrying out the policy and directives of his employers. They were the chief beneficiaries of this money-making machinery.

Intelligence regarding Calderoni's involvement in this narco-political arrangement began filtering in through informants who revealed his close ties to a powerful Gulf Coast trafficker, Juan Garcia Abrego. Garcia had created an important drug trafficking organization during the 1980s, based in Matamoros, across from Brownsville, Texas. After Acosta was killed, Garcia began filling the gap in smuggling services by branching into cocaine, developing connections with the Medellin and Cali cartels. He became one of Mexico's most important cocaine traffickers of the 1990s, carving out a mega-*plaza* and masterminding with his governmental associates a vast cocaine smuggling empire later tagged the Gulf Cartel for its broad reach.

Oscar Olivares Lopez, a former Garcia Abrego lieutenant who had become a key FBI informant, provided the most damaging intelligence against Calderoni. Olivares had at first been a marijuana pilot for Garcia, but had moved up in the organization after killing one of Garcia's rivals in self defense. As a trusted associate, Olivares delivered protection money to the local, state and federal officials involved in Garcia's *plaza* scheme. Olivares also served as an informational channel and interface between protector and protected. After becoming an FBI informant, Olivares played a crucial role in the investigation that led to the indictment of Garcia. He was used as a federal witness against many of the drug kingpin's associates who were later arrested in the United States, and against Juan Garcia Abrego himself when the Matamoros crime lord was eventually tried in the United States on drug trafficking charges.

Early in the American investigation into the Garcia organization, Olivares identified Calderoni as one of those on the receiving end of such payments. And in later FBI wiretaps, Garcia is recorded referring to Calderoni as a "brother." According to one FBI investigative memorandum, Calderoni "facilitated the group's drug activities by providing protection and escorting drugs for the group from inner Mexico to the Mexican/United States border as early as 1983." A further report states that Olivares in the past "paid off Calderoni on numerous occasions at the behest of Garcia and is aware of Calderoni's past criminal involvement with the Mexican mafia." These events occurred before Calderoni's assignment to Ciudad Juarez and his successful raid against Pablo Acosta in Santa Elena.

Using such intelligence as leverage, the FBI hatched a plan in February 1988 to pressure Calderoni into bringing about the arrest of the Matamoros drug trafficker. The FBI gave Calderoni the option of cooperating or facing public exposure of his complicity.

Once presented with his options, Calderoni agreed to assist. The Mexican *comandante*, however, was stymied by the phenomenal amounts of money Garcia was spreading

around for protection—by some U.S. intelligence estimates
a half-billion dollars a year.

In 1991, the relationship between Calderoni and the FBI
intensified when he was assigned as the PGR's liaison at the
Mexican consulate in San Antonio. This transfer came about
after overzealous DEA agents kidnapped a Camarena murder suspect in Mexico, Dr. Humberto Alvarez Machain. The
doctor was suspected of injecting stimulants into the dying
agent to prolong the interrogation and torture at the hands
of Guadalajara drug barons, who included Ernesto Fonseca Carrillo, the uncle of Amado Carrillo Fuentes. After
arranging for his kidnapping, the American agents spirited
the doctor out of Mexico and flew him to Los Angeles to
stand trial. But he was eventually released by a federal judge
who rebuked the American agency for resorting to illegal
means to bring him to justice.

Mexican Attorney General Enrique Alvarez Castillo, himself a suspect in the protection of the very traffickers who
had murdered Camarena, then demanded that the United
States play on "an even playing field" by allowing Mexican
federal agents to be stationed in the United States. Mexico
threatened to throw out the DEA unless the United States
complied.

Having the MFJP in the United States was not an American
idea. But it was an exploitable one. Using the intelligence
handle it now had on Calderoni, the FBI pressured the Mexican *comandante* to obtain the MFJP assignment to San
Antonio. Calderoni was soon behind a desk at the Mexican
consulate, a short distance from the FBI field office that
controlled him.

It was during the stay in San Antonio that Calderoni, under pressure by the FBI to take down Garcia Abrego, began
explaining why this would be a difficult task to carry out:
Garcia, he informed the FBI, was obtaining protection from
the Mexican presidential family. The president's brother,
Raul, was the main source of protection. Calderoni went
into detail, derived from his contacts within the Matamoros
trafficking organization. He told the FBI that Raul Salinas,

for instance, had used his influence to try to help the traffickers buy state-owned stevedore companies that controlled
the dockwork at the Pacific port of Salina Cruz and the Gulf
Coast port of Coatzalcoalcos. Though the deal ultimately
fell through, if successful it would have allowed Garcia's
Gulf Cartel to set up sophisticated maritime smuggling routes.

The Mexican government somehow learned of Calderoni's contacts with the FBI, and the elaborate efforts of the
San Antonio bureau to recruit him as a double agent fell
through. In later talks with the *The New York Times* and
The Wall Street Journal, Calderoni said he believed it was
the FBI itself that brought about his downfall. This came
about after an incredulous official at a higher level in the
FBI discussed his allegations about the Salinas administration with the PGR, the Mexican Attorney General's Office.

The *comandante* was instantly recalled to Mexico and
assigned to an out-of-the-way post in Quintana Roo. When
he learned that President Carlos Salinas de Gortari had personally ordered his arrest, Calderoni defected to the
American camp, ending up in a safe house in San Antonio
under the protection of the FBI.

Given his background and his usefulness to the Mexican
system, Calderoni had reason to aspire eventually to become,
under some future PRI president, Mexico's number one cop
and benefit from all of the opportunities that such a position
offered. But Calderoni was defeated by the truth. He is now
living in self-imposed exile in Texas, comforted by the wealth
he amassed, but fearful of the political class he betrayed.

None of the allegations Calderoni made to the FBI about
the Salinas administration were made public at the time. But
these same allegations began to surface in Mexico following
the assassinations of Colosio and Ruiz Massieu. It is doubt-
ful that these murders will ever be thoroughly investigated,
for the trail would lead to the heart of Mexico's political
darkness; it would cast a searing light on the intentional,
organized and historical involvement of the Mexican political elite with drug trafficking. It would point to the infighting
that broke out over control of these activities within the

Mexican Federal Judicial Police *Comandante* Guillermo Gonzalez Calderoni poses with President Carlos Salinas de Gortari in this 1989 official government photograph, taken after the *comandante* was given an award for the arrest of Miguel Angel Felix Gallardo, one of the most powerful of the Guadalajara drug traffickers. Salinas de Gortari later ordered Calderoni's arrest after learning that the trusted commander had been talking to the FBI about the involvement of the Salinas family in drug trafficking. Calderoni then fled to the United States where he lives today.

Mexican political elite, and show how these factions were little more than Cosa Nostra crime families fighting over turf, crime lords with crowns.

It is an error to think of the involvement of the Mexican governmental system in drug trafficking in terms of corruption, to believe that drug traffickers possess the power to corrupt. Corruption is a phenomenon occurring in democratic nations, when someone in a position of public trust abuses that position for personal gain. It is a deviation from the norm. The people of Mexico have never been in control of anything for most of this century, but rather have been controlled. All positions and all authority emanated from the PRI-party and associated interests. The illusion of democracy was attained through the holding of elections, but opponents were not allowed to win. Strictly speaking, therefore, no public trust existed that could be violated.

What existed was a power arrangement in which a miniscule group had it and the remainder of the population did not. Because it was unaccountable to anyone, the system made use of situations such as drug trafficking to further its primary goal of generating wealth for itself. The system itself was the corruptor through a downward reach, through the sponsorship of organized crime. The traffickers did not buy and intimidate their way in. Rather, they were the ones corroded by virtue of the fact they were allowed to do what they do; they were exploited to generate wealth for their powerful sponsors. Their energies and ambitions were tapped and channeled into the service of their political masters. And when their time was up, the same system that empowered them killed or jailed them and took from them whatever was left.

As with elections, so with drug enforcement. Mexico goes through the motions of dealing with drug trafficking as part of an elaborate deception. It will burn a field of marjiuana in the presence of the media, but only after the tops have been harvested. It will stage public burnings of seized cocaine, but it is more likely to be corn starch inside the packages, the cocaine having long been removed and sold to the favored groups. It will allow DEA agents in the field, but block and frustrate every investigative effort. Its facilitation of drug trafficking pump-primed drug addiction throughout North America, yet it routinely blames the victims and rages and fumes whenever it is accused of involvement. It will offer up a sacrificial lamb, some trafficker whose time has come, as a way of placating the victims. It will even offer up an occasional official. But then business will continue as usual.

The Mexico of today is an illusion, a country where tremendous time and energy is spent in deception, in creating the image of something that has no basis in fact. The truth would bring an end. It therefore attempts to sustain itself through elaborately orchestrated illusions.

These organized criminal assaults against the United States by a governmental system find their origins not only in the greed of a particular political class, but also in the depth of the hatred that existed within the power elite for the United States. A cult of hatred flourished, particularly in the 1960s through the 1980s. It was based in part in the ideological context of the time. But its primary energy came from historical relations, from Mexico's losing status in the territorial conflict of the previous century, and from the economic, cultural, political, industrial and military successes of the north in this century. The animosity is reflected in the epigram made famous by Luis Echeverria, president of Mexico from 1970 to 1976, when he said, "Poor Mexico. So far from God, so close to the United States."

Vengeance became one of the rationalizations for unleashing the exploitation tendency of the Mexican system against the north. When Ernesto Poblano, the turncoat mayor of Ojinaga during the era of Manuel Carrasco, attempted to lure his top PAN administrators, he simply mouthed an argument he had picked up from the PRI system that co-opted him, that trafficking was a tool for "historical vengeance." It is an argument still being used by PRI-politicians and traffickers today. What this system of control and exploitation accomplished over time was to create a juggernaut of crime all along the border that has progressively colonized the American side, created a reactionary incarceration state north of the border and ensured a zone of murder and anarchy on the Mexican side.

There will never be a solution to the problem of drug trafficking and drug abuse in North America without a change in Mexico from a charade democracy into a real democracy. The day the people of Mexico are in control of their destiny, the day presidents, their cabinet members, the powerful in and out of government, are stripped of the privilege and immunity that they have granted to themselves by virtue of being in control of everything, then will it become possible for Americans, Canadians and Mexicans jointly to begin dealing realistically with the soul-destroying, nation-undermining problem of drugs.

Change is slowly occurring. The fact that the PRI-system even allowed the forms of democracy to be practiced in Mexico, if not the content, has given room for the emergence of well-organized opposition groups with leadership hardened and honed by decades of democratic struggle. In 1997, out of fear of a broad internal and potentially violent reaction if it continued engineering the outcome of elections, the PRI-system loosened its grip and allowed a sufficient number of congressional seats to go to opposition parties, creating a power shift. The PRI is now a minority among minorities in the Chamber of Deputies. But a loosened grip is still a grip. Will the next important election of the land—for president—be another rigged event?

Rather than provide helicopters for a pretend drug war, rather than provide Mexican soldiers with Special Forces training at Fort Bragg to continue the pantomime struggle, rather than continuing to be the gullible partners in the Mexican illusion act, the United States would do much better to pressure Mexico over its elections, to push for an end to the PRI system and for the freedom of the Mexican people to select, elect and control their leadership.

Information is a better weapon than bullets. Through the

American federal court system, the United States has brought more truth to the surface than through any other mechanism, and the truth has had an impact in Mexico. The prosecution of some of Camarena's killers, including a brother in law of former Mexican president Luis Echeverria, threw greatly needed light on the Mexican reality. The more recent prosecution of a cousin of Carlos Salinas de Gortari for drug trafficking served justice, and also broader truth.

The United States would therefore do well to pursue investigations into the Mexican ruling class suspected of involvement in drug trafficking—and prosecute regardless of political considerations. Through such actions, the United States obtains justice and the Mexican people gain information to which they might otherwise never have access.

For the same reason, the United States Congress should continue its annual program of certifying Mexico's cooperation with the United States in the war against drug trafficking. This predictable pressure source serves as a lever for helping to crack open the Mexican system. It provides opportunities for informed hearings before committees and subcommittees, placing information and insights onto the public record that might not otherwise get there.

The story of Mexico is a predictable story of absolute power corroding absolutely. It is the story of awesome accumulations of wealth by a miniscule fraction of Mexican society derived through the advantages of power, through the systematic plundering of the wealth of its own people and through the exploitation of weaknesses in the United States. It is the story of a deliberate orchestrating of drug trafficking to flood those neighbors with drugs, for gain but also to satisfy a twisted thirst for vengeance. It is the story of the resulting impoverishment of a potentially great nation whose people are forced out of desperation to flee, bringing about one of the greatest migrations in North American history.

It is a story that is only beginning to be told.

Appendix A

ADMINISTRATIVE

On December 13, 1986, SA 2620-OC was present during a conversation between OSCAR OLIVARES LOPEZ, Mexican Federal Judicial Police (MFJP); Commandante GUILLERMO GONZALES CALDERONE, Cuidad Juarez, Mexico; and MFJP agent First Name Unknown (FNU), Last Name Unknown (LNU), also known as "CHATO".

The source advised that CALDERONE, a former commandante in Nuevo Laredo and Matamoros, Mexico, is a close associate of LOPEZ and of JUAN GARCIA ABREGO, the head of the Mexican Drug Trafficking group in Matamoros, Mexico. CALDERONE, according to the source, facilitated the group's drug activities by providing protection and escorting drugs for the group from inner Mexico to the Mexican/United States border. Even though CALDERONE transferred from Matamoros in approximately 1983, CALDERONE is loyal to GARCIA, and in close contact with the group's activities.

The source advised LOPEZ told CALDERONE he had read an article in the Bu Herald regarding the arrest of some of CALDERONE's agents in El Paso, Texas, who were in possession of cocaine, large amounts of money, and weapons. CALDERONE asked if the paper had attacked him or BETO. LOPEZ replied in the negative. CALDERONE laughed and replied his men had "screwed up", and were involved in the selling of cocaine in El Paso, Texas, when they were arrested; however, the matter had been resolved.

LOPEZ asked CALDERONE if that incident had not tainted him, and CALDERONE replied not him directly in that analysis of the cocaine seized from his agents revealed the substance was not cocaine, and that the matter did look very bad for seven of the agents because they had been arrested. CALDERONE stated that the most delicate situation was that one of the Agents had in excess of $10,000.00, and that he considered damaging.

The source advised LOPEZ asked CALDERONE for some cocaine and CALDERONE advised he did not have any on him because of all the recent problems; however, he had some in Cuidad Juarez, and could get some to LOPEZ by nightfall or the next day. CALDERONE advised he had a man who crossed the cocaine for him into El Paso, Texas.

*T*he following is the complete text of an FBI administrative memorandum dated December 13, 1986, the first page of which is reproduced on the opposite side. A correction was made for the spelling of the name of the focus of this memo—Mexican Federal Judicial Police Comandante Guillermo Gonzalez Calderoni, then commander of the MFJP in Ciudad Juarez.

According to the informant, Calderoni met with a drug trafficker who at one time held an important position in the Juan Garcia Abrego drug smuggling organization in Matamoros. The meeting took place several months before the attack on Santa Elena and the death of Pablo Acosta.

This memorandum and the one that follows on pages 348 to 352 are included here because of their relevance to the book, and also because they are examples of the incalculable number of such documents in existence in U.S. intelligence files. The FBI, DEA, U.S. Customs, Border Patrol, INS, ATF, and CIA, not to mention border state police agencies of California, Arizona, New Mexico and Texas, and local police agencies, have compiled intelligence for decades implicating Mexican police, politicians, bureaucrats, government agencies and the military in organized criminal activities directed against the United States. Such information rarely becomes public knowledge. (Author's note)

Administrative

On December 13, 1986, SA 2620-OC was present during a conversation between Oscar Olivares Lopez, Mexican Federal Judicial Police (MFJP); *Comandante* Guillermo Gonzalez Calderoni, Ciudad Juarez, Mexico; and agent First Name Unknown (FNU), Last Name Unknown (LNU), also known as "Chato."

The source advised that Calderoni, a former *comandante* in Nuevo Laredo and Matamoros, Mexico, is a close associate of Lopez and Juan Garcia Abrego, the head of the Mexican Drug Trafficking group in Matamoros, Mexico. Calderoni, according to the source, facilitated the group's drug activities by providing protection and escorting drugs for the group from inner Mexico to the Mexican/United States border. Even though Calderoni transferred from Matamoros in approximately 1983, Calderoni is loyal to Garcia, and in close contact with the group's activities.

The source advised [that] Lopez told Calderoni he had read an article in the [Brownsville] Herald regarding the arrest of some of Calderoni's agents in El Paso, Texas, who were in possession of cocaine, large amounts of money, and weapons. Calderoni asked if the paper had attacked him or Beto. Lopez replied in the negative. Calderoni laughed and replied his men had "screwed up," and were involved in the selling of cocaine in El Paso, Texas, when they were arrested; however, the matter had been resolved.

Lopez asked Calderoni if that incident had not tainted him, and Calderoni replied not directly in that analysis of the cocaine seized from his agents revealed that the substance was not cocaine, and that the matter did look bad for seven of the agents because they had been arrested. Calderoni stated that the most delicate situation was that one of the agents had in excess of $10,000, and that he considered damaging.

The source advised [that] Lopez asked Calderoni for some cocaine and Calderoni advised he did not have any on him because of all the recent problems; however, he had some in Ciudad Juarez, and could get some to Lopez by nightfall or the next day. Calderoni advised he had a man who crossed the cocaine for him into El Paso, Texas.

Lopez explained to Calderoni he could not cross into Mexico because his name was in the computer in that he is considered a major drug dealer by Calderoni's friends from the Drug Enforcement Administration. Calderoni advised DEA agents were sons of bitches, and considered them a filthy lot. Calderoni advised that he considered both the DEA and FBI a bunch of no good SOBs.

Calderoni asked Lopez how MFJP *Comandante* Joaquin Salvador Galvan of Matamoros, Mexico, was doing. Lopez told him that Galvan does not cross into the United States.

Lopez advised he does not know why Galvan does not cross, although he is aware that he [Galvan] has not crossed since [Juan] Garcia Abrego ceased crossing into the United States.

Lopez asked Calderoni in confidence to determine if there were any arrest warrants for him in Mexico in that recently an aircraft under his name, owned by Garcia, crashed in Mexico during a drug run. Lopez explained that when he had crashed his aircraft during approximately 1983, Garcia had purchased a similar airplane, incorporated Lopez's aircraft tail number, and painted the aircraft similar to Lopez's, and registered it under Lopez's name. Calderoni asked if the plane was ladened with narcotics, and Lopez replied in the negative. Calderoni advised he doubted there was an arrest warrant issued, but would verify the matter. Lopez stated the plane crashed near [Oaxaca], Mexico, and the pilot was his former assistant, Enrique Hernandez. Lopez stated the plane was abandoned, the pilot absconded, the seats were removed, and had auxiliary bladder tanks. Calderoni advised that Mexico did not have a conspiracy law, and even if the plane did have drugs, as long as Lopez was not present he could not be arrested in Mexico.

Lopez told Calderoni he had heard Calderoni had arrested some very heavy people recently. Calderoni advised he had arrested Gilberto Ontiveros and Rafael Aguilar from [Ciudad Juarez], Mexico, who was the equivalent of Rafael Chou when Chou was a *comandante* with the *Dirección Federal de Seguridad* [DFS]. Lopez asked if these persons were members of the Raphael Caro Quintero drug group. Calderoni advised not directly, but had many dealings with the group during Bufalo (a ranch owned by Caro Quintero from which his narcotics operations were coordinated), which was very close.

Lopez advised Calderoni that Emilio Lopez Parra, former DFS *comandante*, has left Matamoros, and is trying to join the MFJP. Lopez advised [that] Parra is the person who is currently taking numerous gifts from Garcia to MFJP director and Mexico's Interpol representative, Florentino Ventura. Lopez commented Garcia was well connected in Mexico and Calderoni agreed.

Lopez advised [that] a person who was very close to him was Adalberto Porte Petit, brother of Luis Octavio Porte Petit, Mexican Attorney General's Office. Lopez commented [that] Adalberto considered his brother a SOB because his brother did not give anyone a break.* Calderoni asked if those were some of the people Garcia was wired with in that they were cousins to MFJP *comandante* Javier Pesquiera Moreno, Sonora, Mexico, who was an intimate friend of Garcia. Lopez advised [that] Moreno is not in good standing with Luis Petit, and that the person who supports the group is Galindo Ochoa (previously identified), Mexican Attorney General's Office.

Calderoni inquired as to how Garcia was doing, and Lopez stated Garcia wanted to see him. Calderoni replied [that] every time he was in town Garcia and his men avoided him. Lopez advised Garcia wanted to send Calderoni a gift. Calderoni advised he would be in his home in Reynosa, Mexico, from December 16, 1986, until the first of the year. Calderoni replied that he would be at the disposition of Garcia at that time, and if Garcia did not come to see him, it was because Garcia did not want to see him.

Lopez inquired what Tomas Morlett was doing in Ciudad Juarez with Calderoni. Calderoni advised Morlett came to see him about some of his [Calderoni's] investigations into the activities of Mexican Customs *Comandante* FNU Villanueva and FNU Parrer (phonetic).

Calderoni explained that when he arrived in Ciudad Juarez the MFJP was a bunch of inactive and corrupt individuals, and the entire city was a no man's land. Calderoni advised that Eduardo, not further identified, was supported by Mexican Defense Chief, General Juan Arevalo Gardoqui, and all of these persons considered themselves untouchable. Calderoni claimed he started to investigate their activities, putting some of them in jail, and that was when Morlett showed up to intercede on their behalf. Calderoni told Morlett to tell these persons to stay out of his way.

---

*This is an allusion to monies owed the attorney general's office for protection, not to penalties for engaging in drug trafficking.

Calderoni advised another heavy involved was FNU Paredes. Calderoni stated, however, he now considered all of these individuals his friends as long as they stayed out of his activities.

Lopez commented that General [Arevalo] Gardoqui was having a lot of problems and that all of the general's problems were being blamed on Carlos Aguilar, Nuevo Laredo, Mexico. Lopez stated Aguilar was addicted to cocaine, was using heroin, and was paranoid, and everyone was staying away from him. The source advised [that] at that juncture, Calderoni dismissed his aide, Chato.

Calderoni advised [that] he was told Aguilar was the person who had killed the two newspaper people in Matamoros, Mexico, and killed his associate, attorney (FNU) Del Vosce (phonetic) in Nuevo Laredo, Mexico. Calderoni stated that no one likes Aguilar, and that the people from Matamoros have no use for him either.

Lopez advised he is very confused because he has at times been told by Garcia to stay away from Aguilar, and then Garcia orders him to contact Aguilar. When Aguilar attempts to contact Garcia, Garcia hides and Lopez is left in a limbo.

Lopez commented he is concerned for Garcia's safety because Garcia is drinking heavily now that he cannot come to Brownsville, Texas, and is frequenting bars. With as many enemies as Garcia has, he is likely to get killed. Calderoni stated that that was true; however, most people were afraid to confront Garcia. Calderoni asked how Garcia got along with Marte Martinez and Enrique Rangel Salinas, and Lopez stated that well but that he considered these people harmless. Calderoni agreed; however, Calderoni stated that these people were well connected in Reynosa, Mexico, like Raul Duran and Manuel Renteria. Calderoni stated Renteria is under arrest in Mexico City.

Lopez advised [that] Duran is a friend of Raphael Arredondo, an ophthalmologist in Brownsville, Texas, and a close friend of Garcia. Calderoni wanted to know if Arredondo is still running around with the Garcia group. Calderoni commented that these are the type of people Garcia needs to be careful with. Lopez disagreed and advised he considered Aguilar the main threat because Aguilar had already demonstrated his capabilities with the killing of newspaper people in Matamoros, and the ones in Reynosa. Calderoni asked if Emilio Quintero, brother of Caro Quintero, had sent men to kill Del Vosce (phonetic). Lopez advised Garcia had sent men to Aguilar to kill Aguilar's associate; however, these people had killed a Mexican state judicial police agent in error in Laredo, Texas. Lopez stated Aguilar thereafter took matters into his own hands and had his partner killed. Lopez advised Aguilar was well connected and a heavy.

Lopez stated he could be in error, but he was aware that Aguilar had connected Garcia and Parra to Ventura (head of the Mexican Federal Judicial Police) and he doubted Garcia could count on Ventura if he [Garcia] went against Aguilar. Calderoni stated that it was possible Aguilar introduced these people to Ventura, but for Lopez not to think that Aguilar was that close to Ventura in that he [Calderoni] was a person very close to Ventura. He continued that Ventura constantly asked him how Aguilar and Parra's activities impacted on MFJP activities. Calderoni stated that, although Ventura was his boss, he also had a social and personal relationship with him. Calderoni stated that Galvan was also close to Ventura; however, not as close as himself. Calderoni stated that Ventura consults him on sensitive matters and as far as comparing the political clout of Ventura and Aguilar, Ventura's connections outweigh Aguilar's.

Lopez asked if Manuel Ayala from Reynosa was still involved with Interpol. Calderoni advised that he was but that he was not worth a damn. Lopez stated he knew that personally because those were the people he initially became involved with in narcotics.

Lopez told Calderoni one of the things he worried about was now that Matamoros Mayor Jesus Roberto Guerra (half brother of Juan Garcia Abrego) is leaving office, he will probably form his own faction. Lopez stated Guerra has already demonstrated malice when he had a former Matamoros police commander, FNU Lopez, killed. Calderoni commented "so what" in that Guerra's main hitman, Brijido Sauceda was killed. Lopez replied in the affirmative and commented that that was part of the plan.

Guerra had planned on Sauceda getting killed to avoid Sauceda's disclosure of Guerra's involvement in contract killings. Lopez opined he doubted Guerra will want to be under Garcia's control in that Guerra considers himself a heavy, and in charge of the city. Lopez advised that Guerra's brother, also known as Gordo, is the person who controls the vice for Jesus Norberto and who also agitates him. Lopez stated both of these brothers want to follow the steps of Juan N. Guerra, and that the only sane one is Pepe Guerra.

Calderoni advised he did not consider Jesus Roberto a threat in that he was not well connected like Garcia. Lopez advised to the contrary and stated ill feeling between Garcia and Guerra already existed.

Calderoni stated that if Guerra wanted to be the *don*, he would have to come out in public, and that this benefited Garcia in that it would take some of the attention away from Garcia's activities.

Lopez and Calderoni agreed that the person everyone needs to be aware of was Garcia's sister, FNU LNU, also known as "La Bebe," who controlled and dominated Garcia, and the Guerra's, including Juan N. Guerra. She is married to Marte Martinez.

Lopez asked Calderoni if drug organizations operated in the city [Ciudad Juarez], and Calderoni advised "yes," ranging from marijuana, cocaine, heroin, barbiturates. He stated he did not have the cooperation of the DEA or FBI, and only had one person he went to see very far from El Paso, Texas. He stated that locally DEA, FBI and others were not worth a damn, and were a bunch of assholes.

The source advised that it was obvious to him that during their conversation with Calderoni, Calderoni was reserved with Lopez. The source opined the reservation was based on the fact that Calderoni and Lopez had not seen each other in over two years, and Calderoni was also uneasy about meeting in a motel room. [End]

Appendix B

Memorandum

To :	SAC, SAN ANTONIO (12C-437)(P) Date 2/22/88
From :	SA ROBERT L. NIXON
Subject :	OSCAR OLIVARES LOPEZ; ET AL; NARCOTICS (C); OO:SAN ANTONIO

     With the relocation of SA CLAUDIO DE LA O's family, on approximately 2/29/88, the San Antonio Division will initiate an operation designed to lure JUAN GARCIA ABREGO to the United States. San Antonio proposes the following scenario:

     SA 2620-D is a reliable source who was the #2 man in the GARCIA MDTO for numerous years and is thoroughly familiar with GARCIA'S criminal activities ranging from narcotics trafficking to kidnappings and assassinations. Most of these activities occurred in Mexico but many of these violations involved conspiracies in the United States.

     In approximately July, 1986 GARCIA and SAUL HERNANDEZ (deceased), a former high ranking member of the GARCIA MDTO, planned the killing of a newspaper publisher, ERNESTO FLORES TORRIJOS (deceased) because TORRIJOS was publishing diatribes against JUAN N. GUERRA, GARCIA'S uncle and recognized godfather of Northern Mexico. GUERRA ordered GARCIA to kill TORRIJOS and GARCIA complied because he knew that TORRIJOS would eventually publicly attack him too. A few months prior to TORRIJOS' killing, SA 2620-D arranged a meeting between TORRIJOS and GARCIA. They attempted to persuade TORRIJOS to "tone down" his attacks on GUERRA and offered him unlimited favors and money. TORRIJOS refused their offers citing his opposition to the wanton killings perpetrated by GARCIA, many of these killings at the behest of GUERRA.

     Thereafter, the source arranged subsequent meetings between GARCIA and TORRIJOS and GARCIA became convinced TORRIJOS would cease publicly attacking GUERRA. However, weeks after his last meeting with GARCIA, TORRIJOS moved *12C - 1/3* his newspaper to a building located across from the residence

2 - San Antonio

RLN:jer
(2)

SA 12C-437

of SAUL HERNANDEZ. GARCIA and HERNANDEZ interpreted this
move by TORRIJOS as a "slap in the face" and on 7/30/86,
TORRIJOS and a female reporter accompanying TORRIJOS, NORMA
MORENO FIGUEROA, were machine gunned in Matamoros, Mexico,
by the GARCIA MDTO.

        The source also reported that during 1983, MANUEL
BUENDIA, a prominent newspaper publisher for the Mexican
newspaper Excelsior was killed in Mexico City at the behest
of President MIGUEL DE LA MADRID. DE LA MADRID assigned
then Dirrecion de Seguridad Fedens(DFS) Director MIGUEL
NASSAR HARO to liquidate BUENDIA. NASSAR ordered two of
his most trusted DFS comandantes RAFAEL CHOU LOPEZ and
TOMAS MORLETT BOURQUEZ (deceased) to carry out the operation.
LOPEZ and MORLETT were closely aligned with GARCIA in GARCIA'S
drug trafficking activities and recruited some of GARCIA'S
hitmen to participate in this operation.

        According to the source, BUENDIA was killed because
he had amassed files implicating President DE LA MADRID'S
misuse of funds and other abuses of powers as President.
Allegedly, DE LA MADRID feared BUENDIA because BUENDIA
had a close relationship with syndicated columnist JACK
ANDERSON who had a strong interest in BUENDIA'S material.
After the killing of BUENDIA, BUENDIA'S office was ransacked
and the files destroyed.

        MORLETT thereafter became closely linked with
GARCIA and SA 2620-D. MORLETT confided to SA 2620-D his
role in the killing of BUENDIA as well as his participation
in the kidnapping/killing of DEA Agent ENRIQUE CAMARENA
in Guadalajara, Mexico.

        The source advised that by the latter part of
1985, MORLETT was considered as one of the key links between
major narcotics Chieftans and corrupt law enforcment officials
in Mexico. The source advised that this power coupled
with MORLETT'S heavy dependence on cocaine turned MORLETT
into a despot and a braggart. MORLETT committed numerous
indiscretions by relating sensitive "Mexican Mafia" secrets
to people who were not considered "trustworthy."

        The source explained MORLETT became paranoid
and suspect of the source when the source and MORLETT accidently
met SA DE LA O at the SHERATON INN, Brownsville, Texas,
and the source described SA DE LA O as being his friend.
MORLETT thereafter started plotting with GARCIA the killing
of SA 2620-D in that MORLETT felt threatened with the revelations
he made to the source.

SA 12C-437

The source explained that CHOU LOPEZ and NASSAR became aware of MORLETT'S indiscretions and cocaine addiction and MORLETT'S assassination was planned.

On 1/27/87, MORLETT and SAUL HERNANDEZ were gunned down at the PIEDRAS NEGRAS RESTAURANT, Matamoros, Mexico, by GARCIA MDTO members. Both GARCIA and CHOU LOPEZ were present during this killing.

SA DE LA O was last contacted by GARCIA on 11/23/87, when GARCIA proposed that SA DE LA O travel to Reynosa, Mexico, to meet with GARCIA and MFJP Comandante GUILLERMO CALDERONI at CALDERONI'S residence. GARCIA described his relationship with CALDERONI was like that of "brothers." Thereafter, GARCIA assigned an intermediary, FRANCISCO PEREZ, to meet with SA DE LA O. During numerous meetings, GARCIA asked SA DE LA O, through PEREZ, to convince SA 2620-D to travel to Matamoros to meet with GARCIA so that they can "iron" out their differences. SA DE LA O has informed GARCIA SA 2620-D resides in El Paso, Texas, but that he contacts SA 2620-D through a relative of the source and does not know the source's exact location.

On numerous occasions, GARCIA has cultivated former acquaintances and associates of SA 2620-D in an effort to locate SA 2620-D with negative results.

As the Bureau is aware, SA DE LA O was last contacted on 1/6/88, by PEREZ and given approximately $40,000 Christmas gift from GARCIA.

It is the opinion of San Antonio that the only way GARCIA can be lured to the United States is for SA 2620-D to threaten exposing GARCIA'S involvement in referenced killings. The source pointed out the killing of BUENDIA is a highly relevant and volatile issue because of vast political pressures that have been exerted on the Mexican Government. As a result of these pressures, over 500 agents headed by Mexico City D.F. Federal Prosecutor RENATO SALES GOSKE have been assigned to resolve the murder. The source stated that MORLETT will in all likelihood be blamed for the killing. Therefore, SA 2620-D will use this issue as a wedge to further incite GARCIA. Additionally, SA 2620-D has been in contact with the wife of ERNESTO FLORES TORRIJOS, AMELIA FLORES TORRIJOS, who currently owns and manages her deceased husband's newspaper El Bravo, Matamoros, Mexico. SA 2620-D will meet with MRS. TORRIJOS in the immediate future and offer to solve her husband's murder.

3

SA 12C-437

SA 2620-D and and handler opine GARCIA will immediately
make the connection of this information to the source.
The source surmises GARCIA will immediately initiate contact
with SA DE LA O to set up a meeting with SA 2620-D. SA
DE LA O will comply and attempt to coordinate a meeting
between GARCIA and SA 2620-D in the United States. If
GARCIA agrees to travel to the United States, all efforts
will be made to persuade GARCIA to "cooperate" with the
FBI and under controlled conditions expose high level corrupt
Mexican officials and set up significant controlled deliveries
of narcotics. If GARCIA refuses, he will be arrested and
an intensive investigation will be initiated to buttress
significant federal/state charges against GARCIA.

        In the event GARCIA does not "bite the bait,"
at a future date, SA 2620-D will arrange a meeting on the
United States side with Comandante CALDERONI. SA 2620-D
has in the past "paid off" CALDERONI on numerous occasions
at the behest of GARCIA and is aware of CALDERONI'S past
criminal involvement with the Mexican Mafia. Additionally,
the source will request CALDERONI bring the source cocaine.
CALDERONI has provided drugs to the source in the past.

        At this meeting with CALDERONI and SA 2620-D,
SA DE LA O will be present. SA 2620-D will follow a scenario
in which he (SA 2620-D) has forced SA DE LA O to investigate
the GARCIA MDTO or risk getting exposed to his agency as
a corrupt agent. This move will enable San Antonio to
guise CALDERONI'S future posture in event he aligns himself
with GARCIA. It is felt CALDERONI would come to SA DE LA O
and detail a plan to neutralize SA 2620-D.

        The meeting with CALDERONI will be handled in
various forms depending on CALDERONI'S disposition. Some
of the strategies are as follows:

        1. Appeal to CALDERONI'S professionalism, emphasizing
GARCIA is a "dead duck," highly unpredictable and a threat
to CALDERONI. Therefore, an offer can be made to CALDERONI
to work hand-in-hand with the FBI in a joint investigation.

        2. Convince CALDERONI that GARCIA'S relationship
with SA DE LA O was a farce and that the FBI is fully aware
of GARCIA'S relationship with CALDERONI and anything short
of total cooperation with the FBI, CALDERONI'S "future"
is at stake as the FBI will deal with him as a co-conspirator.

354

DRUG LORD

SA 12C-437

3. Based on the source's extensive knowledge
re CALDERONI'S past criminal history with the GARCIA MDTO
and his "handle" on CALDERONI, the source will dictate
"terms" to CALDERONI or risk exposure to the Mexican media
re his relationship with the Mexican Mafia.

One of the main requests SA 2620-D will make
of CALDERONI is for CALDERONI to place MFJP Director FLORENTINO
VENTURA in contact with the source. VENTURA and SA 2620-D
are acquainted. The source will attempt to assess VENTURA'S
relationship with GARCIA and enlist VENTURA'S cooperation
in pressuring GARCIA to flee to the United States. The
source advised GARCIA has not personally met VENTURA but
remits large amounts of money and expensive gifts to VENTURA
through EMILIO LOPEZ PARRA, a former MFJP Comandante.

Based on the source's extensive knowledge of
Mexican politics, the source opines that once he details
out GARCIA'S brutal killings, mental instability and the
fact that GARCIA is routinely using VENTURA'S name to insulate
his MDTO activities, VENTURA will perceive GARCIA as a
"liability" and exert pressure on him.

5*

Appendix C

The following is a list of journalists murdered in Mexico since 1988. Few of the murders have been resolved to the satisfaction of independent investigators. The overwhelming majority are believed to have been killed in reprisal for their work exposing governmental crime, drug trafficking and the links between organized criminal activities and the Mexican government. (Source: The Inter American Press Association)

HECTOR FELIX MIRANDA. A political columnist and an editor for the weekly *Zeta* of Tijuana, Baja California, he was murdered on April 20, 1988. A station wagon followed Felix's automobile as he drove to work in Tijuana. The assailant then fired two shots from a rifle at close range.

RONAY GONZALEZ REYES. An editor of the daily *El Mundo de Comitán*, in the state of Chiapas, he was shot to death as he sat at his typewriter at work on July 13, 1988.

LINDA BEJARANO. A television journalist in Ciudad Juarez, she was machine-gunned to death on July 23, 1988, when the automobile in which she was traveling with three other people was riddled with 46 bullets by federal judicial police who fired "by mistake." Only one person survived. The federal agents claimed they had mistaken her car for one being used to transport cocaine.

MANUEL BURGUENO ORDUNO. A former reporter for the newspaper *Noroeste de Mazatlán* and the editor of a political newsletter, he was killed on February 22, 1988, by unknown assailants who broke into his home. It is believed that the murder was connected to his exposés of police abuse and drug trafficking.

ALBERTO RUVALCABA TORRES. A reporter of the newspaper *Novedades de Zapopan*, Jalisco, he was kidnapped on January 19, 1989 by three individuals armed with a machine gun as he rode in a taxi. He was found dead the next day.

EZEQUIEL HUERTA ACOSTA. An editor of the magazine *Avances Politicos* of Saltillo, Coahuila, he was murdered in 1989 in the city of Guadalajara allegedly by drug dealers.

ELIAS MARIO MEDINA. A former editor of the newspapers

El Sol de Durango and *El Sol del Norte*, he was shot to death in Durango on June 28, 1989.

VICTOR MANUEL OROPEZA. Writer for the *El Diario de Juárez* and a homeopathic doctor, he was stabbed 14 times in his office on April 28, 1989. Three suspects were arrested but later released. No motive has been established, but Oropeza was a noted critic of the Mexican political system.

ALFREDO CORDOVA SOLORZANO. He died June 9, 1990, three days after he was shot at home in Tapachula, Chiapas, by unknown gunmen. He had covered drug trafficking and had written pieces critical of state authorities. He was founder and publisher of his five-year-old Chiapas newspaper *Uno Más Dos*. He had been attacked and beaten before.

JUAN CARLOS CONTRERAS and MIGUEL ELOY GIL SOTO. Reporters for *El Nacional* and *La Opción*, they were murdered in Nogales, Sonora, on August 26, 1991, allegedly by drug traffickers.

GABRIEL VENEGAS VALENCIA. He disappeared on October 11, 1991, after finishing work at his television station and was found dead four days later. Venegas covered the labor beat, often reporting on strikes and labor disputes.

JESSICA ELIZALDE DE LEON. She was killed at her home in Ciudad Juarez, Chihuahua, on March 14, 1993, by an unidentified assailant who came to her home with a bouquet of roses and then shot her twice in the head. The journalist, who worked on the news program, *Notiactualidades* of 106 FM, had been investigating police matters.

PEDRO LANGARICA MIRELES. A freelance writer, he was beaten and then strangled to death on November 20, 1993, in Navojoa, Sonora. No one was ever arrested, but it is believed the murder was committed by drug traffickers.

JESUS NUNEZ SANCHEZ, a reporter and columnist, ROBERTO MANCILLA, a reporter, and JOSE HERRERA CANAS, a photographer, were murdered in 1993 in Mexico.

JOSE AGUSTIN REYES. A correspondent for the newspaper *El Heraldo* and the radio network *Raza*, he was gunned down in his offices in La Paz, Baja California, on March 16, 1994. His partially burned body was dumped at a nearby ranch.

JOSE MARTIN DORANTES. Managing editor of the weekly newspaper, *Crucero*, he died after he was shot five times by at least two persons in front of his house in Cuernavaca, Morelos, on June 6, 1994. The 30-year-old editor managed to fire his own weapon, but apparently did not hit his attackers.

JOSE LUIS ROJAS MERA. Murdered June 7, 1994.

ENRIQUE PERALTA TORRES. A journalist of *La Unión de Morelos*, he was murdered on July 6, 1994.

OSCAR AYALA PEQUENO. A photographer for the afternoon paper *La Prensa de Reynosa*, Tamaulipas, he was shot to death on November 21, 1994. His murderer, a former prisoner who had just been freed from jail, Octavio Trevino Perez, was later arrested. The murder appears to have been related to the victim's journalistic activities.

DANTE ESPARTACO CORTEZ. A photographer for the Tijuana daily, *El Mexicano*, he was machine-gunned to death outside his home in Tijuana, Baja California, on June 18, 1995. The crime appears to be linked to drug traffickers.

RUPERTO ARMENTA GERARDO. An editor of the newspaper *El Regional de Guasave*, Sinaloa, he was beaten to death on February 5, 1995. It is suspected that his assailants may have been police agents.

CUAUHTEMOC ORNELAS OCAMPO. Editor of the magazine *Alcance* in Torreon, Coahuila, he has been missing since October 4, 1995. He is presumed to have been kidnapped and murdered.

EDGAR FEDERICO MASON VILLALOBOS. A freelance writer who wrote about economic issues for a variety of publications. He was murdered November 29, 1996, in Cuernavaca, Morelos. Assault is the motive given by police for the murder. No suspects have been arrested.

ABEL BUENO LEON. Editor of the weekly newspaper *Siete Días* in Chilpancingo, Guerrero, he was murdered May 20, 1997.

BENJAMIN FLORES GONZALEZ. Editor of *La Prensa*, a daily newspaper in San Luis Rio Colorado, Sonora. He was murdered July 15, 1997. Gunmen fired at him with an assault rifle when he was within steps of the front of the newspaper, then fired into his head as he lay on the ground. His murder was attributed to the publication of investigative reports about drug trafficking and corruption.

VICTOR MANUEL HERNANDEZ MARTINEZ. A reporter for the magazine *Revista* of Mexico City, he was murdered July 26, 1997.

Additionally, FERNANDO BALDERAS, his wife YOLANDA FIGUEROA, daughter PATRICIA, 18, and sons PAUL, 13, and FERNANDO, 8, were murdered on December 6, 1996. Each had been bludgeoned to death at their residence in Mexico City. FERNANDO BALDERAS, a crusading journalist, was publisher of *Fourth Estate*, which specialized in exposing corruption in Mexico. His wife, Yolanda, had just published a book called *The Boss of the Gulf*, a book about Juan Garcia Abrego. (Author's note)

Index

ORDER FORM

Drug Lord, the Life and Death of a Mexican Kingpin
ISBN: 0-9664430-0-4
$14.95

Spanish translation:
El Zar de la Droga, la vida y la muerte de un narcotraficante mexicano
ISBN: 0-9664430-1-2
$14.95

Erkki Alanen

By Mail: **Demand Publications**
                   2608 Second Avenue, Suite 2450
                   Seattle, WA 98121
                   Send check or money order

By Telephone: Call toll free: 1 (888) 622-7311
                   Credit card: Visa, M/C, American Express, Discover

On Line: www.amazon.com
                   (check other on-line bookstores too)
                   All major credit cards

Cost per single copy is $14.95 plus $3.95 for shipping and handling. Add $2.00 for shipping and handling for each additional copy. For information about institutional or retail discounts, please call our toll-free number.

Visit our website: www.druglord.com